CORNERSTONE

In *Cornerstone: Encountering the Spirit of Christ* in the Catholic School, Dr Sultmann has provided a lively contribution to Catholic educators, a deep grounding of the Catholic schools' theological base and their imperative for creative, faith-filled cultural transformation.

Sr. M. Paul McCaughey, O.P. Coordinator
Catholic Educational Leadership Program, DePaul University College of Education

Every professional needs books on their shelf (or in their computer) that map the terrain of their discipline. Cornerstone provides Catholic educators with a map that is as detailed as it is true. Every page is filled with a commitment to mission and a faith that evokes the best of what we have in our tradition and in our hearts to serve. Cornerstone provides a sure guide and strong encouragement to build Catholic school communities permeated by faith, hope and love.

Dr Paul Sharkey, Director Identity and Mission Catholic Education Office
Archdiocese of Melbourne

A timely publication in that it addresses the key issues around Catholic distinctiveness for teachers and leaders in Catholic schools. Mission and vision feature strongly in a book which encapsulates a sacramental vision of the Church, espoused so strongly by Pope Francis. This book is an essential read for all involved in the governance, leadership and teaching ministry in all Catholic schools, called to live Pope Francis' vision of a Church called to be a Church where all are welcome and where distinctiveness is respected and convergence for the common good is proposed.

Professor John Lydon
St Mary's University of Twickenham and University of Notre Dame Indiana

Its content and method are so outstanding that it deserves to become a resource for both beginning-teachers and for conscientious seasoned teachers engaged in professional development. It might also find a place in theological schools and training colleges as a text for studies of the foundations of religious education.

Reverend Dr Brian Gleeson CP
Lector Emeritus, Systematic Theologian and author

Martin Buber characterised our lives as encounters, dialogues and relationships. An experienced and respected educator Bill Sultmann brings the reader into conversation with the Catholic tradition, the scriptures, theologians, educators and modern thinkers in this thoughtful exploration of the nature and mission of Catholic education in our current context. This is a rich and valuable resource for graduate students, teachers and those interested in knowing more about the Church's understanding of education and the philosophy of the Catholic school. A marvellous combination of reflection and resources providing the reader with treasures both new and old.

Reverend Dr Christopher Monaghan CP
President, Yarra Theological Union, University of Divinity

The wisdom and deep insights in this book are indispensable to those who serve, support, govern and lead in Catholic systems and schools, and in all faith-based schools who profess a philosophy centred on the Gospel of Christ. The key themes are grounded in and inspired by an authentic and transparent spirituality of engagement, the universal presence of the Spirit in relationships, and the presence of God in all things. This book is for all who are engaged directly or indirectly in the governance, leadership and educative practises in Catholic education, including those involved in the academic leadership and teacher preparation programs for Catholic educators within tertiary institutions. This book is a shining light that will become a beacon of hope and possibilities for Catholic leaders and educators who are grappling with challenges and problems within contexts of disruption, uncertainty and rapid change. I recommend it without qualification.

Professor Emeritus Patrick Duignan
Australian Catholic University

The pages of this meticulous, scholarly document breathe a Spirit of Hope and Joy for new possibilities and renewed life for leaders and teachers in Catholic schools. At a time when the Catholic Church is struggling to reclaim its identity and mission for the future, Catholic schools are invited to renew and re-imagine their identity, by encountering the Spirit of Jesus Christ alive, present and active in their midst. This scholarly presentation is a "must read" for all leaders and teachers in Catholic school communities.

Dr Joe McCorley, OAM
Former Executive Director, Queensland Catholic Education Office, and Chairperson (Queensland College of Teachers)

Catholic educators will appreciate Dr Sultmann's incisive analysis of contemporary thinking and issues driving mission, identity and ministry within Catholic schools. His explanation of the essence, practice, characteristics and fruits of ministry will encourage many to be reawakened to life in the Spirit. This book challenges all to an awareness of developments in neuro-science which could change the way we teach Religious Education, yet remains full of practical hints and deep reflections based on one's own experiences.

Dr Elizabeth Dodds RSC
Chair, Faith Formation and Religious Education Standing Committee
National Catholic Education Commission

Third century fresco of the Catacomb of Callixtus – the Good Shepherd.

The Joy of the Gospel fills the hearts and lives of all who encounter Jesus [1]

CORNERSTONE

Encountering the Spirit of Christ in the Catholic School

William Sultmann

COVENTRY PRESS

Published in Australia by
Coventry Press
33 Scoresby Road
Bayswater Vic. 3153
Australia

ISBN 9780648360131

Copyright © William Sultmann 2018

All rights reserved. Other than for the purposes and subject to the conditions prescribed under the *Copyright Act*, no part of this publication may be reproduced, stored in a retrieval system, or transmitted in any form or by any means, electronic, mechanical, photocopying, recording or otherwise, without the prior permission of the publisher.

Scripture quotations are from New Revised Standard Version Bible: Catholic Edition, copyright © 1989, 1993 National Council of the Churches of Christ in the United States of America. Used by permission. All rights reserved worldwide.

Cataloguing-in-Publication entry is available from the National Library of Australia http:/catalogue.nla.gov.au/.

Word Processing by Worthy Secretarial Services

Design and layout by Shayla Melrose

Printed in Australia

DEDICATION

Congregation of Passionists and their ministries within Oceania[2]

ACKNOWLEDGEMENTS

Heartfelt appreciation goes to my family; Noelene Sultmann, Clare and Cam Stewart and their children William, Joseph and Amelia for their acceptance of a passion that has been long in the making and demanding in the obsession.

The development of this work draws from multiple privileges, opportunities and relationships; all of which have been gifts of the Spirit. In addition, the text advances earlier writing supported by Mr Martin Scroope, Reverend Dr David Pascoe, and Associate Professor Denis McLaughlin; together with a series of more recent research papers in collaboration with Associate Professor Ray Brown, Professor Br David Hall, and Dr Geraldine Townend.

The finalisation of this resource has been supported by friends, colleagues, practitioners and theoreticians. To this supportive and generous group I am deeply appreciative. In particular, gratitude is extended to Professor Brother David Hall FMS, Reverend Dr Brian Gleeson CP, Dr Margaret Lee, Dr Barry Donaghue CFC, Mr James Willcox, Ms Judith Gardiner, Dr Geraldine Larkins RSJ and Ms Louise Cosgrove for their willingness to comment on the evolving content and presentation of the manuscript. In addition, the generous reviews by esteemed colleagues; Sr M Paul McCaughey OP, Dr Paul Sharkey, Dr Elizabeth Dodds RSC, Professor John Lydon, Professor Emeritus Patrick Duignan, Reverend Dr Christopher Monaghan CP, Reverend Dr Brian Gleeson CP, and Dr Joe McCorley are much appreciated. Finally, particular thanks is extended to Mrs Maureen Worthy for her unfailing advice and assistance with editorial and word processing, Mrs Shayla Melrose for design and layout expertise, and to Mr Hugh McGinlay (Editor) for his faith and commitment to publishing this work.

---

2 Proceeds directed to the Passionists Heart Foundation

CONTENTS OVERVIEW

INTRODUCING THE NARRATIVE   1

CHAPTER ONE
Knowing his story: Foundations in faith   9

CHAPTER TWO
Walking his way: A spirituality of engagement   45

CHAPTER THREE
Telling his truth: The prophetic mission of the Catholic school   70

CHAPTER FOUR
Living his life: Leadership as Christian praxis   109

CHAPTER FIVE
One garment: Ministry as integration   150

CHAPTER SIX
To experience is to know: Open the window and let in the world   198

EPILOGUE: LIVING AGENDA   215

REFERENCES   216

APPENDIX 1
Catholic School Formation Index (CSFI)   245

TABLE OF CONTENTS

ACKNOWLEDGEMENTS	I
CONTENTS OVERVIEW	II
TABLE OF CONTENTS	III
FIGURES AND TABLES	VIII
ACRONYMS OF CHURCH DOCUMENTS	IX
GLOSSARY OF TERMS	X
FOREWORD	XIII
INTRODUCING THE NARRATIVE	1
Intentions	*1*
Why cornerstone: the fertile question	1
At our best	1
Why now?	2
For whom?	3
The next lane	3
Text parameters	*4*
Chapter framework	4
A personal journey	5
Distinguishing features	6
Beginning with the 'end in mind'	7
CHAPTER ONE	9
KNOWING HIS STORY: FOUNDATIONS IN FAITH	9
INTRODUCTION	9
Reflection	*9*
At a glance	*9*
Focusing story: "Getting one's top button done up"	*10*
From your experience	*10*
THEMES AND MAIN IDEAS	10
Graced and gifted	*10*
Meaning and purpose	11
Identity and identity	12
Identity in God and systems of belief	13
Journeying in faith	15
Revelation of God	*17*
Judeo-Christian tradition	17
Revelation of God in Christ	18
Teacher of divine wisdom	19
Kingdom vision	21
Kingdom living	23
Spirit of Trinity	25

TABLE OF CONTENTS

Vatican II	*28*
Context and signposts	28
Compass for the new millennium	29
Impact of the Council	30
Church today	*32*
Social and cultural context	32
Religious context	34
Catholic school: Christ as cornerstone	37
INTEGRATION	**41**
Executive Summary	*41*
Reflection: "Whom are they talkng to Sister?"	*41*
Questions	*41*
Activities	*42*
CHAPTER TWO	**45**
WALKING HIS WAY: A SPIRITUALITY OF ENGAGEMENT	**45**
INTRODUCTION	**45**
Reflection	*45*
At a glance	*45*
Focusing story: "Don't you want to know my name?"	*45*
From your experience	*46*
THEMES AND MAIN IDEAS	**46**
Living Spirit	*46*
Life as a sacred whole	46
Spirituality in the everyday	49
Being present	50
Mysticism	51
Sacramental living	*53*
Sacramental consciousness	54
Sacraments as expressions of life	54
Discipleship	*55*
Universal call	56
People of God	57
Discipleship metaphors	58
Missionary discipleship	*60*
A new myth for mission	60
Discipleship in the Catholic school	63
INTEGRATION	**65**
Executive Summary	*65*
Reflection: "Is that Jesus?"	*66*
Questions	*66*
Activities	*67*

TABLE OF CONTENTS

CHAPTER THREE — 70
TELLING HIS TRUTH: THE PROPHETIC MISSION OF THE CATHOLIC SCHOOL — 70

INTRODUCTION — 70
- *Reflection* — 70
- *At a glance* — 70
- *Focusing story: "Go back and tell John"* — 71
- *From your experience* — 71

THEMES AND MAIN IDEAS — 71
- *Humble beginnings to established service* — 71
  - In the beginning - denominational schools — 72
  - A century of Religious — 74
  - Post-conciliar era — 75
  - Beyond the crossroads — 78
  - International perspectives — 79
  - The Australian context — 80
- *A distinctive philosophy* — 84
  - Agency of Church — 84
  - Learning as liberation — 86
  - Aims, models and principles — 87
  - Signposts from Vatican II — 88
  - Post-conciliar emphases — 90
- *Constants in context* — 94
  - Mission alignment — 96
  - Christian anthropology — 96
  - Engagement typology — 97
  - Constants and characteristics — 100
  - Purpose, goals and the 'elevator pitch' — 102

INTEGRATION — 104
- *Executive Summary* — 104
- *Reflection: "You are that tree"* — 104
- *Questions* — 105
- *Activities* — 105

CHAPTER FOUR — 109
LIVING HIS LIFE: LEADERSHIP AS CHRISTIAN PRAXIS — 109

INTRODUCTION — 109
- *Reflection* — 109
- *At a glance* — 109
- *Focusing story: Pervasive Spirit* — 110
- *From your experience* — 110

THEMES AND MAIN IDEAS — 110

TABLE OF CONTENTS

An expansive and challenging canvas — 110
- Leadership: Images and paradigms — 111
- Myths and memes — 114

Leadership movements — 116
- Leadership characteristics — 116
- Leadership behaviours — 117
- Leadership in context — 117
- Leadership forces — 118
- Leadership as co-responsibility — 120
- Leadership for learning — 121
- Leadership and ethics — 123
- Leadership and purpose — 124
- Leadership and Institute models — 126

Leadership as Christian praxis — 127
- Church life as sacrament of Christ — 127
- Sign and instrument: summary characteristics — 129
- Touchstones of Christian leadership — 130
- Christian leadership practices — 131

Leadership and transformation — 132
- Personal transformation — 133
- Relational transformation — 135
- Educational transformation — 138
- Organisational transformation — 140
- "What do we know for sure?" — 144

INTEGRATION — 146
- *Executive Summary* — 146
- *Reflection: Service and communion at the table* — 147
- *Questions* — 147
- *Activities* — 147

CHAPTER FIVE — 150
ONE GARMENT: MINISTRY AS INTEGRATION — 150

INTRODUCTION — 150
- *Reflection* — 150
- *At a glance* — 150
- *Focusing story: Jigsaw* — 151
- *From your experience* — 151

THEMES AND MAIN IDEAS — 151
- *Oneness of mind and Spirit* — 151
  - Thriving in the new normal — 152
  - Mind: the brain and body relationship — 154
  - Mind and spirit relationship — 156

TABLE OF CONTENTS

Ministry	165
Professional vocation	166
Five-star aspirations	167
Spirit encounters	169
Legends in the Spirit	171
Fruits of the Spirit	174
Prayer and meditation	176
Living consciously	179
"Why was it so?"	181
Ministry: Perspective and capabilities	181
Researching capabilities	184
A metaphor for capabilities	191
Gauging priorities	193
INTEGRATION	194
Executive Summary	194
Reflection: The essence of ministry	194
Questions	194
Activities	195
CHAPTER SIX	198
TO EXPERIENCE IS TO KNOW: OPEN THE WINDOW AND LET IN THE WORLD	198
INTRODUCTION	198
Reflection	198
At a glance	198
Focusing Story: Piercing the cocoon	199
From your experience	199
THEMES AND MAIN IDEAS	199
Glance again	199
Known for what?	200
Responding personally	201
Stepping up and stepping out	204
Why as a basis for how?	205
ENGAGING HOLISTICALLY	206
Conclusion	208
A dynamic tradition	208
Blessing in a sacred place	209
An unfinished symphony	210
Reflection: "No more fences"	211
Activities	212
EPILOGUE: LIVING AGENDA	215
REFERENCES	216
APPENDIX 1: Catholic School Formation Index (CSFI)	245

FIGURES AND TABLES

FIGURES

Figure 1.	Service as a dynamic and interconnected process	5
Figure 2.	Encounter as formation	6
Figure 3.	Stages of faith development	16
Figure 4.	The metaphor of cornerstone in Scripture	38
Figure 5.	Alignment with the person and message of Christ	60
Figure 6.	Mission expression through discipleship	61
Figure 7.	Spirituality and the Catholic school	65
Figure 8.	Facilitating authentic human growth	87
Figure 9.	Aims, models and principles of Catholic schools	88
Figure 10.	A typology of Catholic school mission	98
Figure 11.	Christian praxis leadership principles	131
Figure 12.	Shifts for personal transformation	134
Figure 13.	Personal integration through life in the Spirit	158
Figure 14.	Expressions of the Spirit in the culture of the Catholic School	160
Figure 15.	Five-star characteristics of a Catholic school educator	169
Figure 16.	Fields of engagement and interaction in processes of formation	189
Figure 17.	Formation elements integral to Catholic school mission	191
Figure 18.	Encountering the Spirit of Christ in the Catholic school	206

TABLES

Table 1.	International challenges for Catholic Education	79
Table 2.	Structural shifts and principles underpinning Vatican II	89
Table 3.	A summary of 'calls' to Christian Education from Vatican II	90
Table 4.	Themes and concepts of the conciliar and post-conciliar period	95
Table 5.	Constants and characteristics of Catholic school mission	101
Table 6.	Purpose and goals of the Catholic school	102
Table 7.	A summary of student outcomes	103
Table 8.	Characteristics of a parallel leader	120
Table 9.	A summary of leadership responsibilities	126
Table 10.	Leadership for mission in the Catholic school	132
Table 11.	A continuum of leader behaviours	136
Table 12.	A shared wisdom model for inter-personal engagement	138
Table 13.	Traditional to contemporary educational perspectives	139
Table 14.	Shifts in organisational transformation	143
Table 15.	Ministry impulses from the *Joy of the Gospel*	170
Table 16.	Dispositions of a Spirit centred consciousness	180
Table 17.	Discourse data relevant to the practice of ministry	185
Table 18.	Examples of ministry capabilities within generic formation fields	190

ACRONYMS OF CHURCH DOCUMENTS

MAGISTERIAL DOCUMENT	LATIN NAME	YEAR	ACRONYMS
The Christian Education of Youth	Divini Illius Magistri	1929	DIM
Dogmatic Constitution on the Church	Lumen Gentium	1963	LG
Constitution on the Sacred Liturgy	Sacrosanctum Concilium	1963	SC
Pastoral Constitution on the Church in the Modern World	Gaudium et Spes	1963	GS
Decree on the Mission Activity of the Church	Ad Gentes Divinitus	1965	AGD
Declaration on Christian Education	Gravissimum Educationis	1965	GE
The Decree on the Apostolate of the Laity	Apostolicam Actuositatem	1965	AA
Dogmatic Constitution on Divine Revelation	Dei Verbum	1965	DV
Evangelisation in the Modern World	Evangelii Nuntiandi	1975	EN
The Catholic School	N/A	1977	TCS
Redeemer of Humankind	Redemptoris Missio	1979	RM
Lay Catholics in Schools: Witnesses to Faith	N/A	1982	LCIS
The Religious Dimension of Education in the Catholic School	N/A	1988	RDECS
Christ's Faithful People	Christifideles Laici	1989	CL
Catechism of the Catholic Church	N/A	1994	CCC
The Gospel of Life	Evangelium Vitae	1995	EV
Jesus Christ and the Peoples of Oceania: Walking His Way, Telling His Truth, Living His Life	Lineamenta	1997	LI
The Catholic School on the Threshold of the Third Millennium	N/A	1998	CSTTM
The Church of the New Millennium	Novo Millennio Ineunte	2001	NMI
Ecclesia in Oceania: Post Synodal Apostolic Exhortation	N/A	2001	EO
Love of God	Deus Caritas Est	2005	DCE
Educating Together in Catholic Schools: A Shared Mission Between Consecrated Persons and the Lay Faithful	N/A	2007	ETCS
Hope Saves	Spe Salvi	2007	SS
The Word of God in the Life and Mission of the Church	Verbum Domini	2010	VD
The Light of Faith	Lumen Fidei	2013	LF
The Joy of the Gospel	Evangelii Gaudium	2013	EG
Educating to Intercultural Dialogue in Catholic Schools: Living in Harmony for a Civilization of Love	N/A	2013	EID
On Care for our Common Home	Laudato Si	2015	LS
Educating to Fraternal Humanism: Building a Civilization of Love 50 years after Populorum Progressio	N/A	2017	EFH
On the Call to Holiness in Today's World	Gaudete et Exsultate	2018	GEE

GLOSSARY OF TERMS

Alignment	The congruence between structure, people, systems, emotions, intellect and values that create stability, balance and interactive harmony.[3]
Catechesis	Education in faith of children, young people and adults which includes especially the teaching of Christian Doctrine.[4]
Christian formation	A process of encounter with the person and message of Christ at three interdependent levels: faith, life and culture; person, school and system; and head, heart and hand.[5]
Culture	Commonly referred to as "the way we do things around here," it incorporates personal witness, relationship dispositions, organisational structures, and traditions, expectations, relationships, processes, and structures.
Dialogue	The ability to listen, share, inquire and reflect in a discussion which entails a free flow of meaning between people.[6]
Encounters	Experiences that engage thoughts, feelings and actions which are invitational, developmental, personal, relational, collegial, vocational, and in the ultimate sense, potentially transformational.
Encounters with the Spirit of Christ	Encounters awakened through attentiveness to the Spirit in the formal and informal, the ordinary and the extraordinary, the infrequent and the everyday experiences of life.
Evangelisation	A process of sharing the Gospel, the Good News, derived from the Greek word, *Evangelium*.[7]
Formation	The development of the whole person and the community through experiences that integrate faith, life and culture. It is characterised by intentionality, engagement, interdependence and reflection and impacts knowledge, affect, and behaviors.[8]
Formation assumptions	Formation which builds on the nature of the individual (biological determinants) and the innate search for meaning (spiritual determinants).
Formation capabilities	The outcomes of formation in knowledge, skills, behaviours and dispositions.
Formation fields	Generic arenas of development incorporating such areas as the personal, relational, professional, and communal nature of the Catholic school.
Holistic Catholic education	The informal and formal curriculum of the Catholic school, defined by the content it teaches, the processes it uses and its environment.[9]
Identity	The characteristics of mission as influenced by the religious, social, economic, environmental and political influences within the community.
Learning community	People who share a common purpose, collaborate and draw on individual strengths, respect a variety of perspectives, and actively promote learning and learning opportunities.[10]
Mind	The oneness of the brain and the body. The element of a person that enables them to be aware of the world and their experiences, to think, and to feel.[11]

[3] From *Building Effective Relationships to Drive Excellent Performance and Alignment. Three Frames Workbook*, Queensland Government, March 2001.
[4] *Catechism of the Catholic Church*, para. 5.
[5] National Catholic Education Commission document, *A Framework for Formation for Mission in Catholic Education*, March, 2017.
[6] From *Educating to Fraternal Humanism. Building a Civilization of Love 50 Years after Populorum Progressio*, 2017.
[7] Pope Francis address to the Pontifical Council for promoting new evangelisation, (2017).
[8] From National Catholic Education Commission (2017), A Framework for Formation for Mission in Catholic Education.
[9] See Groome, T. 1996.
[10] Kilpatrick, Barrett & Jones, 2003, p. 11.
[11] Dr Joe Dispenza, 2012.

GLOSSARY OF TERMS

Ministry	Pastoral action formally endorsed by the Church which entails quality professional practices which aligns with the vision of Christ.[12]
Mission	Witness and practice, within and beyond the Catholic Church, in contributing to the work of God already present in the world.[13]
New evangelisation	The presentation of the Gospel through language, story, processes, commitments and ardor that advance being Church in the new millennium.[14]
Quantum	In physics, a quantum (plural: quanta) is the minimum amount of any physical entity involved in an interaction.
Quantum field	A theoretical framework for constructing quantum mechanical models. These models are of subatomic particles in particle physics.
Quantum mind	The quantum mind or quantum consciousness is a hypothesis that posits a connection between consciousness, neurobiology and quantum mechanics.
Quantum thinking	A paradigm of thinking that has shifted away from stability, order, uniformity and equilibrium towards a new order of instability, disorder and disequilibrium. It also denotes a new form of thinking that goes to a new level.[15]
Relationships	Interactions between and among individuals and within groups.
Religion	The duty of offering God genuine worship, individually and collectively, without force and in contradiction to personal conscience.[16]
Religiosity	Engagement in religious activities and thinking, personal and communal prayer, and participation in religious rituals integral to a community of faith.[17]
Religious education	Attending to the nature and role of the transcendent through the systematic study of religious traditions inclusive of their history, doctrines and rituals.[18]
Religious education in context	Formal religious instruction; the religious dimension of the overall curriculum; the religious life of the school; and school culture.[19]
Religious educator	One who encounters to varying degrees, formal religious instruction; the religious dimension of the curriculum; the religious traditions of the school; and, culture in relationships, organisational structures and system processes.[20]
Religious life of the school	The expression of religious culture through prayer, sacrament, liturgy, ritual, story and symbol.
Spiritual	The natural dimension to life that includes thinking and feeling about transcendence; human values; love and care for self and others; sense of stewardship for the earth and its flora and fauna; the aesthetic.[21]

12 From McBrien, *Ministry: A Theological Pastoral Handbook*.
13 Stephen Bevans SVD, 2013 in the Keynote Address: Partnering with the Missionary God.
14 From Porteous, J. 2008.
15 Definitions of quantum, quantum mind and quantum field by Chopra, *Quantum Healing*, 1990.
16 *Catechism of the Catholic Church*, paras. 2105 & 2106.
17 From Rossiter, 2015.
18 From Groome, T. 1980.
19 National Catholic Education Commission statement on Religious Education, 2018.
20 From Hall & Sultmann, 2018. *Formation for Mission: A Systems Model for Advancing the Formation of the Religious Educator Within an Australian Context*.
21 From Rossiter, 2015.

GLOSSARY OF TERMS

Spirituality	The consistent application of one's Spirit to the circumstances and relationships of life and living.
System	The overall model and associated sub-systems that underlie complex situations and enable discernment of high from low leverage opportunities.[22]
System of Catholic Education	The organisational entity that operates within the authority of the Church and incorporates the governance, management and services of schools and educational entities.
Teaching as profession	The professional response which carries the expectations of the profession, school and community.
Vocation	Drawn from the Latin word 'vocare' meaning to be called, and involving a commitment to action in keeping with a view of life and living.
Vocation to teach in the Catholic school	A vocation to teach within a Catholic Christian faith context that involves a commitment to the shared moral purpose of the school.[23]
Wave theory	In physics, a wave is an oscillation accompanied by a transfer of energy that travels through medium (space or mass).

---

[22] From Senge, P., 1990 (p. 69).
[23] From Burford, C., 2017. *Leading Self and Leading Communities*.

FOREWORD

Cornerstone: Engaging the Spirit of Christ in the Catholic School is a welcome addition to the growing body of literature on identity, mission and ministry within the Catholic school. It is a reflective, integrative, practical and contemporary work which draws its inspiration from the Letter to the Ephesians on the dignity and status of Christians, "... you are members of the household of God, built upon the foundation of the apostles and prophets, with Christ Jesus himself as the cornerstone" (2: 20-22).

The text's pervasive theme reinforces what should be understood as front-and-centre in the raison d'être of the Catholic school. To this end the author has succinctly summarised its scope:

...the expression of ministry as a spirit-driven force, focused on the kingdom vision of Christ as a spirituality of engagement, serving a prophetic mission, and leadership which holds at its centre a moral purpose. These characteristic 'faces' of the Spirit, are the 'doors' and 'windows' through which the cornerstone (Jesus Christ) is engaged in the Catholic school.

The work is a highly relevant application to the Catholic school of the age old principle crisply and incisively enunciated by Professor Gerald O'Collins SJ "What we *do* with the Church will rest ultimately on what we *think* about Jesus."[24] The particular angle on Jesus in which the writer engages his readers from start to finish, is as "living stones" connected to him as the "cornerstone" of the whole edifice. This connection is again summarised in the author's words:

the text ... is about pointing to or awakening something that is already present, operative in known and unknown ways and always looking like development, communion, joy, hope and forgiveness. It begins with the presumption of good people doing good things and seeks to engage, name, celebrate and enact this Spirit with gratitude, relationships and intentionality in all manner of ways and places.

The text is acknowledged by scholars, leaders, practitioners and theologians. I am particularly drawn to and aligned with the conclusions of Fr Brian Gleeson CP who notes that "Its content and method are so outstanding that it deserves to become a resource for both beginning-teachers and for conscientious seasoned teachers engaged in professional development. It might also find a place in theological schools and training colleges as a text for studies of the foundations of religious education." In this light, personally, professionally and in view of the La Salle Academy's commitment to formation as integral to learning and scholarship, I am delighted and privileged to introduce this significant contribution to colleagues and friends in ministry.

Professor Brother David Hall FMS (Dean, La Salle Academy, ACU)

24 From *What are They Saying About Jesus?* 1977: viii, New York: Paulist Press.

INTRODUCING THE NARRATIVE

Intentions

The view of Sydney from the top of the harbour bridge offers a different perspective from the one experienced on the ground. The 'bridge view' permits an appreciation of the landscape from a wider panorama. Such is the goal of an introduction; to offer a different but complementary perspective without getting into the detail of the overall narrative. In this light, the introduction frames intentions and introduces the parameters for what follows.

Why cornerstone: the fertile question[25]

Manuscripts typically start with a single idea and usually a blank page. For this work, the fundamental starting point, the fertile question, explores what is understood by the statement "Christ is the cornerstone[26] of the Catholic School" (TCS, 1977, para. 33). The blank page represents an opportunity to examine this through the mission and ministry of the living stones who complete the "new temple dedicated to the Lord" (Ephesians 2:19-22).

The metaphor of cornerstone invites the response as to how the life and message of the invisible Jesus is mediated through the visible lives of his followers. The selection of the sub-title: 'Encountering the Spirit of Christ in the Catholic School' introduces the notion that it is through the Spirit of Christ that the community of the Catholic school draws its life and imagination. This is an imagination that seeks to become present and responsive to the Spirit of Christ in ways that are authentic, comprehensive, personal and practical.[27]

At our best

The text invites reflection, discussion, integration, collaboration and action by the living stones within the Catholic school. While service describes the characteristic focus of mission for all educators; the prism of this service is through the Spirit of Christ.[28] The text elaborates that the community of the Catholic school is therefore 'at our best,'[29] when it knows and integrates the Christ story as a basis for meaning and purpose; when it engages his Spirit present in self, others, and creation; when it values, manifests and models mission in accord with the Gospel;

---

[25] From Harpaz (2005): a fertile question is 'open, supports assumptions, rich, connected, charged and practical.'
[26] Cornerstone is a metaphor used interchangeably with foundation stone. It holds preference because it implies not only a base for the new building, but is able to shape and direct the placement of other stones.
[27] Christ is the cornerstone of the educational experience within all faith-based schools centred in the Christian tradition.
[28] The concept of prism is drawn from a keynote address by Dr Paul Sharkey at the Catholic Leadership International Symposium, Melbourne, 2017.
[29] The phrase 'at our best' is drawn from the writing on educational leadership by Don Willower as introduced by Charles Burford when developing the concept of 'shared moral purpose' within the Catholic school, 2017.

when leadership is a sign and instrument of Christian discipleship; and, when ministry integrates these dimensions and finds expression in the multitude of situations within and beyond the Catholic school.

Encounters are the occasions where the Spirit of Christ can be awakened in the formal and informal, the ordinary and the extraordinary, the infrequent and the every-day experiences of the Catholic school. They constitute the places where the personal, relational, professional, and communal elements of the Catholic school can be enlivened by the Spirit. They are the experiences that are impossible to predict or plan. They are manifested by being spiritually awake, offering welcome and trust, and engaging people, situations and opportunities through openness, reflection, empathy and capability. These encounters for personal and professional development are not to imply inadequacy within the individual, group or community. Rather, "Capacity and adequacy are already present and are foundational to the nature of service to which all are called."[30] Individuals and communities are graced and gifted and so engage the experience of service as whole people who already contribute to a developing and flourishing humanity. The on-going process is therefore one of deepening and expanding pathways and horizons in the mystery and opportunity that faith offers.

Why now?

The once trusted and traditional institutions of banking, politics, sport, the arts and the Church are now publicly regarded as less trustworthy and more open to scrutiny. The impact on the person and community is evident in a loss of hope and confidence. This is compounded by the absence of a foundational compass point to offer security and direction within what is a chaordic world, a place of needing to bring order from chaos.[31] Within Australia, the place of religion is argued to be no different. The community echoes a cacophony of multiple and often discordant voices whereby the challenge to re-imagine and reclaim identity within the context of faith becomes highlighted.[32]

The invitation to encounter Christ is to engage a Christian response to life and living. It is to find new life through a coherent and integrated perspective informed by Christ who brings together perfectly the dimensions of the divine and the human. It is a process that is Paschal in its rhythm to life for it calls for naming 'what deaths,' 'what resurrections,' and 'what life' might be engaged in the everyday.[33]

---

30 The concept of adequacy for mission was discussed by Dr Doug Ashleigh in the open forum within the Catholic Leadership International Symposium, Melbourne, 2017.
31 Chaordic is a term used by Dee Hock to describe the contemporary age.
32 Archbishop Mark Coleridge, *Catholic Mission and Identity Symposium*, October 26, 2017.
33 Ronald Rolheiser OMI in the Audio series: *Against an Infinite Horizon: The Finger of God in Our Everyday Lives*. 1995.

It is awakening a consciousness which contributes to a 'new world' in ways that give meaning and purpose to a challenging reality. It is to function with integrity based on the Gospel of Christ.[34]

The question posed by 'the rich young man'[35] to Jesus (Matthew 19:16-30) is not dissimilar to the question that an educator might ask at some point. The response to the contemporary question is the same as the response of Jesus. The invitation to encounter the Christian life is the opportunity for personal and community growth. This is the 'kingdom,' the life to the full as Jesus describes it "I came that they may have life, and have it abundantly" (John 10:10). It is the means for happiness and completeness "I have said these things to you so that my joy may be in you, and that your joy may be complete" (John 15:11). It is the development of a meaning system and a personal relationship with Christ in ways that are life-giving, life-wide, life-long and life-enabling. It is an invitation to know more, experience more, give more, and so be more.

For whom?

The text is primarily for graduate students' intent on education, research and formation within the tradition of the Church and the philosophy of the Catholic school. The material is relevant also to those who serve within, support, and govern the Catholic school and wish to pursue a deeper interest in its foundations and practices. In addition, the content has significance for all faith-based schools who proclaim a philosophy centred on the Gospel of Christ.

Pope Francis confirms the Gospel is for the baptised and unbaptised, for all who would engage the living Spirit of Christ. "The joy of the Gospel is for all people: no one can be excluded." This is the attitude of a Church that desires inclusiveness, a place where no one defines the boundaries of God's mercy and where the people of God are seen as the primary source of a missionary impulse (EG, para. 119).[36]

The next lane

As I began to piece together the ideas for this work, I soon realised that the sources being drawn upon would be familiar to many educators, particularly those who had been in the service of Catholic Education for some years. Nonetheless, I persisted, if for no other reason than my own search for meaning and for some integration of the literature with the experience of life.

---

34 The concept of integrity: to observe, obey and integrate in order to 'bridge the gap' was highlighted by Archbishop Mark Coleridge in a video address to Principals when commenting on the essence of Leadership and Governance, 2018.
35 The economic status of the person asking the question (Matthew 19:16-30) is not specifically identified although the story is conversationally shared as one involving a 'rich young man'.
36 Drawing from the reflections of St. John of the Cross (1542-1591), a Spanish mystic and Roman Catholic saint, Ronald Rolheiser (2014) speaks of three stages to Christian discipleship: the essential, getting one's life together; the mature, through generating life for others; and the radical, giving life away in and towards one's death and final years.

Mindful of this goal, I was conscious of who 'might be in the next lane' and the wealth of personal experience and perspective that each draws upon.

I have a friend, an outstanding athlete who, on medical advice, recently transferred his exercise regimen from the road to the pool. I can still hear Ron's recollection of that first day when his swimming coach invited him to "Show us what you've got." The circumstances were truly moving because in the adjacent lane were swimmers of legendary status; none other than Kieran Perkins, double Olympic champion and world record holder, training with Hayley Lewis, Commonwealth champion and world record holder in freestyle distance swimming. Hence, as this text begins I feel a bit like Ron in that the material, however personal, professional and limited, stands alongside the volume of the inspirational works of the Church and the reflections of multiple commentators, members and supporters.

Text parameters

Sacred scripture, Vatican II, and the Bishops of Oceania signal insights and challenges into what service and encounter might look like within the Catholic school. In particular, the Synod of Bishops special assembly in Oceania in 1997 drew attention to engaging the world through manifesting the Spirit of Christ by "walking his way, telling his truth, and living his life" (John 14:6). It is out of this paradigm that *Cornerstone: Encountering the Spirit of Christ in the Catholic School* has been framed.

Chapter framework

The text comprises six chapters. Knowing his story: Foundations in faith; Walking his way: A Spirituality of engagement; Telling his truth: The prophetic mission of the Catholic school; Living his life: Leadership as Christian praxis; and, One garment: Ministry as integration. The final chapter, To experience is to know: Open the window and let in the world, reinforces the challenge to engage the Spirit within and beyond the school community.

Each chapter is introduced with 'a reflection', 'at a glance,' a focusing story, and questions which build an awareness from lived experience. Themes and main ideas are subsequently developed and integrated through an executive summary, a short reflection, discussion questions, and activities which echo the content of the chapter.[37]

---

[37] The process of learning: Acquisition, Assimilation and Application correlates with the work of Duncan McNulty, 2016 when presenting 'designing (effective) curricula 101' within Australian Catholic University.

The overall presentation seeks to develop the paradigm of Christ as the cornerstone of the Catholic school by arguing that the school community (living stones) is a place of service where foundations in faith underpin spirituality, mission, and leadership, and where ministry is the basis of the integration of these dynamic and interconnected elements through the action of the Spirit (Figure 1).

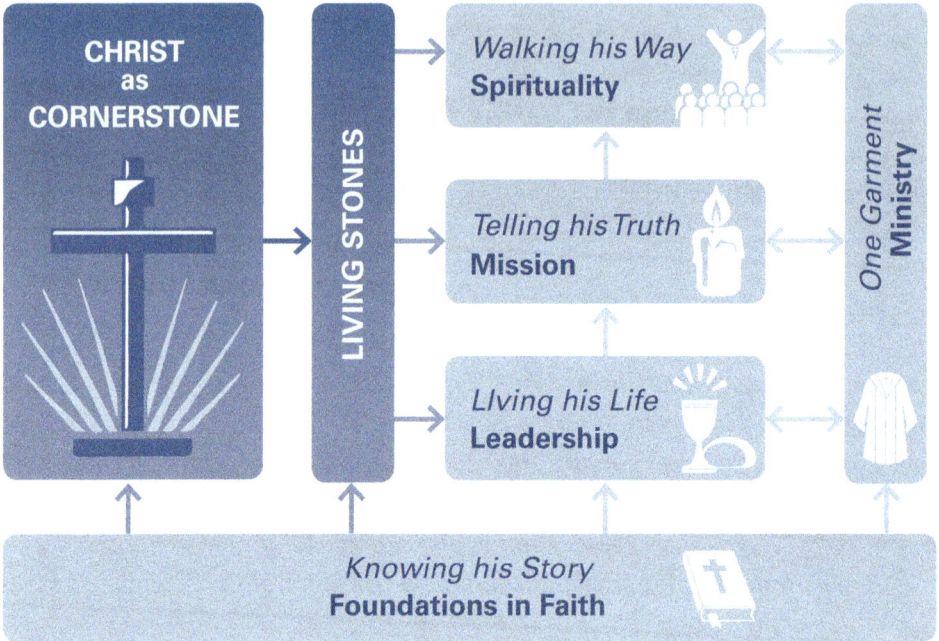

Figure 1. Service as a dynamic and interconnected process

A personal journey ———

A key assumption of the text is that ministry in the Catholic school is manifested within a diverse community where relationship and dialogue mirror respect and openness. Encounters in this context do not presume baptism into a Christian community nor the practice of a Catholic faith tradition. Rather, encounters arise from enacting the school's moral purpose. They provide for continuing formation as knowledge is shared, experiences are engaged, and outcomes of a transformative kind become evident (Figure 2).[38]

---

[38] The importance of formation for understanding and nurturing belief is evident in the Prime Minister John Howard statement "If you don't believe you can't persuade" taken from D. Furse (Ed.) *Howard: The art of persuasion.*

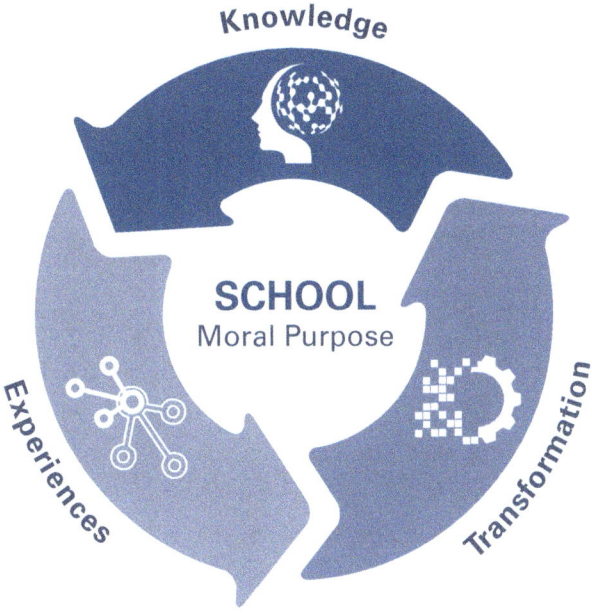

Figure 2. Encounter as formation

A challenging remark about the precedence of personal perspectives came from my daughter Clare. While the comments were offered in casual conversation, they underlined what is fundamental to the educative process. She simply said "So dad, who really cares about what you are thinking, writing and offering? Haven't you got the message that people have their own ideas and experience, may not be really interested, and will follow their own instincts?" In this light, the presentation of ideas is not a goal in itself but a means for inviting reflection and dialogue in ways that connect with experience. The text does not set out 'to convert' but to acknowledge that reflection, wisdom and change arises through the work of the Spirit in forms that balance theory with practice and in ways that are deeply personal, largely unknown and with outcomes often beyond expectations.

Distinguishing features

Commentary on the mission, life and culture of the Catholic school is voluminous and inspirational. In this context, the question as to how this text might be different, and by implication be of some value, can and should be asked. The response ultimately rests with the 'end user' although the intention of the work is to offer particular points of emphasis. Essentially, the text seeks to expand on professional practice as shaped by a Catholic Christian foundations; explore this meaning system through spirituality, mission and leadership; and, promote ministry that integrates professional practices and is supported through formation of generic capabilities.

Beginning with the 'end in mind'

Practitioner scholars speak of beginning any project, essay, or intention by 'keeping the end in mind.' This is the basis for planning, aligning and integrating a sequence of reflections leading to desired outcomes. The end in mind simply represents those 'end points' of most significance.

The summary of Christ's teaching in the Beatitudes represent 'the end in mind' in matters of engaging the Spirit of Christ in the Catholic school. They are the magna carta of what constitutes living discipleship. They are the far goals of human flourishing when aligned with the cornerstone of Christ.

> *Blessed are the poor in Spirit, for theirs is the kingdom of heaven.*
>
> *Blessed are those who mourn, for they will be comforted.*
>
> *Blessed are the meek, for they will inherit the earth.*
>
> *Blessed are those who hunger and thirst for righteousness, for they will be filled.*
>
> *Blessed are the merciful, for they will receive mercy.*
>
> *Blessed are the pure in heart, for they will see God.*
>
> *Blessed are the peacemakers, for they will be called children of God.*
>
> *Blessed are those who are persecuted for righteousness' sake, for theirs is the kingdom of heaven.*
>
> *Blessed are you when people revile you and persecute you and utter all kinds of evil against you falsely on my account.*
>
> *Rejoice and be glad, for your reward is great in heaven, for in the same way they persecuted the prophets who were before you* (Matthew 5:1-12).

An extended meditation by Pope Francis (2018) begins with the significance of the Beatitudes as the basis of discipleship. The series of homilies speak to the nature of existence and the priority of the Spirit over the material. The path of 'happiness' is explored through narration of experiences lived and celebrated in accord with the message of Christ. This is the path that "We too can travel with the grace that Jesus gives us" (Francis, 2018, p. 2). It is 'the Christians identity card' (GEE, para. 63), the expression of encountering and responding to the Spirit of Christ in the Catholic school.

CHAPTER ONE
Knowing his Story: Foundations in faith

Chapter Outline

INTRODUCTION	9
Reflection	9
At a glance	9
Focusing story: "Getting one's top button done up"	10
From your experience	10
THEMES AND MAIN IDEAS	10
Graced and gifted	10
Meaning and purpose	11
Identity and identity	12
Identity in God and systems of belief	13
Journeying in faith	15
Revelation of God	17
Judeo-Christian tradition	17
Revelation of God in Christ	18
Teacher of divine wisdom	19
Kingdom vision	21
Kingdom living	23
Spirit of Trinity	25
Vatican II	28
Context and signposts	28
Compass for the new millennium	29
Impact of the Council	30
Church today	32
Social and cultural context	32
Religious context	34
Catholic school: Christ as cornerstone	37
INTEGRATION	41
Executive Summary	41
Reflection: "Whom are they talkng to Sister?"	41
Questions	41
Activities	42

CHAPTER ONE
Knowing his Story: Foundations in faith[39]

INTRODUCTION

Reflection

"The theme chosen for the Special Assembly for Oceania was: *Jesus Christ and the Peoples of Oceania, Walking His Way, Telling His Truth, Living His Life.* The theme is inspired by the words of John's Gospel where Jesus refers to himself as *the Way, the Truth and the Life* (John, 14:6), and it recalls the invitation which he extends to all the peoples of Oceania: they are invited to meet him, to believe in him, and to proclaim him as the Lord of all. It also reminds the Church in Oceania that she gathers together as the People of God journeying on pilgrimage to the Father. Through the Holy Spirit, the Father calls believers - individually and in community - to walk the way that Jesus walked, to tell all nations the truth that Jesus revealed, to live fully the life that Jesus lived" (EO, para. 8).

At a glance

Knowing his story, exploring and relating to the person and message of Jesus is foundational to the mission, life and culture of the Catholic school. The story of Christ provides the vision, the ground for being and doing for individuals and the community in relationship with God, each other and all creation.

Foundations in faith incorporate a disposition to life as gift; faith as a natural search for meaning; identify Christ as the perfect revelation of God; and Christian life as an encounter and commitment into a 'way of life' which connects with God and with God's creation. The chapter identifies God's very being as truth and love and Jesus as the embodiment of divine wisdom. Drawing from Scripture and the Second Vatican Council, emphasis is given to the kingdom proclaimed by Christ and expressed within the vision and mission of the Catholic school.

---

[39] The common understanding of what is believed within the Catholic Christian tradition (CCC, para. 185).

Focusing story: "Getting one's top button done up"

A clerical friend,[40] famous for his 'one-liners,' would often ask about "one's top button being done up?" While the image of putting on an article of clothing and ensuring the buttons correspond with their respective button holes is familiar to many, the application of the image in this instance related to the extent that a person had developed an image of God. Getting the top button in place, establishing one's image of God, was considered important to engaging in formal ministry.

The invitation to explore an image of God more fully, 'getting the top button done up' is not an attempt to achieve a final or absolute position on the nature of God, but it is a challenge to reflect on Christ in relationship to ministry. In summary terms it is the process of considering 'work' and the workplace of the Catholic school from the perspective of faith, and seeking to know, feel and behave in ways that mirror what is commonly believed. It is carrying out a role that is reflective and being open to a progressive awakening that connects life with the presence of the Spirit. It is the process of establishing the background and foreground of life in the Spirit that empowers the 'living stones' to become more than stones.

From your experience

1. How natural is it to reflect upon the source of meaning and purpose in life?
2. How do you see the significance of Christ to what God desires for God's creation?
3. How might a relationship with Christ present itself?

THEMES AND MAIN IDEAS

Graced and gifted

How often do we consider just how lucky we are? We're not talking here of luck based on winning the lotto, or having a good day at the races, but rather the good fortune of just being alive. Tony Robbins, the renowned social analyst and commentator on personal effectiveness talks of people who are never fully happy. For some, he says, it is always a matter of "my next million, my third car, a beach house, the ultimate promotion, a new business venture." In other words, what one has is never enough.

---

40 Reference is made to Reverend Jeff Scully, now deceased, who was 'gift' to many.

However, for others, just being alive, waking up and being given another day is an absolute bonus; one for thanksgiving and reverence as the experience of life in whatever form is welcomed. This is seeing the richness of life as gift and living out this appreciation with a mentality of abundance.

Personal experience often reinforces how precious the gift of life is. On a customary walk to a McDonald's restaurant in Kings Cross, Sydney, adjacent to where my wife, daughter and I were living at the time, I experienced three powerful reminders of life as gift in a period of no greater than forty minutes. On the way to the restaurant I was explicitly invited by a member of the oldest profession to become a client. It was apparent that she was old before her time, despondent and desperate, indicative of a life that was unfolding on the streets. Having arrived at McDonald's and regaining some composure, I began my coffee and pancakes. It was not long before a woman next to me asked for a few gold coins for a cup of coffee. I passed them to her only to discover that 'she' was a 'he.' Not believing these two happenings could be topped, as I made my way to the door, an inebriated person arrived to beckon someone inside. While brandishing a knife, a weapon Crocodile Dundee would have been proud of, he made everyone aware of his intentions towards one of the customers "Come out here you !@#$% and I will slit your !@#$% throat."

Meaning and purpose

The 'big' questions: Who am I? Where have I come from? What must I do? With whom do I share the journey? Where am I going? What can I hope for? - dispose all to a process of reflection on life and one's place within it. Humans are blessed with the capacity to stand back and look upon themselves, as if in a mirror, and so stretch their knowledge, satisfy their need for identity and provide a sense of meaning about self. This ability and desire to seek and find answers is not restricted to a religious search but is argued to be an essential and non-negotiable part of human nature.[41]

The search to inquire into one's deepest self and place in creation is a quest for meaning that is integral to the completeness of self, to becoming whole. As a natural search, it is integral to being authentically human. The questions that emerge are focused on whether there is something or some other that is responsible for life, what might be the nature and extent of this being, and what models exist to provide some guidance? It is a process of being religious, looking to the deeper purpose in life and asking questions as to the place of self and one's relationship with the Creator.

---

41 It is said to be part of our DNA (Bishop Michael Putney, 2010).

> *Religiosity, in its broadest sense, is a quest for meaning ... to know, understand and experience fullness as part of the completeness of self ... the task of those involved in religious formation is to facilitate the recognition of something already present, rather than attaching or integrating a religious consciousness that is external or extra* (Maria Clara Lucchetti-Bingemer, 2001).[42]

The role of faith and reason in exploring meaning is a topic that holds much controversy along with "much ignorance, prejudice and plain hostility" (Ormerod, 2010, p. 2). While the debate can be attributable to notable works such as *The God Delusion* and the optional role of religion articulated in *A Secular Age*, there exists a growing disillusionment with formal religion and is characterised as "A new secularism thrashes tradition" (Kelly, 2017). The argument is made that Christianity and accompanying personal and social communities are under threat, being eroded by an 'array of forces; the march of secularism and the rise of a progressive alternative morality.' The conclusions of Kelly are that society is in a state of confusion and what it means to be virtuous is now conflicted and different across the workplace, church and community. The implication is that the search for meaning will inevitably be more necessary, more demanding and more complex. Nonetheless, the search presents as 'not going away' with the challenge to explore, confirm and live one's identity in the context of a diversity of approaches and within an overall changing context.

Identity and identity

Identity is a common term used in Catholic schools. It is often heard in association with mission, ethos, tradition and culture and is also applied to roles within social groups. One's activities as a leader, administrator, teacher, or school officer for instance are described in terms of identity. As well, in the wider social arena it is commonplace to talk of one's identity as child, spouse, partner, father, mother, friend, coach and so on. In this light it is conceivable to have multiple identities. However, for the Christian, one's deepest identity is who one is in relation to God and God's revelation. True identity therefore blossoms from deep within; the other multiple and socially accorded identities are the roles played in life.

Pierre Teilhard de Chardin SJ comments on the core of Christian identity as that we are not human beings having a spiritual experience, but spiritual beings having a human experience.[43] For Teilhard, one's core identity lies in the spiritual dimension of self.

---

42 Keynote address provided a discussion of religious consciousness as integral to the makeup of humankind. The position presented was that religious education should build on the basic religious inquiry already present in humankind.
43 Pierre Teilhard de Chardin SJ was a French philosopher and Jesuit priest who trained as a paleontologist and geologist and took part in the discovery of Peking Man.

While individuals possess multiple identities within life; mother, son, teacher, husband; one's core identity rests in being made in the image and likeness of God. Notwithstanding the significance of the Spirit of God manifested in self; it is in and through the multiple identities within life that God can be experienced. In the words of Marianne Williamson (2004, CD), one's core of identity, the capital I, is "I am as God created me ... know who you are and why you came ... we are the children of God ... I am mind, love and Spirit and that lasts forever ... this is the path home; the memory we have when we wake up from our sleep and remember who we are in God." The argument is made that what is most crucial to a life of fulfilment is the activation of interiority where the spiritual self is found, in contrast to unreflective living which gives primary attention to the needs of the ego and the avoidance of the now.[44]

An understanding of identity can be evident in the language of conversation. For instance, in the context of disappointment with a job application, a mentor was reported to have said to the unsuccessful applicant "Well, are you physically injured in any way?" 'No' was the reply; and then the further comment came "It's only your ego that is hurt; remember that you have a deeper identity than what your 'job' suggests." A similar appreciation of identity is given by Wayne Dyer from his early days of writing. Interested in 'how he was being perceived by the public,' he would ask his wife about the progress of his book on the 'best seller list.' The response was, "Wayne you are not on the best seller list, your book is."

Identity in God and systems of belief

The nature of one's deepest identity in God and the systems of belief which characterise this relationship have been synthesised into three basic positions: indifference to God; acknowledgment of God and religious practice; and, a trusting abandonment to God (Rohr, 1992). These ways of thinking, feeling and behaving in relationship to God are not necessarily independent, predictable or sequential as each is impacted by a host of personal, social, educational and community influences that shape human maturation.

An indifferent view about one's identity in God entails neither a positive nor negative approach to the existence and a relationship with God. In this view, the response of the individual to life is orientated to the self and the importance of self-reliance. 'Good times' would be regarded as emanating from hard work or simply good fortune, and 'bad times' a consequence of some lack of prediction and expectation. Life would essentially be seen as a series of experiences calling for personal intervention and planning.

---

44 The conclusions of the social psychologist, Martin Seligman (2007), affirm the significance of factors other than the material for personal happiness. In Seligman's view, meaning and service are more critical than possessions, prestige and power. Similarly, Tolle (2004; 2005; 2006), discusses the foundation to happiness residing in one's essence or stillness.

It would entail living life as if God did not exist, being reliant totally on self and others, aggregating possessions, and building relationships as a basis of security, connection, personal advancement and communal obligation.

A second perspective on one's identity in God entails a level of acceptance that God exists and hence some form of religious observance is relevant. This may arise from a need to recognise the 'bigger picture,' to give thanks, or even to prepare oneself for the spiritual journey and life hereafter. Religious observances would be important and potentially directed to ensure one's personal situation is secure. It is an attitude that when 'the chips are down,' personal struggle and self-reliance need to be forthcoming and that reliance on God's abundance in covering all contingencies is more the ideal than the real. This second position for the Christian entails recognition of God and God's revelation in Christ, while falling short of accepting God into the very fabric of one's personal and communal existence.

A third perspective on personal identity in relationship to God views one's life as a gift from God and perceives all that happens as a bonus. With this mindset, very little can disappoint, as life itself has been the 'lottery prize,' and all that constitutes life is merely a further manifestation of this gift within a universe that is held together by a benevolent God. It is a belief system centred on trust, experience and hope. It manifests itself in being ready to surrender and discern life's events, rather than planning and controlling the present or the perceived future. The consequences of this 'letting go' are evident in a lack of anxiety about life, in peacefulness and genuine happiness, and pursuing religious observance as a means for engagement with God.

The fullness of spiritual identity is found in this third position: the acceptance of a benevolent universe under the authority of a gracious God. This system of belief allows one's personal identity to be shaped by God's graciousness and one's giftedness to be seen as a mirror of this goodness. Instead of defining one's self in terms of physical appearance, wealth, status, occupation or personal ability, one can lay claim to being a child of God on a journey with God and ultimately to a place of full union with God. Religion is the process of deepening this belief and spirituality as a means for activating it. It involves a journey towards a conscious and subconscious realisation that God will suffice, that all will be well, as one is loved into being and loved into growth (Rohr, 1992).

A view that life is a gift from God, and that within life the individual moves towards a greater good is one that Christian tradition holds as foundational.[45]

---

[45] *The Catechism of the Catholic Church* (para. 313) identifies the scriptural justification for this position, while Article 1, paras. 51-53, introduce God's plan of loving goodness.

This view reflects a belief about God's graciousness and the presence and action of the Holy Spirit as a life-giving force at the heart of human life. This is grace, the constant outpouring of God's unconditional love. It means that we are receivers before we are givers, and, despite our imperfections, we are a gift from God, totally loved by the Creator who journeys with us. It invites keeping in perspective the needs of the ego and looking with the eyes of faith at the unfolding experiences that life provides. The giftedness of life offers the opportunity to celebrate this gift and to value challenges as opportunities for reflection and new learning in the Spirit.

Journeying in faith

Journeying in faith is not something that is linear, ordered or predictable. Rather, the journey of faith is most likely chaotic. It stops and starts, resigns and re-joins, changes with age and speeds up and slows down. It is a life-long journey, rather than a conducted tour. It is a journey that all make, and one that needs and deserves support through the models that might be imitated and the messages that are integrated. Central to journeying in faith is support at appropriate developmental stages, with continued learning and re-learning as maturation unfolds. These perspectives become apparent at different stages of life's journey and are considered never fully completed.

There are at least three stages in the journey of faith for the journeying Christian. While these are presented sequentially, they are also interactive and cumulative. The stages entail a pattern of movement from a 'simple consciousness' of the faith story to a stage where it is examined in more depth, 'complex consciousness,' to a final level of 'enlightenment' (Rohr, 1992). The process of faith development involves a progressive deepening of faith at each stage until everything can be held in balance and life and relationship to the Creator is understood as being 'okay.' This is a place where anxiety is replaced by trust, fear by hope; a place where the love of God can be seen and shared, where the cardinal virtues of faith, hope and charity are both means and endpoints to a holistic Christian life (Figure 3).

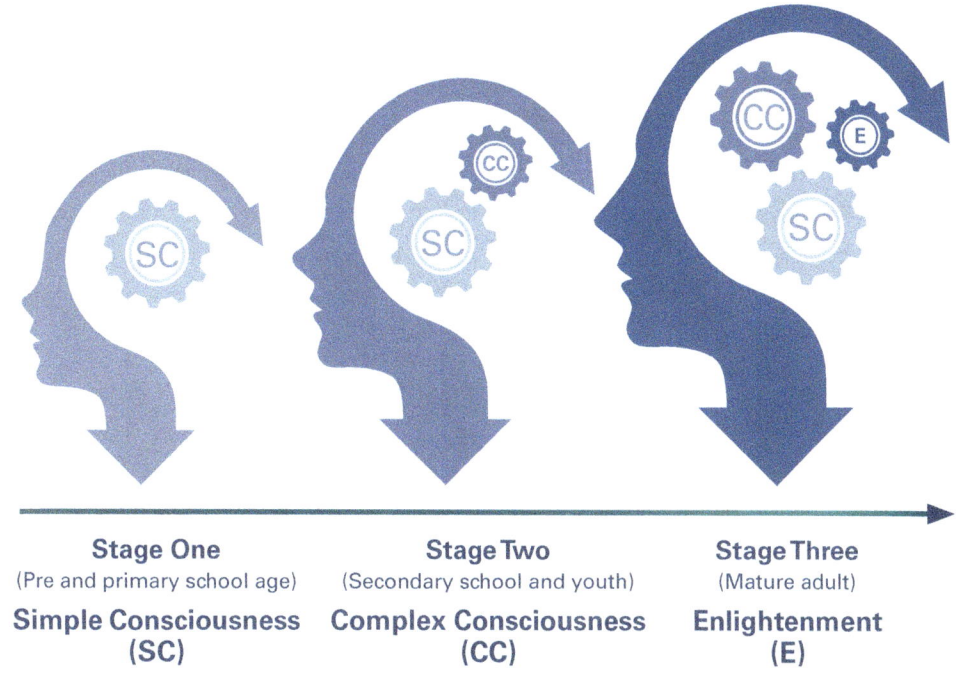

Figure 3. Stages of faith development

The concept that faith development unfolds in stages suggests that its content and educative processes can be understood, planned and supported. For example, growth in simple consciousness occurs when the breadth and simplicity of the faith story is shared at home and in the early and primary years of school or associated parish catechesis. The secondary school or parish youth involvement become significant in the exploration and development of this story when students engage their complex consciousness and personally interrogate the belief system they have come to know.

As well, contemplative space and time also need to be available so that the growth in knowledge and understanding can move out of the head and into the heart; leading to a growth in relationship with all that is. Significantly, faith formation is not over when adolescents leave school as further growth can arise through a multitude of youth and adult education and prayer experiences.[46] Central to the journey is the continuing examination of God's revelation, the centrality of Jesus and the capacity and intention of a faith community to keep this message relevant and supported.

---

46 Dr David Tacey, *Mind the Gap: Youth Spirituality and Formal Religion*, Catholic Education Magazine, November, 2001, provides a thoughtful discussion on the spirituality of the young and formal religion. His argument is that spirituality is flourishing and yet its interface with formal religious observance is still to be developed.

Revelation of God

Judeo-Christian tradition

The Catechism of the Catholic Church (CCC, para. 42) states that an understanding of God is restricted by reason and the ability to communicate a Mystery that involves "The inexpressible, the incomprehensible, the invisible, and the ungraspable." However, within the limits of human understanding, Christians believe that God has been revealed throughout history, particularly in the story of the Jewish people and fundamentally in the person and message of Jesus.

God's very first command is recorded in the Judaic Scriptures as "Be fruitful and multiply, and fill the earth and subdue it, and have dominion over the fish of the sea and over the birds of the air, and over every living thing that moves upon the earth" (Genesis 1:28). This revelation highlights the gift and challenge given to the Israelites as they journeyed and committed progressively to a covenant relationship with their one true God.

Jewish belief presents the image of God as the transcendent being and the One who is everywhere, immanent. This understanding images God as an unimaginable being who is totally beyond and independent of reality, while also advancing that God can be observed in the beauty and expanse of creation. In this light, a balanced view is needed as the adoption of only one perspective on God would be to lose sight of the whole. For instance, the image of God as the transcendent other can lead to an image of God as distant and aloof, and, as such, contribute to thinking that God is "Out there, watching over, looking down on us" (Morwood, 1997, p. 10). Alternatively, the view of God as immanent also possesses limitations as it views God as being so tied up with creation as to restrict God's reality to that of creation only.

An image of God that is more holistic can be observed in the John O'Donohue presentation on the '*Divine Imagination*' (1997). Here, an integrated perspective is advocated so that the transcendent is always present, with the responsibility being left to individuals to pursue a deepening of an already existing connection. The challenge becomes the acceptance of God's continuing presence and contemplation of God beyond this relationship. Such a position reflects a tradition within the Catholic Church, one that is founded on God as Mystery "The ultimate participant, dynamic in movement, participation and relationship" (Richard Rohr, CD, 2017).

> *What if we were to view God and creation not as two orders but simply as a conceptual order of being that is thoroughly interrelated? Could we think of God as divine, uncreated implicate order of being, the endless depth, movement, process and relatedness*

> *of being? ... We could conceive of God and creation as interrelated divine and creative energies. Could we not think of God not as other to the world but as the inner dynamic of the world, that is the world within God?* (Ilia Delio, 2011, p. 33).

Christian Scriptures identify God as love (1 John 4:8) and it is out of God's love that humankind has come to an understanding that "God's very being is truth and love" (CCC, para. 231). Through love, God freely and reciprocally interrelates with all creatures in a manner that respects their dignity, their core identity.

In this way, all are related to one another, and the divine presence can be seen in all things (CCC, para. 41). The significance of this belief is evidenced in the Letter of Saint John "God is love, and those who abide in love abide in God, and God abides in them" (1 John 4:16). Love is inscribed in the human heart. Humankind is challenged to recognise and attend to the Spirit of God in life, so that life is infused with love, and living is disposed to all that is holy.

> *The entire activity of the Church is an expression of a love that seeks the integral good of humankind: it seeks evangelisation through Word and Sacrament, an undertaking that is often heroic in the way it is acted out in history; and it seeks to promote humankind in the various arenas of life and human activity. Love is therefore the service that the Church carries out in order to attend constantly to humankind's sufferings and needs, including material needs* (DCE, para. 19).

Revelation of God in Christ

Christian Scripture interprets Jesus as the full embodiment and incarnation of divine wisdom. Jesus is identified as the 'power and wisdom of God' (1 Corinthians 1:23), the perfect revelation of the Father, God in human form (Colossians 1:15-29). Jesus is the ultimate disclosure of God in human history, and it is in his life that Christians come to believe in and understand the essence of what it means to be authentically human in relationship to God.

> *Christ is both the mediator and perfect realisation of this mystery: He is Priest, Prophet, Alpha and Omega. It is in him, above all, that God deals with 'people'[47] as his friends, having spoken to them on many different occasions and in many ways. He is the Word of God through whom all things are created; in his incarnation, the whole of humanity is called to peace, to intimate communion with God in a bond of universal love which embraces all creatures* (Australian Episcopal Conference, 1970, para. 5).

---

47 The original quotation uses the term 'men'. As appropriate 'men' has been replaced by 'people'.

Christ is presented as Saviour and Lord (Acts 16:30-31), the hope for life and eternity (Romans 10:8) and the one in whom strength is found through the action of the Spirit (1 Peter 1:5). As with the woman at the well (John 4:10-14) it is Christ who offers the world a new form of life-giving 'water,' a form of spiritual sustenance that is at the core of human life and lasts forever. It is his imagination that provides vision and it is his invitation to proclaim and share his story (Matthew 28:19) that shapes mission and ministry.

In short, "the Church was founded to spread the Kingdom of Christ over all the earth" (AA, para. 2) and it is in Christ that the Church's apostolate draws inspiration, the fruitfulness of which depends on the relationship that people have with Christ (AA, para. 4).

> *Incarnation should be the primary and compelling message of Christianity. Through the Christ (en Christo), the seeming gap between God and everything else has been overcome "from the beginning" (Ephesians 1:4, 9). Incarnation refers to the synthesis of matter and Spirit. Without some form of incarnation, God remains essentially separate from us and from all of creation. Without incarnation, it is not an enchanted universe, but somehow an empty one* (Richard Rohr, meditation, 2018).

The centrality of Christ to the maturing Christian is described in the invitation by the author of Hebrews "Let us keep our eyes fixed on Jesus, on whom our faith depends from beginning to end" (12:2). Moreover "In many and various ways God spoke of old to our ancestors by the prophets; but in these last days he has spoken to us by a Son ... He reflects the glory of God and bears the very stamp of his nature" (Hebrews 1:1-3). Writing some decades later than Paul, the author of John's Gospel also records the centrality of Christ in the dialogue between Jesus and Philip "Have I been with you all this time, Philip, and you still do not know me? Whoever has seen me has seen the Father" (John 14:9-10).

> *Following Christ and united with him, Christians can strive to be imitators of God as beloved children, and walk in love by conforming their thoughts, words and actions to the mind... which is yours in Christ Jesus, and following his example* (CCC, para. 1694).

Teacher of divine wisdom

Conventional wisdom is that which people know to be correct, whereas divine wisdom offers a 'narrow way' (Matthew 7:13-14), one that 'leads to life.' This 'way' is captured in the Scriptures through a weaving together of short sayings (aphorisms) and stories (parables). The sayings and stories evoke the imagination and invite the reader into a place and time where interpretation and transformation become possible. It is in the actions and words of Christ that the divine response to a host of human situations can be observed. It is in the interpretation of these responses that the followers of Christ draw insight as to beliefs and behaviours that are congruent with the Gospel.

> *This call to follow Christ establishes Christian life as not "A religion of the book: Christianity is a religion of the Word of God, not of a written and mute word, but of the incarnate and living Word," one to be "Proclaimed, heard, read, received and experienced as the word of God* (VD, para. 7).

The life and teaching of Jesus reflect the nature and circumstances of his time. Christian Scripture, therefore, is to be interpreted within this context and said to include three discrete phases; three lenses on the literal word: the original social and cultural milieu of Jewish culture within which Jesus was immersed; the Apostolic tradition in which eyewitnesses continued to teach and reflect upon his life; and through the continuing reflection of the body of believers throughout the ages (Brown, 1986). The full revelation of Jesus is therefore drawn from what the immediate, subsequent and on-going communities were able to discern as they looked back in the Spirit to what was taught and written. Maher, (2017a) draws similar conclusions about text interpretation (hermeneutics) and speaks of the triad of interpretation: the intention of the author; the actual content of the text; and, the experiences and pre-suppositions of the receiver. Whatever the approach that might be applied to the Scripture, the means by which the final text has come down in history reflects several layers of interpretation which entail at least the original teaching, the remembered teaching, the interpreted teaching, and the final teaching in the recorded text.[48]

The images that Jesus applied to awaken human consciousness drew from his lived experience (Wilkins, 2018) and incorporated the familiar symbols of water, light, shepherd, vine, door, gate, bread and wine. Ultimately, his disclosure to Thomas as being the Way, Truth and Life to the Father confirmed his relationship to the Father and his conviction about his ministry. Through sayings and stories he revealed God as gracious and called followers into a 'way' which connects with God and God's creation. This was the subversive wisdom of Jesus which undermined traditional reliance on family, wealth, honour, purity codes and religiosity for salvation, and offered a new perspective to events and situations in a fashion that reinforces God's wisdom for guiding life.

---

[48] The levels of interpretation are offered by Hugh McGinlay, Editor.

The living centre of faith is Jesus Christ. Only through him can 'people' be saved. It is from him that they receive the foundation and the synthesis of every truth. In him they find a 'key' the centre and destiny of 'people' and of all human history ... the Church must preach Jesus Christ to all 'people' and it must do this in such a way that all Christians adhere to his divine person and to his teaching to the extent that they live the whole of his "mystery" (Australian Episcopal Conference, 1970, para. 57).

In the past, the idea that only through Jesus can people be saved was interpreted as a necessity to become a Christian; often, and more specifically, a Catholic Christian. However, what it really entails is living as Jesus lived and relating as he related, with the entity he called 'Alaha' in Aramaic, with all other human beings and with all else that is.

Kingdom vision

The evangelist Mark records the first words of Jesus as "The time is fulfilled, and the Kingdom of God has come near; repent, and believe in the Good News" (Mark 1:14). Similarly, Luke (4:18) introduces the public ministry of Jesus with the words from Isaiah "The Spirit of the Lord is upon me, because he has anointed me to bring good news to the poor. He has sent me to proclaim release to the captives and recovery of sight to the blind, to let the oppressed go free, to proclaim the year of the Lord's favour." This was the dream of Jesus, a vision of a kingdom in which the presence of God would be reflected in the totality of life.

Jesus announced, lived and inaugurated for history a new social order that is an actual alternative ... and an alternative that he said is inevitable ... by the promise and grace of God. He called it the reign or Kingdom of God. It is the subject of his inaugural address, the majority of his parables and clearly the guiding image of his entire ministry. It was also the reason that he was killed (Richard Rohr, 1996, p. 3).

The central message of Jesus is that God is active in the world, transforming aspects of human existence and bringing about liberation. This liberation enables a sense of self, personal relationships, political and social order, and our relationship to the living God (Edwards, 1987, 1990; Nolan, 1987, 2006). The message of Jesus is a call to have life. The call is to be children of God, to be fellow creators with Jesus in the work of God "So if anyone is in Christ, there is a new creation: everything old has passed away; see, everything has become new" (2 Corinthians 5:17).

The literature and audio presentations of Richard Rohr recount two central themes of the kingdom vision of Jesus. The first involved the role played by God who he addresses as Father; and the need for personal conversion in order that the kingdom become a reality in personal and communal life.

The key figure in the life of Jesus was that of his Father. This central compass point was clear and unquestionable for him. It was a reality, which was not an idea or a theory about anything, but a person, a thoroughly reliable and lovable person. The kingdom preached by Jesus was therefore based on a God who is experienced personally; someone whom Jesus teaches should be imitated, enjoyed and loved. The God of Jesus was the God who loved graciously and lavishly. This is argued to be a love that is creative, redemptive and reconciling, the mark of which is unity in the presence of diversity (Riley, 2009).

The kingdom evoked by Jesus is founded on the fatherhood of God for all; a concrete expression of God's universal love that was not only announced by Jesus but also lived authentically by him. Jesus crossed boundaries in his expression of a social order that would add quality to the life that defined his spiritual and social environment. He challenged contemporaries to look to the totality of life so that the created order could be seen as a gift and promise of God's continuing love and presence in all things. This was something that was achievable, present already in many forms, but not yet fully realised. It was able to be manifested in the lives of individuals and in the varying social, communal and institutional structures that governed and supported community life.

The second core theme of a kingdom vision announced by Jesus was conversion through a process of *metanoia*. Drawn from two Greek terms, *meta* (going above or beyond) and *noia* (incorporating a new mind-set), *metanoia* is a call to go beyond the interests of knowing and relying on self to a relationship and a reliance on God. The process of *metanoia* is the challenge to be born again, to be spiritually converted whereby the power of God is accepted and trusted within the journey of life (Rohr, 2012).

The *metanoia* sought by Jesus called for a complete turnaround of worldviews. Conversion became a process of transformation. It was a transformation that involved "More than occasional observance to the sacred to a level where God begins to penetrate the conscious and subconscious and hence really touches a person deeply and comprehensively" (Rohr, 1996, p. 7). It is said to be a process that is neither superficial nor without effort.

> *Until you've moved to a level of prayer and surrender where God and grace are allowed to invade the subconscious - not just conscious - it really doesn't matter in some ways what your conscious belief systems are. Until you get God into the subconscious where your deep agendas are touched and freed, your formal religion doesn't make a lot of difference ... until you meet a benevolent God and a benevolent universe, until you realise that the foundation of all is love, you will not be at home in this world (Richard Rohr, 1996, p. 117).*

Kingdom living

Matthew (Chapter 13) presents seven parables about how social and cultural processes might be understood and lived in accord with a kingdom vision of life. The Kingdom of God is like the sower who scattered seed on differing places of growth, the influence of the weeds on that which is sown, the growth of the mustard seed, the yeast that enhances life, the treasure and the pearl that are worth striving for, and the net which draws both good and worthless fish. The behaviour of those who pursue this kingdom is also identified (Matthew 5:3-12) as those who are gentle, sorrowful, merciful, hunger for justice, peacemaking and are pure in heart. The kingdom is evidenced by the son who returns home and is welcomed, seen in the feeding of the hungry, the clothing of the naked, the visitation of the sick, and the release of those in bondage. The kingdom is advanced as a place where love and justice prevail and where wholeness, prosperity, physical health and security are desired outcomes.

Jesus used the criterion of quality relationships for measuring the prevalence of the kingdom. Rohr (1996) argues that when a social order allows and encourages, and even mandates, good connection between people and creation, people and events, people and people, people and God, then you have a truly sacred culture: the Reign of God. This would not be a world without pain or mystery, but simply a world where people and creation would be connected and in communion.

> *It is all about union and communion, it seems, which means that it is also about forgiveness, letting go, service and lives of patience and simplicity. Who can doubt that this is the substance of Jesus' teaching? He makes right relationships desirable, possible and the philosopher's stone by which everything else is to be weighed and judged (Richard Rohr, 1996, p. 9).*

The ministry of Jesus reveals the presence of the reign of God, the possibility of being in harmony with the life-force of the universe, in the ordinariness of life, the familiar activities of daily living. It is concerned with the recognition and exercising of Spirit which is continuous, pervasive, dynamic and powerful. "The Gospel is much more a process than a product, a modus operandi more than a structure, a person more than a production. It is a way of being in the world that will always feel like compassion, mercy and spaciousness." (Rohr, 1996, p. 13).

The kingdom is both a desired outcome and a present reality. It is a process of how to go about life and observing the presence of God already in life. It invites a movement from a mind-set that is narrow, self-centred and static to a position that is vast, outwardly focused and dynamic. It is a way of looking at the world and a way of operating in the world. It is not about prescription of what to do, but a description of what life might be like if a kingdom imagination were to be lived out. This is the challenge taken up across the history of the Christian faith and revealed in the Christian living of known and unknown saints. It is centred on God's action in life, the betterment of the whole through the lived expression of love.

For Jesus the Kingdom of God was not an intimate spiritual reality, but a transformation that involved the whole of life and of people. Jesus declared emphatically that the reign of God was for the poor. He was looking at people who lived in humiliation in their villages, defenceless against the powerful landowners, he knew the hunger of those children; he had seen peasants crying in helpless rage (Jose Pagola, 2011, p. 112).

Commentary on the kingdom vision of Jesus, specifically its impact on the cultural and religious context of the first century, suggests that Jesus was far from being a naive idealist who died for a cause with little or no relevance to the circumstances of the world of his time or those of our current age. Rather, Jesus is said to be a clear-eyed person who was able to understand the heart of the human condition and was offering the human race the only possible way of "Breaking out of the endless cycle of hate, domination and greed" (Robinson, 1997, p. 28).

The vision of the kingdom provides the blueprint of what it means to live in accordance with the Spirit of Jesus. Within a Catholic school context, the kingdom dream shapes the purpose, goals, curriculum, processes and educational outcomes that are significant to the community as much as it would direct the behaviour of the individual, group and community. In this way, the school exists to advance the kingdom and is itself a beacon as to what a kingdom community might look like.

The Reign of God is not about churchiness at all. It has everything to do with everything. In fact, as we listen to Jesus, Jesus' images and examples, it appears that it is the world of house and field and job and marriage where we are converted to right relationship. The secular has become the place where we encounter the true sacred. It is the unexciting world of details, diapers and 'women who have lost one dime' (Luke 15:8-10) that appears to offer the teachable moment for Jesus (Richard Rohr, 1996, p. 19-20).

Spirit of Trinity

Living Christ's presence in the world is the experience of interpreting the kingdom vision and operating in the world as if one possessed the 'mind of Christ' (Philippians 2:5). It is becoming awake to the Spirit of Christ through participation, observation and reflection. It is described as 'participatory knowledge' (Rohr, 2004), a level of awareness that presumes connection through being open to the dynamic Spirit of Christ operating within self, others and the world. It is encounter and engagement with the Mystery of God which finds its deepest expression in the relationship of the Father, Son and Spirit; the relationship named as Trinity.

The distinction between 'knowing about' and 'experiencing' the Spirit is developed by Richard Rohr (2004) in his reflection on the theology of Trinity narrated in the text of Catherine LaCugna's work, *God for Us*. While describing the reflection as the 'ultimate presumption,' Rohr stresses that the doctrine of the Trinity is 'paramount and foundational' to the life of the Christian. Trinitarian life, he advances, is central to the expression of love which involves 'perfectly receiving and perfectly giving' the life of the Spirit, a life that is found in relationship, intimacy and communion. It is the flow of the Spirit that moves through creation and hence to "Live a perfectly holy life, the life of a saint, would be to never stop that flow" (Rohr, 2004, CD). In this light, Rohr adds that the flow has very little to do with the person, but rather is the initiative of the Spirit.

The response of Christians to the life of the Trinity is simply to 'receive the love, believe the love, allow the force to come to you and flow out of you'... If God is moving in the world, to blow new life into it, to differentiate it, to renew it, then that is where we are driven. This draws the Christian into works of justice and co-creation, and generates one's direction in life as emanating from surrender, trusting, yielding and allowing (Richard Rohr, 2004, CD).

A discussion of the Trinity through images of triangles, circles, shamrocks; to articulate the unimaginable, is said to "either partially work or they don't work for us at all." Within this challenge, Eric Alleume OMI argues that "the best explanation of the Trinity is to think about two friends who have had a falling out." Living the Trinity can be demonstrated by showing love and compassion in practical and relevant ways. "Buy a packet mix chocolate mud cake, bake your cake and take it over to your friend. When the door opens begin with an apology and say "So I'd love to share this cake with you; if you could make the cup of tea!" That's the Trinity: "love, compassion, reconciliation: the exchange of love through action; all working together! If you just have love, it doesn't have the same effect. Feeling compassion by itself ... won't work either."

Over centuries, lots of metaphors have been used to explain the Trinity. I prefer one that was presented by St John Damascene (also known as St John of Damascus, Syria). John was an 8th century bishop. He suggested that we think "of the Father as a root, the Son as a branch, and the Spirit as a fruit, for the sustenance of these three is one." This is simply stating that God has been revealed to us as Father, the root which sustains life, Jesus (Son), the Word of God who grafts us to that life as branches (cf. "I am the vine; you are the branches," John 15:5), and Spirit, the fruit of God's love in everyone, binding us all together in love (Julian McDonald CFC, 2017).

The response to God as Trinity is observed through right relationships in community. The mystery of the Trinity invites trust in God as Father and Creator; a relationship with Jesus as brother and redeemer; and a personal connection with the Spirit of love and truth that advocates and sustains life. Significant to an appreciation of God as Trinity is the acceptance of the doctrine as a human attempt to explain the unexplainable but nonetheless, an extraordinary offering of how God might be understood in human terms. Notwithstanding the challenges of explaining belief through doctrine, what Catholic teaching presents is that the essence of God, as Trinity, is found in love (DCE); love which is freely given, experienced and shared. This is the participatory knowledge of God to which Richard Rohr refers and about which relationship and reflection provide the appreciation.

Christological catechesis is Trinitarian Catechesis ... Jesus Christ introduces us into the Mystery of God the Father, the Son and the Holy Spirit. Revealing himself as the Messiah and the Son of God he has revealed at the same time the Father and Holy Spirit. The God whom we must recognise and bless is "The Father of Our Lord Jesus Christ"

> *who has chosen us in Christ to be his sons and daughters who in him has given us the Spirit of adoption, the pledge of our inheritance and salvation* (Australian Episcopal Conference, 1970, para. 82).

Living the theology of Trinity is summarised by our relationships with God and with one another; "relationships that are meant to take us on a journey of transformation. We will be transformed as we open our hearts and minds to God's Spirit whose love and hope for the world will be reflected in the love and hope that shine through our living in very ordinary and unassuming ways" (McDonald, 2017). Living the life of the Trinity involves the expression of God's love through The Word of God (Jesus), the life of the Spirit, and the engagement by Christians in everyday life. Just as God's love poured out to those who gathered at Pentecost, so too does God's power come to those who desire to live the 'way' of Jesus in contemporary times.

The National Geographic magazine coverage of the life of Jesus pursues the archaeological evidence surrounding the Scripture passages that narrate his life and context. Beginning with a statement as to his identity as a religious reformer, a social revolutionary, and an apocalyptic prophet, the subsequent review of archaeological evidence by Kristin Romey concludes "That to believers, the scholar's quest for the historical, non-supernatural Jesus is of little consequence. That quest will be endless, full of shifting theories, unanswerable questions and irreconcilable facts. But for believers, their faith in the life, death and resurrection of the Son of God will be evidence enough" (Romey, 2017, p. 64).[49]

> *Since the earliest days of the Church, Christians have gathered in communities of different kinds, expressing their faith in liturgy and sacrament, in friendship and service, whether in households, hospitals, prisons, schools, or church buildings. Drawing on the gospel for inspiration, these communities still today express the presence of Jesus in the world in unique ways. Each anticipates a new order of personal relations in living out a gift and vision of community that imitates its foundation in Christ, embodying self-giving love and gratitude* (Mercy Partners Theological Framework, 2018, p. 3).

---

[49] For some researchers, Romey's comment could be regarded as incomplete. Work by researchers such as Jose Pagola, John Dominic Crossan, and Neil Douglas-Klotz *(The Hidden Gospel: Decoding the Spiritual Message of the Aramaic Jesus)* is very helpful in coming to appreciate what Jesus was trying to do and to convey.

Vatican II

Context and signposts[50]

The revelations of Science, the knowledge explosion, and the 'cry' for liberation and meaning within a complex and connected world within the first half of the twentieth century were profound. Within this new age, the Second Vatican Council was initiated.[51] In the broadest of terms, it was a process of interpreting the message of Jesus within changing times, a process that "constituted the greatest shift ever in Christian thought" (Morwood, 2007, p. 7).

Vatican II was a landmark Council for the Church, a time that precipitated incredible change and blessings on the Church as it journeyed mysteriously in the world.[52] Vatican II (1962 - 1965) was an experience at which, for the first time, the Local Churches (Archdiocesan and Diocesan) across the world came together. Some 2600; Cardinals, Archbishops and Bishops gathered in prayer and reflection to look back and dream a future within the context of the modern world. Outcomes included four constitutions, nine decrees, and three declarations.

Maher (2017) argues that Vatican II had its beginnings at least one hundred years earlier. The first Vatican Council (1869 - 1870) left open the desire for reform that the Church was seeking in response to the modernist crisis. This gave rise to continuing reactions from theologians who presented reform in courageous terms.[53] Moreover, in the period from approximately 1930 to 1960, a new Theology *(Nouvelle Theologie)* focused on engaging the modern world, particularly in the aftermath of two world wars, rampaging nationalism and a new scientific awakening; the age of Einstein. It was a movement spearheaded by the French theologian Yves Congar who sought to have Theology inform a Church on the 'primacy of the pastoral'; the value of experience in revealing the incarnate God through engaging 'the signs of the times.'

The propositions of the *Nouvelle Theologie* were reinforced in the opening address to the Council by Pope John XXIII. The emphasis for reform was centred on *Resourcement* and *Aggiornamento*. The French term *Resourcement* spoke to the process of 'looking back' at the tradition and drawing from its riches, while *Aggiornamento*, the Italian concept for 'bringing up-to-date,' considered these riches in light of the modern world.

---

50 The metaphor of signpost is offered by Anthony Maher (2017a) as a means for identifying influences on Vatican II.
51 The Second Vatican Council was convened by Pope John XXIII in December 1959, began its formal deliberations in 1962, and was concluded by Pope Paul VI in 1965.
52 Pope John Paul II in his encyclical *Novo Millennio Ineunte* (2001) argues that the Second Vatican Council was a source of significant richness to the Church, much of which is still to bear fruit. Moreover, *The Dogmatic Constitution on the Church* of the Second Vatican Council described this Church as the people of God, journeying to holiness in a way that is characterised by mystery.
53 The example provided by Maher is that of Reverend George Tyrrell SJ who petitioned for reform but was silenced and excommunicated.

This was the dual challenge for the Church to look inwards *(Ad Intra)* and look outwards *(Ad Extra)* as she journeyed in relationship with people and culture. In this context, Faggioli (2017) argues that the opening speech to the Council Fathers was one of the most influential addresses in Church history. It was the time for identifying a new beginning for the global Church; discerning a role in the modern world that looked more like being servant than institution.

The Ecumenical Council will surely be, even more than a new and magnificent Pentecost, a real and new Epiphany, one of the many revelations which have been renewed and are continually being renewed in the course of history, but one of the greatest of all (Pope John XXIII, 1962).

Compass for the new millennium

Vatican II ushered in significant change from the pre-conciliar era. The intention of the Council to be pastoral, non-condemnatory and open to new learning (GS, para. 44) gave it a style defined by horizontal as well as vertical relationships, service over control, openness to change, inclusiveness and active participation (Rush, 2009). It offered a vocabulary of inclusion and collegiality along with an emphasis on dialogue about mission (GS, para. 92), and full, conscious and active participation (SC, para. 14). Clearly, the Church emanating from Vatican II was sustained by its reliance on tradition but equally awakened to its full and active life in the Spirit.

The Second Vatican Council (1962–1965) challenged elements of Catholicism unquestioned since the 18th century. Pope John XXIII intended this to be a 'council of opportunity,' to bring the Church 'up to date' in a dynamic and fast changing world. Over four years the Council culminated in 16 documents that marked a profound shift in the ways of the past (Burke Family Trust, 2009, p. 1).

The literature emanating from the Second Vatican Council is regarded as 'normative' in terms of the overall volume of material provided by the teaching arm of the Church, the Magisterium. Pope John Paul II contended that this literature had lost none of its brilliance and provides "A compass by which we can take our bearings in the century now beginning" (NMI, para. 57). The final form of the deliberations revealed the Council's vision for the Church as being "A sacrament or instrumental sign of intimate union with God and the unity of all humanity" (LG, para. 1).

Impact of the Council

The impact of Vatican II is evident in ritual and Christian living. The liturgy of the Eucharist now uses the language of culture, emphasises the gathering, is particularly attentive to Scripture and encourages involvement by those present. The domestic Church of the family is now less disposed to traditional expressions of Catholic life (e.g., Rosary, Catholic social organisations), religious artefacts and conformity to observances. Moreover, the community of the Church is much less engaged in outward and triumphal activity and is now more focused on dialogue and partnership with other faith traditions in service and prayer. The contemporary Church is more inclusive in its outreach and broader in its emphasis as to where the presence of God can be found. It is a Church that concentrates on mission and communion while it journeys as a pilgrim people, engaged with the world in an endeavour to be 'salt, light and leaven' in accord with the Reign of God and the mind of Christ.

Some twenty years on from the closure of Vatican II, Pope John Paul II announced an extraordinary session of the Synod of Bishops to reflect on the "Experience, meaning, implementation and effects of Vatican II" (Dulles, 1985, p. 5). Not wanting to distance the Church from Vatican II outcomes, Pope John Paul II declared of the Council and its effects that it "Remains the fundamental event in the life of the contemporary Church... the constant reference point for every pastoral action" (Dulles, 1985, p. 3). Notwithstanding this, Dulles adds that, for many Catholics, the Council had precipitated controversy. For some it went too far, while for others the changes were not enough to alter "Absolutistic changes and antiquated hierarchical structures" (Dulles, 1985, p. 5).

The Council of the Synod determined that the central theme emerging from the Council was that of the Church and that this should be examined in terms of its self and in relation to other realities. Clearly, the challenge of the Council was towards renewal, but equally it needed to be attentive to its own tradition in matters of the Word of God (Scriptures), sacramental structure and its dogmas (Dulles 1985, p. 9).

The themes of the Synod are captured explicitly in the encyclical, *Christifideles Laici* (Christ's Faithful People, 1989). Not only are the milestone statements of Vatican II reinforced, but an elevated consciousness among the laity is also sought. Baptism was reinforced as the basis of Christian vocation and dynamism and described as the 'sacrament of faith' with fundamental aspects of regeneration in Christ. "The life of the Son of God, unites us to Christ and his Body, the Church, and anoints us in the Holy Spirit, making us spiritual temples." This is a consciousness of not just belonging to the Church, but of being the Church (CL, para. 26).

Unquestionably the Church today is very different because of Vatican II. One story used to illustrate the underlying nature of this change is captured by reference to the actions of the Popes prior to and after the Council. Customary as it is for the Pope to visit and contemplate within the Vatican Gardens, the typical nature of this presence prior to the Council was to be private and self-reflective. In this context those tending the gardens would not engage in any form of dialogue with the Pontiff. This was not the case for Pope John XXIII who convened the Council and heralded a new Spirit. For Pope John, exchange was encouraged and dialogue promoted. The actions symbolised the self-renewing Church as being open in its dialogue with the agenda of the world.

The changing worship and social patterns of the Church have been likened to living in a house while it is being renovated.[54] The core structure is present, the foundations, outer walls, general floor plan and so on, but so, too, are there indicators of a house under repair. Commentary on this social and spiritual upheaval suggests that the process of 'renovation' and the period of destabilisation are not over (Lennan, 2001).

Change in the Church arising from Vatican II is comprehensive. However, the debate continues as to the extent and pace of this change. In a reflective and challenging presentation of the 'forces' involved in Vatican decision making, media speculation suggests that the continuing and somewhat 'controversial reforms of Pope Francis may destroy him' (Livingstone, 2017). The report argues that while Pope Francis is committed to reform, some senior Cardinals believe that too much has been lost. Evidence for the alarm is cited in a landmark speech in Germany where the Cardinal Prefect of the Congregation for Divine Worship and the Sacraments said the Church had renounced its centuries-old heritage. "Political Europe is rebuked for abandoning or denying its Christian roots. But the first to have abandoned her Christian roots and past is indisputably the post-conciliar Catholic Church" (20 April, 2017).

Andrew Brown in *The Guardian* makes the point that "the most senior clergy in the Church believe that the Pope is flirting with heresy" (2017). The present crisis is regarded as the most serious instance of Church division since the 1960's when conservatives in France under Archbishop Lefebvre wanted to break away. Significantly, the Pope is steadfast in his commitment to dialogue and his engagement within and beyond the Church. In a book called *Honest Interviews: A pastoral risk*, Pope Francis expresses his wish for a pastoral approach "that knows how to insert itself into the conversations of people, that knows how to dialogue" (McElvee, 2017). This he contends is foundational to mission, is exemplified in the Catholic school and will grow.

---

[54] Reverend Professor Richard Lennan, 2001 when addressing the Diocesan assembly of Toowoomba used the image of a house under repair to illustrate the nature of the emerging directions for Church.

Our world has become a global village with multiple processes of interaction, where every person belongs to humanity and shares the hope of a better future with the entire family of peoples ... Catholic educational institutes are called, in the front line, to practice the grammar of dialogue that aims to encounter an appreciation of the cultural and religious diversities. Dialogue, in fact, educates when a person relates with respect, esteem, sincerity in listening and expresses self with authenticity, without obfuscating or mitigating identity nourished by evangelical inspiration. We are encouraged by the conviction that the new generations, educated in a Christian way to dialogue, will come out of the school and university classrooms motivated to build bridges and, hence, to find new answers to the many challenges of our time (Pope Francis, 2017).

Church today

Social and cultural context

Brian Swimme, an evolutionary cosmologist, refers to the contemporary era as being "big news in a million years" (2008). It involves a movement away from frameworks that once had provided a sense of certainty, even security, into what, at first glance, appear to be 'turbulent waters.' Moral, ethical, economic, organisational, ecclesial and political issues appear so complex and difficult that they present as being beyond control. What was once regarded as 'cut-and-dried' is being regarded increasingly as open-ended, challenging and near impossible to manage. This contemporary situation is said to constitute an upheaval of enormous proportion, a boiling over of chaotic forces which impact all, cannot be avoided and are of the order of change heralded by the agrarian and industrial revolutions (O'Murchu, 1995).

The experience of social and cultural change has been described as "Something is dying in our world and something is struggling to be born." Furthermore: "Whether in politics, economics, physics, medicine or spirituality, we can feel the ground beneath us is shifting; old certainties are falling apart, and fresh possibilities surface at an accelerating pace" (O'Murchu, 1995, p. 6). It is in the human domain of existence; one's self, relationships, family, school, workplace and wider community, that the effects of a new socio-political and cultural context are being experienced. The effects can be seen in a crisis of values, with results observed in subjectivism, moral relativism and nihilism. It might also be said, specifically in the developed world, that values of consumerism, materialism and secularism are pervasive. The effect of all this is not in the future, not independent of the Church or Catholic school, but is being experienced already.

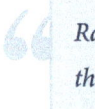
Rather than prospects of development for all, we witness the widening of the gap between the rich and the poor, as well as massive migration from underdeveloped to highly developed countries. The phenomenon of multiculturalism and the increasingly multi-ethnic and multi-religious society is at the same time enrichment and a source of problems. To this we must add, in countries of longstanding evangelisation, a growing marginalisation of the Christian faith as a reference point and a source of light for an effective and convincing interpretation of existence (Congregation for Catholic Education, 1998, para. 1).

The essence of contemporary society as being postmodern is characterised by Feeney (1997) as society demonstrating a sense of exhaustion, a loss of feeling and meaning, possessing minimal expectations and hopes, and a desire to make fun of things that are serious. The optimal postmodern society is one that experiences and even overcomes these pressures and is at a point where new meaning is sought. However, the directions and destinations still remain unclear and, if there is anything that is concrete, it is that society is in some form of perpetual transition. In this context, basic questions emerge: What are 'normal' patterns of life? What is truth, and where can it be found? Without some establishment of these parameters, individuals are said to be disposed towards a 'pick and choose' mentality with a strategy of avoidance and an associated loss of the opportunity to build and reinforce identity.

The experience of living in a postmodern world is felt deeply by all, but especially by young people who engage a world of diversity within a community undergoing transformation. For the young, the task of finding one's social and personal identity becomes a process of exploration in search of possibilities that sustain and give life. As one mother noted the comment from her adolescent daughter: "I feel like I am a butterfly; privileged to be free on the one hand, and yet exposed to choice and decisions I am so unsure about." The remark imaged the experience of many and captured the essence of a postmodern generation in search of meaning in a world of instability.

In a culture of computers and cars and personal independence ... the planet is in orbit, the country is in orbit, families are in orbit. This is a people who move from place to place. Everything is in flux. Everybody is going somewhere for something else. Everybody is scrambling. Everybody is straining and stretching to get more of something, more things, more security, more status, more power ... what we have lost is the sense of who we are and where we belong in the universe and what that means for everything we do (Joan Chittister, 2003, p. 11).

The living of the Paschal Mystery and the creation of a kingdom-centred community "where God writes the agenda for the Church" (O'Murchu, 1995a, p. 121–122), calls for conversion; a continuing response in faith to the gift of the Spirit. Just as the context of the first Christian communities was characterised by constant change and unceasing challenge, so too is contemporary culture confronted by influences that distract from a life in the Spirit.

The response in faith, the imagination of the Good News of Christ, by the early Church was a call to holiness. It was this same message and response that the Extraordinary Synod of Bishops confirmed as the focus of the Second Vatican Council. It is the call to the pilgrim Church to take up the invitation of Christ to "go into the world and preach the good news" (Mark 16:15) while drawing hope from the promise: "I am the bread of life. Whoever comes to me will never be hungry, and whoever believes in me will never be thirsty" (John 6:35).

> *Dogma carries little weight or relevance for the masses crying out for fresh hope. In their world preaching Christ or teaching Christ carries no long term meaning: being Christ to them is what will make a difference. And being Christ to the other is not a rational option of the head but an emotional, inspired response from the heart. At the end of the day it is love rather than truth that endures* (Diarmuid O'Murchu, 2005, p. 15).

Religious context

Christianity continues as the world's largest religious group with 34 per cent of the world's population. Growth is projected in countries outside of Europe, particularly in the developing regions of Africa, Asia and Latin America. Projections are that by 2050, approximately three quarters of Roman Catholics will live outside Europe and North America with increases of 146 per cent in Africa, 63 per cent in Asia, 42 per cent in Latin America and the Caribbean, and 38 per cent in North America. Meanwhile, Europe will experience a six per cent decline in its Catholic population.[55] Notably, while Christians worldwide will grow in number, Hugh McKay predicts that China will contain the highest number of Christians, and Islam will overtake Christianity as the most popular religion world-wide.[56]

The profile of Christianity in Australia is undergoing change of a dramatic nature. The most recent data from the Australian Bureau of Statistics (ABS) census in 2016 revealed that the percentage of Christians fell to 52.2 per cent, with the Australian Catholic community now 22.6 per cent; down from 25.3 per cent six years ago.

---

[55] Projections are drawn from the Population Reference Bureau in commentary on The Changing Demographics of Roman Catholics.
[56] Data provided by Hugh McKay, 2018.

Moreover, while 60.3 per cent of Australians report an association with some religion, some 31.1 per cent indicated 'no religion' and the remainder of respondents simply did not complete the optional question on the census report. The percentage of respondents in the 'none' category rose dramatically from a base of 22.3 per cent six years ago.

Complementing ABS population data, research by Powell and Pepper (2016) into religion and spirituality in Australia drew more precise conclusions about changing religious attitudes and practices. The data revealed:

- About six in ten (60%) Australians believe in God or Spirit or Life Force;
- About a quarter of Australians (25%) report a mystical or supernatural experience;
- About four in ten Australians (40%) believe that religion is good for society;
- About four in ten Australians (40%) believe that religious faith shapes life's decisions;
- Three in ten (30%) of Australians say they pray or meditate at least once a week; and,
- Less than a fifth of Australians (< 20%) say they attend religious service once a month.

The extrapolation of religious trends within the Catholic Christian population of Australia by Robert Dixon (2017) speaks of change as being consistent and continuous. The Catholic population will grow but is expected to fall in percentage terms with significant dis-identification being recorded as 'no religion.' Ethnic changes will be increasingly evident and a decline in Mass attendance is predicted. Reductions in the number of Priests will be steady and continue to be augmented by overseas support; while the presence of Religious Sisters and Brothers will become negligible. Moreover, attitudes and practices are expected to reveal continuing shifts and become most noticeable in the practice of the Sacraments, beliefs, and social attitudes. One response, Sheridan (2017), argues that Australia is becoming an atheistic nation and is best described in terms of "the eclipse of Christianity."

For a time, we will continue to live off the declining ethical and cultural capital of our heritage of 2000 years of Christianity and more than 3000 years of the Judeo-Christian tradition. But as British writer Arnold Lunn once remarked, we are living off the scent of an empty vase. As we cut ourselves off ever more comprehensively from the roots of our civilisation, our civilisation will be damaged (Greg Sheridan, August 2017).

The decline of religion within Australia has pointed to the value of respectful dialogue, particularly for those who might be nominated as 'cafeteria Catholics' and for whom discernment and participation are processes of election not obligation (Brennan, 2018). Moreover, the value of selecting 'the right bits over the wrong bits' (Craven, 2018) and the importance of common good over individualism, inclusion over exclusion, and the amplification of what unites over what divides (Perry, 2018) were given prominence within a national forum. The questions of 'where to start and what to do' were responded to in terms of 'starting with God and the nature of the human being,' giving preference to people as people and not as a statistic, and promoting encounter as a face to face engagement; 'without raised voice, categorisation, stamping of feet, or entering into battle' (Coleridge, 2018a).

A further informed and passionate discussion of the place of religion in society was evidenced in the open forum discussion within the Dialogue Australia Network (DAN) meeting of April 2018. Acknowledgement was given to the changes in beliefs and practices with the challenge to educators being "Is there space in your classroom for God; how do you demonstrate your values; and, would the world be a lesser place without religion?" Commentary across the conference argued for a disposition of living critically as a process of giving meaning to life, and, negating the goals of acquiring 'more' as leading to happiness or higher levels of satisfaction (Singer, 2018). The discussion of personal, religious, educational, social and professional experiences were noted as not particular to Australia, with the conclusion of ten years ago remaining current.

> *Whatever is 'going on' is going on everywhere in the western world. In Australia, for example, research indicates that 95 percent of students educated in Catholic schools have no regular participation in Catholic worship within twelve months of leaving school. In the United States 90 percent of Catholics believe they can dissent from Church doctrine and still remain good Catholics. In England, Ireland, and across Europe regular attendance at Sunday worship has dropped dramatically* (Michael Morwood, 2007, p. 15).

Notwithstanding changing patterns and practices of engagement, the Church today is called to be integral to life as it promotes an openness to dialogue and withdrawal from the barricades which separate. For Maher (2017a), it is a Church that is challenged to be inclusive, true to its message and socially just in its processes. It is the lived imagination of a joyful and hope filled servant, contributing to and being enriched by the world in which it serves. Aligned with the vision of the Church in the Modern World (GS, para. 39) the Church continues to be engaged through looking at the agenda of the world (the signs of the times), and being responsive through mission, especially in relation to the poor.

> *I want a Church which is poor and for the poor. They have much to teach us ... Each individual Christian and every community is called to be an instrument of God for the liberation and promotion of the poor* (EG, paras. 198 & 187).

Summarising the nature of the Church espoused by Pope Francis, Faggioli (2017a) outlines three macro trends: the movement of the Church from institution to mission; from predominantly European to a global body; and, from exclusiveness to inclusiveness. The vision of Church expressed by Pope Francis is a Church where all are welcome, where distinctiveness is respected, and where convergence for the common good is proposed. The image of Church as a polyhedron (EG, para. 236) conceives this Church with multiple relationships and yet possessive of a universal character. It is a Church where Christ is at the centre and where the mercy of God is experienced. It is a Church where all can minister acts of mercy and where mercy can be understood in sacramental terms by being a sign and an instrument of God with us.

The expectations of affiliation and confidence with respect to religion in Australia is commented upon by Hugh McKay (2018) who makes the point that while religion is declining in terms of its significance within society, there are signs of contradiction. He cites that 90 per cent of non-Church goers like to have a church building within their local environment; enrolments in faith-based schools are increasing; and, religious affiliation still provides a sense of belonging that inspires, encourages and motivates. Clearly, the 'glass is not half empty' and there exists hope in people, structures and processes that continue to invite engagement and give witness to the message of Christ.

Catholic school: Christ as cornerstone

The social environment of the Catholic school is a concrete reality of Church life, a fertile field where the model and message of Christ is taught and experienced. While not the sole environment for evangelisation, it is, nonetheless, a significant pastoral initiative of the Church throughout the world. John Sullivan,[57] the acclaimed commentator on Catholic schools, describes Catholic schools as 'places like no other.' While distinctive and inclusive, they are places of privilege and encounter where the Spirit of Christ inspires and gives meaning to mission, life and culture.

---

57 John Sullivan is Professor of Christian Education, at Liverpool Hope University.

Metaphor in Scripture

The metaphor of cornerstone is argued to possess a history of significance for both the Israelites and for the community founded by Jesus.[58] For the nomadic tribes of the early nation of Israel; 'stones' provided shelter and protection from the elements and were a source of comfort and safety for the community who moved and lived in relationship to their God. For the followers of Jesus, the metaphor offers a similar experience of relationship and exists as a symbolic reminder of Jesus, the Christ, as foundational to a new community informed and supported by his living Spirit.

The centrality of Christ to the life of the Church is evidenced in Scripture as Christ being the foundation stone of the new temple (John 2:18-21); and manifested by the 'living stones' who constitute the new spiritual temple (1 Peter 2:4-6; 1 Corinthians 3:16). Saint Paul develops the metaphor in his letter to the Ephesians (2:19-22) by making the connections among those who precede, come after and are gifted by the Spirit of Christ. "You, too, are built upon the foundation laid by the apostles and prophets, the cornerstone being Christ Jesus himself. He is the one who holds the whole building together and makes it grow into a sacred temple dedicated to the Lord. In union with him you too are being built together with all the others into a place where God lives through his Spirit" (Figure 4).

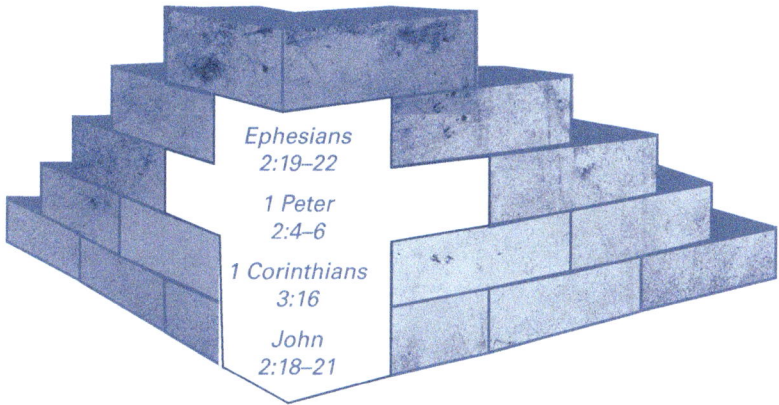

Figure 4. The metaphor of cornerstone in Scripture

The unfolding relationship between Jesus and his disciples is seen throughout the Gospel, and, in particular, achieves a poignant emphasis in the passage from Luke (19:39-40). The scene records the journey of Jesus into Jerusalem and the exchange with those who challenge him about his disciples creating unrest. The response by Jesus is that if his disciples become silenced, then even the 'stones would cry out.'

---

58 Commentary from Bishop William Morris in the introduction to the multimedia package, Cornerstone.

It is against this background that the metaphor is extended to reveal the activity and significance of the wider group of 'living stones' who live and proclaim his person and message. It is a proclamation that captures the three integrated elements which define the new community: 'stones,' the living followers; their 'cry,' of conviction and passion; and 'out,' through teaching and witnessing to the Lord.

The metaphor of cornerstone provides a means of seeing the centrality of Christ in the multiple and connected 'new temples' that gather in his name. The metaphor evokes a spread of conclusions about the relationship of Christ to those who follow him, and in the context of this text, speak to the nature of the mission, life and culture of the Catholic school. In this light, the following observations are offered as initial reflections:

- A cornerstone is laid on foundations;
- A cornerstone gives direction and shape to a new construction;
- A cornerstone is complemented by other stones;
- A cornerstone projects what other stones might look like when combined with it;
- A cornerstone is the touchstone for the authenticity of other stones.

Christ is the cornerstone of the Catholic school. His person and revelation give shape and meaning to this 'new temple of the Spirit.' To borrow from the language of architecture, the elevations of this new temple can be drawn from the words of Christ "I am the way, the truth and the life." These are the perspectives that the Synod of Bishops in Oceania chose as the characteristic 'elevations' of what discipleship might look like within entities committed to Christ. Within the text, these elevations are elaborated upon through a discussion of spirituality, mission and leadership. They are the perspectives that manifest the expression of discipleship within and beyond the Catholic school.

Cornerstone to liquid gold

The significance of the relationship of the Catholic school to the person of Christ has been likened to the need that Australia possesses for water (Bathersby, 2010).

Australia is an old and largely arid country with an expansive centre and a population distribution which is situated primarily along its coastline. As the journey is made to the 'heart,' the striking realisation about the Australian landscape is that every city and small town is situated on a water supply of some form. As well, even in the most remote and expansive grazing properties, the local water supply is the dominant feature of the landscape, usually in the form of a deep and not yet dry part of a meandering riverbed. The necessity for water for the existence and continuance of life is obvious. A feature of the most remote of settlements, even those which appear to possess no noticeable water, is the presence of windmills, pumps, drains and open pipes which serve to draw water from below the earth's surface. The accession of water from artesian and sub-artesian basins offers a continuing source of refreshment, invisible at first glance, but ever-present to those who would seek to draw from it.

Project Catholic School reinforced the foundation of the Catholic school as being centred in the Spirit of Christ. Christ was advanced as fundamental to the Catholic school as water is to human existence. The presence of water and its life-giving properties is symbolic of how a Catholic school might draw from the Spirit of Christ. It is the 'stream' from which individuals and communities draw their direction and sustenance. It is the resource which sustains and provides for continuing grace. It is the gift of God which not only reveals the life of the Creator, but is one of the means by which the Creator enters life. It is a metaphor that is ancient as it is new.

Blessed are those who trust in the Lord, whose trust is the Lord. They shall be like a tree planted by water, sending out its roots by the stream. It shall not fear when heat comes, and its leaves shall stay green; in the year of drought it is not anxious, and it does not cease to bear fruit (Jeremiah 17:7-8).

Extending the image of water as 'liquid gold' an imagination goes to the 'travel' of this water in the isolated regions of Australia. Literally, the influence of the wet season is such that the largely flat and dry land is transformed into an inland sea which creates a supply of water for thousands of miles both above and below the known landscape. As a continuing image, is it conceivable to expect that the Spirit of Christ, like the impact of rain on the outback, may reach out and serve the landscapes beyond the local and immediate? Can the Spirit of Christ be so broad that it serves to manifest the graciousness of God and God's revelation in Christ in people and places beyond the school? Can the Spirit of Christ be such that its influence is able to transform and nourish the potential that is in all, the gifts which serve to provide uniqueness and dignity, the building blocks for accessing life to the full?

For Christians, the complete expression of what it means to be fully divine and authentically human is found in Jesus. The first-century Latin phrase, *Christianus alter Christus* (Christians are another Christ), gives expression to the relationship between Christ and his followers. For Christians, it is the message and person of Jesus that provide the shape and direction for living. Christ is the cornerstone around which a 'new temple', a new gathering, is formed. It is he who constitutes that metaphorical 'liquid gold' that serves to offer guidance and support in times of change and challenge.

INTEGRATION

Executive Summary

The pastoral context for Catholic schools is shaped by foundations in faith which encompass life as a gift, a natural search for God, the revelation of God in Christ, the wisdom of the tradition and specifically of Vatican II, and, the continuing presence of Christ through the life of the Spirit. Those who constitute the Catholic school community, the living stones aligned with the cornerstone, are invited to share in this Spirit and so nurture their own formation and grow in awareness, conviction and activation of a kingdom way of life. This is the meaning system that is proposed to offer joy, hope, and oneness to a world in search of integrity and purpose.

Reflection: "Whom are they talkng to Sister?"

The occasional remark from a student can be a powerful reminder as to what cannot be taken for granted when sharing the faith. The context for this particular 'lesson' was a small Catholic boarding school, known for its outreach and care, particularly to the young. The time was mid-year, and the circumstances, an innocent question from a seven-year-old, who, up to that time, had been a recipient of home schooling. Subsequent to admission to the boarding establishment and, after two days of familiarisation with the ritual of formal evening prayer, the boy's question came in response to observing fellow students reciting aloud their night prayers. On the third evening, still uninformed as to the basics of the evening ritual, the boarding student felt compelled to ask 'Whom are they talking to Sister?' The question stunned Sister. In one sense, this was the most reasonable of inquiries, yet it came as a shock. The experience of saying prayers had become so routine for the majority, that its fuller explanation for those not initiated had been missed.

Questions

1. **Head:** What image/s of God inform/s your life and practice within the Catholic school?
2. **Heart:** What metaphors for the Catholic school hold most appeal?
3. **Hand:** What supports your life as a living stone within the mission and culture of the Catholic school?

Activities

Theme: Attitude is important "so pick a good one"

Goal: Living life abundantly

Task: First consider and then share with a colleague or friend your response to the characteristics of living an abundant life identified by Dr Wayne Dyer (2016).

- *A tendency to think and act spontaneously rather than on fears;*
- *An unmistakable ability to enjoy each moment;*
- *A loss of interest in judging other people;*
- *A loss of interest in interpreting the actions of others;*
- *A loss of interest in conflict;*
- *A loss of the ability to worry;*
- *Frequent, overwhelming episodes of appreciation;*
- *Contented feelings of connectedness with others and nature;*
- *Frequent attacks of smiling;*
- *Susceptibility to the love from others and the uncontrollable urge to extend it.*

Theme: Trust in God through prayer

Goal: "Refer it to the manager"

Task: Consider the image offered by Richard Rohr when referring to God as 'a shop manager' who graciously accepts referrals from 'front counter people.' The image promotes a prayerful, trusting and personal relationship to God and involves five steps:

- *R (Receive):* Graciously receive the concern that comes to mind;
- *R (Respect):* Experience the concern in its fullness (thought, affect and behaviour);
- *R (Refer):* Acknowledge the graciousness of God and refer the concern with trust;
- *R (Rejoice):* Give thanks for the presence and action of God;
- *R (Re-join):* Become attentive once more to the 'graced' present moment.

Activities

Theme: Relationship Stories

Goal: Explore personal story in relationship to story of school and story of Christ

Task: Participants go 'aside' to reflect individually and collectively on one's personal story in relation to the school and Christ stories.

- *My Story:* Reflecting, journaling and sharing of one's own story in terms of spiritual growth and religious affiliation;
- *Our Story:* Facilitated sharing of the story of the school: charism, history, mission, people, highlights and hopes;
- *The Story:* Sharing and encountering personal and school stories as they interface with the universal story of Christ.

Theme: Opening the doors

Goal: Imaging Church

Task: Vatican II heralded that the 'windows and doors' of the Church were to be opened. What would you see as most significant to the Church as she engages a changed and changing social and cultural context? The reflection can be supported by considering:

- *What of the old is no longer life-giving?*
- *What of the present gives joy and hope?*
- *What is struggling to be born in the Spirit of Christ?*

CHAPTER TWO
Walking his way: A spirituality of engagement

Chapter Outline

CHAPTER TWO	45
WALKING HIS WAY: A SPIRITUALITY OF ENGAGEMENT	45
INTRODUCTION	45
Reflection	45
At a glance	45
Focusing story: "Don't you want to know my name?"	45
From your experience	46
THEMES AND MAIN IDEAS	46
Living Spirit	46
Life as a sacred whole	46
Spirituality in the everyday	49
Visible witness	49
Presence	50
Mysticism	51
Sacramental living	53
Sacramental consciousness	54
Sacraments as expressions of life	54
Discipleship	55
Universal call	56
People of God	57
Discipleship metaphors	58
Missionary discipleship	60
A new myth for mission	60
Discipleship in the Catholic school	63
INTEGRATION	65
Executive Summary	65
Reflection: "Is that Jesus?"	66
Questions	66
Activities	67

CHAPTER TWO
Walking his way: A spirituality of engagement

INTRODUCTION

Reflection

"Going on further Jesus saw two other brothers, James the son of Zebedee and John his brother, in the boat with Zebedee their father, mending their nets, and he called them. Immediately they left the boat and their father, and followed him" (Matthew 4:21-22).

At a glance

Walking his way invites an awareness of the abundance of God's life and grace within self, others and creation. Christian spirituality is a response to this awakening. It is what faith looks like in attitudes, commitments and behaviours in relation to God's gifts.

The chapter explores spirituality through being attentive to life as a sacred gift and conversion to the Spirit of Christ within everyday life. Spirituality is expanded through themes of presence, mysticism, sacramental consciousness and participation. Metaphors of priest, prophet, and king are introduced to characterise spirituality, and discipleship is developed as an intentional response within the mission, life and culture of the Catholic school.

Focusing story: "Don't you want to know my name?"

During a visit to an isolated school, I had an opportunity to attend an early childhood centre comprising students from four to five years of age. Usually, visits of this nature involve some engagement with the students. However, on this particular occasion, I was a little rushed and was only able to manage a chat with the teacher. Probably sensing my need to move on, a young boy came up to me, pulled the leg of my trousers and asked "But, don't you want to know my name?"

Getting to know people, experiencing even the smallest aspect of their person and circumstances, is an expression of care and recognition of dignity. The interaction is, at one level, normal human behaviour, but, when prompted by the Spirit of God, the interaction becomes elevated to an experience of the Divine. In short, life can be an endless engagement of the ordinary and not-so-ordinary, or it can be this same experience seen with the eyes of faith and as an expression of the spiritual in self and others.

From your experience

1. How do I personally express my beliefs and values in the day-to-day life of the Catholic school community?
2. How can the Church's sacramental life support my engagement with the sacred in life?
3. How might my spirituality be integrated, sustained and applied within the community of the Catholic school?

THEMES AND MAIN IDEAS

Living Spirit

Saint Paul challenges the early Church in Rome to a new spirituality: "For those who live according to the flesh set their minds on the things of the flesh, but those who live according to the Spirit set their minds on the things of the Spirit. To set the mind on the flesh is death, but to set the mind on the Spirit is life and peace" (Romans 8:5-6). To be open to the Spirit is to discern the movement of the Spirit in oneself and in life. It is typically described as spirituality; a recognition of the presence of God in all of life and the associated response of 'leaning into life' as a consequence of this awareness.[60]

Life as a sacred whole

The almost entrenched separation of the sacred and the secular is said to have been associated with Christianity for almost two millennia.[61] The beginning of the first millennium in the then known world was so influenced by Greek philosophy that coming to an understanding of God (theology) was dominated by Greek thinking.

---

60 The phrase 'leaning into life' is one used by Dr Barry Donaghue CFC when leading a course in spirituality within James Cook University.
61 An expanded discussion of the sacred and secular differentiation, particularly from an historical perspective, is provided by Dr Elizabeth Dreyer, 1998.

Christian thought drew from the Greek world the concept that elements of human experience are arranged in two categories, with a clear preference of one over the other. Important concepts such as soul-body, mind-heart, spirit-matter and reason-feeling were separated and became the subject of theological and philosophical reflection. Further, the world itself was viewed hierarchically, with Spirit at one end and matter at the other. In the 'Christian appropriation of this world view, God was imaged at the top of the ladder' (Dreyer, 1998, p. 3) and the sacred was separated from the secular.

The dualism of the spiritual and so-called secular is precisely what Jesus came to reveal as untrue and incomplete. Jesus came to model for us that these two seemingly different worlds are and always have been one. We just couldn't imagine it intellectually until God put them together in one body that we could see and touch and love ... What an amazing realisation that should shock and delight us! (Richard Rohr, 2018).

The discernment of God in self, others and creation is a progressive awakening to beauty, goodness and truth. In simple terms, it is a path to experiencing God in all of life. It means being involved; thinking about, feeling and engaging fully the circumstances of life and living and finding the presence of God in the reality of what exists. It draws on the belief that experiences and creation reveal the sacred and that it is by being attentive and responsive to these that the Divine is encountered. It is a form of engagement that makes only limited sense if it is isolated from everyday life of the family, work, relationships, recreation, and care of the environment and is restricted to particular times, places, or days of the week.

Faith must be integrated with the rest of life, so that a Christian's life will not be broken into separate segments, but will display a profoundly unified character. Any divorce of faith from life represents a grave risk for the Christian, especially at certain stages of growth, or at times 'people' are faced with certain concrete tasks (Australian Episcopal Conference, 1970, para. 53).

The fathers of the Second Vatican Council spoke of the artificial separation of life into the sacred and the secular when they argued that 'the split between the faith that many profess and their daily lives deserves to be counted among the more serious errors of our age' (GS, para. 43). Describing the role of the Church in the modern world as *Gaudium et Spes* (Joy and Hope), the Council captured the essence of the Church's work as integral to life, a means for sharing joy and hope, a mission of continuing the message of God's love and dream for the world expressed by Christ.

The practice of being attentive to the Divine has been described as taking care of the soul (Moore, 1994), and, as a theology of the Holy Spirit and Divine immanence (Tacey, 1998, p. 17). To take care of the soul goes beyond an intellectual assent to the presence of God in self and others to incorporate a process of uncovering the magnificence of God in the events that shape daily life. It is seeing the sacred in all things and taking time to marvel and learn from the experience. It is reliant on the totality of the self; the physical, intellectual, emotional, behavioural and spiritual, reaching out and being awakened and touched by experience. Soul care entails 'being' and becoming attentive in ways that allow the whole person to live every moment of life with accelerated awareness, appreciation and inquiry. It is an integrated, non-dualistic way of connecting the whole person with the whole of life.

> *The importance of realising Christianity as a nondual spiritual path is that it frees our souls to continue their natural maturation in Spirit by honouring, attending to, and coming to understand the actual experiences of this life. We can slowly begin to realise that the essential qualities we long to experience such as compassion, strength, peace - are of the very fabric of our Being. Perhaps above all, we can discover the freedom of being alone as Being because we no longer search out there for something else to save us from our true selves. We are always already of Being (Kevin G Forrester, 2018).*

Taking care of the soul necessitates 'letting go' and 'being free' to respond to experiences within community. It is fundamentally a process of being open to the movement of the Holy Spirit. Put another way, care of the soul entails 'leaving behind,' or not even planning directions, in order to be free to discern what the spiritual life might be suggesting. Thus, the concept of faith moves from being a belief, which tends to be fixed and unchanging, to a position, whereby faith is almost always a response to the presence of the Holy Spirit.

> *The deepest level of communication is not communication, but communion. It is wordless. It is beyond words, and it is beyond speech, and it is beyond concept. Not that we discover a new unity. We discover an older unity. My dear brothers, we are already one. But we imagine that we are not. And what we have to recover is our original unity. What we have to be is what we are (Thomas Merton, 1975, p. 308).*

At the centre of Christian spirituality is a trusting attitude towards God's presence and action of grace in the world. If God is not seen as a benevolent being, and one's existence as stemming from and growing in God's love, then life is a solitary experience, with personal needs being met solely by self. Relationship, interdependence and mutual love do not enter such a formula for living. Conversely, conversion to a kingdom view of the world involves a commitment to Christ and acceptance of the goodness of God in the unfolding of creation. This mindset recognises that life is a gift, one constantly changing for the good, and that one's journey in life can be embraced for growth. This is a dynamic cooperative interplay between Divine and human action, the creation of a continuing set of interactions, improvements and re-directions as life unfolds for the better.

I was amazed when a Professor of Theology imaged the Spirit of God by reference to his grandfather's free-range chickens. The expansion of the image included a reflection on the Spirit as immeasurable, uncontainable, and unpredictable in its manifestations, as distinct from being definable, caged, and predictable. Unlike factory chickens, his grandfather's chickens were free, adventurous and contented to operate in a multiplicity of locations. This grounded image conveyed that living in the Spirit is not about identifying and consolidating a 'factory like approach' to encountering the Spirit. Rather, it is more about pointing to or awakening something that is already present, operative in known and unknown ways and typically looking like development, communion, joy, hope and forgiveness.

Spirituality in the everyday

A spirituality of the everyday has its roots in the early Church. The early followers of Jesus formed a community around a belief and commitment to his way. The followers of Jesus were people called, not only to Jesus, but also to a new relationship with one another and the Father whom Jesus proclaimed as Father of all. This early Church endeavoured to be a sign and an instrument of God's abiding presence and love. Within this tradition "Christian communities could be seen and heard" (Cooke, 1983, p. 69). Membership entailed conversion to Christ through Baptism, reception of the Pentecostal gift of the Spirit, celebration of the Eucharist, and an operative communitarian love.

Awe came upon everyone, because many wonders and signs were being done by the Apostles. All who believed were together and had all things in common; they would sell their possessions and goods and distribute the proceeds to all, as any had need. Day by day, as they spent much time together in the temple, they broke bread at home and ate their food with glad and generous hearts, praising God and having the goodwill of all the people. And day by day the Lord added to their number those who were being saved (Acts 2:43-47).

As with the early Church, the contemporary Church is called to be people of God actively nurturing and witnessing the love of Christ. This engagement takes root in the everyday events of life and allows the Church to be present and instrumental in a multitude of places and circumstances where presence value adds to life and living (LG, para. 33). The longstanding goals of the Church of being teachers and witnesses to the faith (*kerygma and martyria*), exercising a service for the good of all (*diakonia*), being and building community (*koinonia*) and engaging in celebration of prayer and worship (*leitourgia*) characterise a spirituality that entails fullness of life for Christians in the world (DCE, para. 25).

Being present

God's abiding presence within the world and the response by Christians is captured in a reflection that Dick Westley believes holds the key to God's presence and humankind's response. "I have called you to live out your lives in the presence of one another, and I pledge myself to live out my life in your presence" (Westley, 1996, p. 5). Being present stems from an outpouring of love and involves not only 'being there,' not only 'being with.' It is both of these and, most importantly, 'being there for' (1996, p. 11).

> *The human face, the yes, the smile, the look and the glance are invitations and expressions of the Spirit. A tone, a word, a phrase and a sentence, are also powerful indicators and means for exchange in the spiritual life. Physical handshakes, helpful hands and caring hands are all means of experiencing one's support, which reflects the revelation of God* (Dick Westley, 1996, p. 11).

The challenge, privilege and opportunity to make real the presence of the Spirit in everyday life is elaborated by Gerard Hughes in his discussion of the 'God of surprises.' It is in the unpredictability of the world that the God of surprises is experienced, and it is in our own efforts to understand our reality that God is to be found. The view leads to the conclusion that "He is no longer remote and out there, no longer dwells only in tabernacles and temples of stone, but we meet him smiling at us in our bewilderment, beckoning to us in our confusion and revealing himself in our failure and disillusionment as our only rock, refuge and strength" (Hughes, 1994, p. ix).

> *If the God who wants to enter into a bond of personal relationship is the Creator of heaven and earth, it implies that our being confronted with the world, existence with this world, is going to teach us more about the living God than the world alone can teach us, more than merely that God is the Creator of all things* (Edward Schillebeeckx, 1963, p. 6).

Becoming attentive to the Divine is to listen to the ordinary, being present to the immediate moment, and developing a sense of obedience and compassion. Listening to the ordinary is being attentive to the seemingly trivial, with the idea of seeing the holy; being present to the moment entails being able to withstand the pressures of the moment to take time to secure a sense of grace in the present; developing a sense of obedience involves aligning one's life with the will of God; and nurturing compassion flows from realising the depth of one's own brokenness before entering into the frailty of life experienced by others. In summary, attentiveness to the Divine involves being present to self, others and creation in ways that balance contemplation with action underpinned by love.

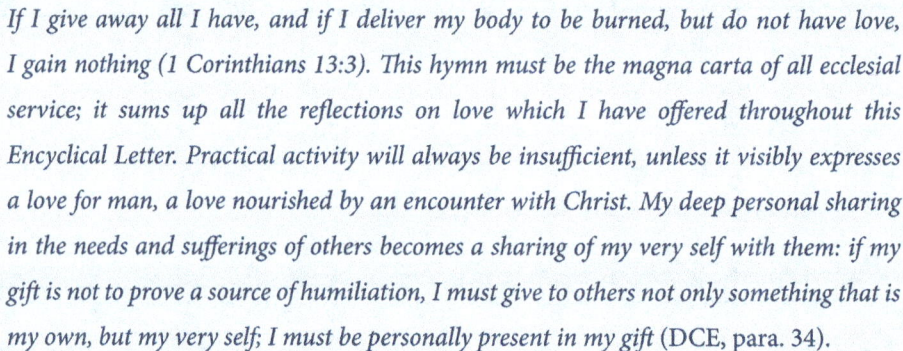

If I give away all I have, and if I deliver my body to be burned, but do not have love, I gain nothing (1 Corinthians 13:3). This hymn must be the magna carta of all ecclesial service; it sums up all the reflections on love which I have offered throughout this Encyclical Letter. Practical activity will always be insufficient, unless it visibly expresses a love for man, a love nourished by an encounter with Christ. My deep personal sharing in the needs and sufferings of others becomes a sharing of my very self with them: if my gift is not to prove a source of humiliation, I must give to others not only something that is my own, but my very self; I must be personally present in my gift (DCE, para. 34).

Being attentive to the possibilities of engaging, sharing and experiencing love and truth within the many environments of life is at the heart of mysticism. Where presence creates the opportunity for engaging the Divine, mysticism involves the intentional practice of looking deeper for the presence of the Spirit. It is a process that reflects on the real, asks why, and explores meaning as if God was fully active in the process, event or relationship under consideration.

Mysticism

Mysticism is a word that often draws a response of 'not me,' or, 'that's only for the very holy.' The mystics of the Church are commonly thought to be those who have frequented hermitages, lived in times past or been dedicated to life as Priest, Sister or Brother. However, the practice of mysticism is open to all as the sacredness of life is observed within the experience of the ordinary and every day. As Christian faith teaches, God already permeates all that we are and do, and mysticism is the act of becoming aware of this presence. Mysticism is becoming awake to the movement of the Spirit already present within the sacredness of creation.

The practice of mysticism is said to incorporate three basic processes. The opening of self on a daily basis and accepting the good times and the bad from a God who is lovingly called Mystery. This disposition begins with shedding control, prejudices and predictions and recognises that there will inevitably be a need for trust, forgiveness, and fidelity to conscience, service, and Gospel living. The second element of mysticism is again a resolution: resisting dualism so as to engage the Divine in all ways, times and experiences. The third component to mysticism extends this principle of not separating God from life to a view of Church as also not being separate from the realities of family, social experience or work (Dreyer, 1998, p. 3-5).

Classical theism has so stressed God's independence and absoluteness ... that love hardly seems to be God's essential quality or characteristic. Whitehead[62] was insistent that the concrete reality of God is found in concrete nature rather than in the more abstract aspects of the divine nature. Love cannot be known except in relationships, in being affected as well as affecting, in sharing and participating. God is the cosmic Lover who tenderly, luringly, persuasively, faithfully, indefatigably, inexhaustibly (for God's caring never comes to an end) relates to, cares for, and brings all possible good out of the world (Ilia Delio, 2011, p. 35).

The art of mysticism necessitates the ability to become unencumbered, detached from the slavery of inflexible thinking, the security of possessions, and the pursuit of needless ambitions. In a similar vein, Richard Rohr talks of the encumbrances of the three P's of power, possession and prestige. Whatever the terms used, the point being emphasised is that unbalanced influences from material, personal and interpersonal 'gods' are potential barriers to engaging the presence of the one true and everlasting God though being awake.

If you want to reach a state of bliss, then go beyond your ego and the internal dialogue. Make a decision to relinquish the need to control, the need to be approved, and the need to judge. Those are the three things the ego is doing all the time. It's very important to be aware of them every time they come up (Deepak Chopra, 2018, AZ Quotes. 519463).

Growth in mysticism begins with an acceptance of the need of God and a growing humility regarding God's place at the centre of life. It is summarised by the ability to be patient as the love of God is allowed to permeate and shape the interactions and responses to events and circumstances. It is basically

---

62 The reference is made to Alfred North Whitehead who addressed change in an evolutionary world. His process theology is based on the notion that change is integral to God, because God is love.

realised through being open to the goodness and truth of God and allowing this to resonate with the goodness and truth that reside within. It is an experience of God with God. It is the spiritual experience of beginning with and acknowledging the gift of 'an empty cup' and allowing it to be accepted, understood and advanced. It is the capacity to become amazed at the presence of God in life and develop a sense of wonder at self and the world. It involves a response of accepting and drinking from the cup of life and doing so with grace, relationship and depth of reflection.

It is a privileged experience to participate in a prayer group. On one occasion members elaborated on their understanding of God, the images that accompanied that understanding, and the personal relationship they had developed with God. One group member who had been committed to prayer, church attendance and good works throughout her life spoke up. "I never see God, and as for a personal relationship, I have no idea what you are talking about." It wasn't long before others in the group expanded on what they meant. "I see God in the beauty of my garden;" "the sunset and the stars are my way of being reminded of God's glory;" "the openness of my children, their simple and strong love sustains me."

Awe and amazement are characteristics of mysticism. They entail recognising love in deeds that are motivated by selfless interest, seeing the truth in statements that confront injustice, or being attentive to the Spirit of love and forgiveness that is able to transcend personal hurt. Just as the first Disciples of Christ were amazed at the nature of his person and action, so too can others be amazed and celebrate the expression of Christ-like, Spirit centred behaviours that attest to the presence of God in all things.

There are only two symptoms of enlightenment, just two indications that a transformation is taking place within you toward a higher consciousness. The first symptom is that you stop worrying. Things don't bother you anymore. You become light hearted and full of joy. The second symptom is that you encounter more and more meaningful coincidences in your life, more and more synchronicities. And this accelerates to the point where you actually experience the miraculous (Deepak Chopra, 2018, AZ Quotes. 561248).

Sacramental living

Sacramental living is becoming attentive and celebrating life in ways that experience every moment of life with heightened awareness, appreciation and inquiry. Living sacramentally draws from the significance of presence and mysticism and highlights the importance of community as the principal place in which the life of God can be encountered and shared.

Sacramental consciousness

The goal of seeing the Divine in all things signals a relationship with God at the centre of every moment of every day: a conscious disposition to live in 'the constant womb of God' (Boevre & Bloechl, 1999). This form of relationship is depicted by Karl Rahner (1971) as sacramental consciousness. Not unlike 'taking care of the soul,' it is seeing the sacred in all things and taking time to marvel and learn from the experience.

A sacramental vision sees every moment as an incarnation of heaven's promise. Daniel O'Leary (2008) describes these multiple and seemingly endless and ordinary experiences as a 'breeze that blows open the heart.' They come and go with the only imperative being to be alive to the experience. It is a time "when the veil parts between the two worlds we contain – our inner desire for a divine destiny and the hard reality of our present circumstances" (O'Leary, p. 142). It is as if a 'sacramental shutter' is thrown open and the experience of something special lifts us into another realm. For some it may be the smile of a child, the song of a bird, the vastness of a landscape or the scent of a flower. Whatever the experience, for a moment in time, this new imagination transforms and takes us into a new being and offers a tiny inkling into the experience of heaven.

Sacraments as expressions of life

When the Church gathers for liturgy, she does so in response to the mystery of encountering God in the world. The Church sacramentalises this larger liturgy of the world, of the week, of the ordinary and the everyday, by means of its rituals.

The purpose of the Sacraments to the life of the Church is "To sanctify... to build up the body of Christ and, finally to give worship to God" (CCC, para. 1123). The Sacraments are called sacraments of faith because they nourish and express faith and "Touch all the stages and all the important moments of Christian life" (CCC, para. 1210). In short, "What faith confesses, the Sacraments communicate" (CCC, para. 1692).

The Sacraments are the signs and instruments by which the Holy Spirit spreads the grace of Christ, the head, throughout the Church which is his body (CCC, para. 774). Ultimately, however, Sacraments cannot be fully defined nor perfectly understood. They offer mere windows into the Mystery of God. The original Greek word applied to these liturgical celebrations was *mysterion*.

The word sacramentum is derived from *mysterion* and refers to the visible sign of the hidden reality of salvation (Cooke, 1983, p. 5).

The relevance of a sacramental life to the everyday and the ordinary is depicted by Ruddiman (1999, p. 160) in her commentary on the Sacraments as being 'the Catholic way.' Sacramental rites not only provide assurance that God is present to the community; they also reinforce that there are responsibilities and values which connect with this gift of grace. Karl Rahner SJ advocated a revolution in thinking in regard to the nature and the pervasiveness of Sacraments and identified the power of the Sacrament to reflect and celebrate God's life in the world. "Instead of seeing them as a spiritual movement outward of the Sacramental action to an effect in the world, we should look for a spiritual movement of the world toward the Sacrament" (Rahner, 1971, p. 227).

The contrast of interpretations as to the place of Sacraments in the lives of Catholic Christians has been captured by images. Within a colloquium of the Irish Theological Association, Sean Fagan describes a traditional view as encompassing a 'petrol pump' mentality which is founded upon a need to "Supply different graces to meet different needs" (Fagan, 1976, p. 264). A characteristic response to this interpretation is to give attention to questions about how often and how much, rather than to see the Sacrament as an encounter with Christ which has an intimate relationship with Christian living. It is this latter interpretation that gives significance to the continuing presence of God in the world and the role of the Sacrament as providing high points, peak moments of special insight and celebration of the oneness of faith and life.

The Catholic Church celebrates seven Sacraments: Baptism, Confirmation, Eucharist, Penance, the Anointing of the Sick, Holy Orders and Matrimony. These are grouped into the Sacraments of Christian Initiation (Baptism, Confirmation and Eucharist), Sacraments of Healing (Penance, and The Anointing of the Sick) and the Sacraments at the service of communion and the mission of the faithful (Holy Orders and Matrimony). The correlation between the stages of natural life and the stages of the spiritual life (CCC, para. 1210) gives added impetus to the Sacraments as being integral to faith formation and spiritual expression.

Discipleship

The challenging words of Dietrich Bonhoeffer on discipleship are as relevant today as they were in a time of reflection and definition for the Church in pre-war Nazi Germany. "Discipleship is commitment to Christ ... Discipleship without Jesus Christ is choosing one's own path. It could be an ideal path or a martyr's path, but it is without the promise ... So the call to discipleship is a commitment solely to the person of Jesus Christ ... a gracious call, a gracious commandment" (Bonhoeffer, 2003, p. 59). This encounter with, and invitation by Jesus dispose a response that is not 'cheap grace' but 'costly grace.' "Costly grace is the Gospel which must be sought again and again, the gift that has to be asked for, the door at which one has to knock. It is costly, because it calls to discipleship; it is grace because it calls us to follow Jesus Christ" (2003, p. 45).

Universal call

The call to discipleship is a universal call, an encounter, invitation, privilege and responsibility that has appeared continuously throughout history. It is seen in the call to the chosen people of Israel, in the call to the patriarchs and the prophets, in Christ's call to the disciples, and is evident in the 2000 years since the Church has responded in Christian faith. It is a call to a way of being in the world that challenges conventional expectations and promises a life of relationship to God and God's creation that signals wholeness and happiness.

Scripture records the words of Jesus "Come follow me" (Matthew 4:19); "I am the Way, and the Truth, and the Life" (John 14:6); "I am the vine, you are the branches" (John 15:5); "Go therefore and make disciples of all nations" (Matthew 28:19). The message is clear. The invitation to Christian discipleship is centred on an encounter and a non-coercive relationship with a master teacher, a Rabbi, and an associated way of living that reflects integration and commitment. It is not a discipleship that entails worship, but discipleship that enables a new way of looking at and being in the world. A way that is taught and witnessed in practices that give meaning, purpose and direction to life and living.

The call to discipleship within the Christian Scriptures can be seen in the Gospels of Mark and John. The first call to follow Christ in Mark is observed in the encounter when Peter and Andrew are challenged to abandon their trade and take on a new vocation (Mark 1:17). Soon after, James and John join the group and leave their immediate duties to see what Jesus offers. This first call is said to be 'a break with business,' (Moses & Lizzio, 2011), an invitation to move from the predictable and traditional to the unexpected and new.

The second call recorded by Mark "If anyone wants to become my followers, let them deny themselves and take up their cross and follow me" (8:34) depicts Jesus as calling people to a form of discipleship that holds both blessing and cross. This is the paradox of denying oneself in order to move into a life of God's love. It calls for a response that goes beyond recognition, curiosity and interest in things that are different, to a level where the challenge of the Gospel holds privilege and new life born of sacrifice.

The third call to discipleship in Mark (16:7) comes after the crucifixion when the women visit the tomb of Jesus and are invited to find him in Galilee.

This is the invitation to experience the risen Christ within the community. This is the expression of discipleship through engagement with the Spirit already active and supportive within community in known and unknown ways. The Spirit of the risen Christ is first to be found in Galilee where relationship, knowledge, memories and lived experiences of Jesus are so prevalent.

The opening chapter of John's Gospel (1:35-42) also demonstrates discipleship arising from the power of encounter with Jesus. The first is when two disciples of John the Baptist hear John refer to Jesus as 'the lamb of God.' The announcement stirs their interest and leads to an encounter which prompts the question "What are you looking for?" (v. 38). The exchange results in them spending time with Jesus and subsequently leads Andrew to invite his brother, Simon, into a similar encounter. The call by Jesus to others, Philip and Nathaniel, soon follows and the company of disciples begins to be formed.

> *For the first three centuries all followers of Jesus Christ saw each other as equals although people had various roles in the Christian church (e.g., apostles, preachers, teachers, healers, speakers in tongues). They all wore the dress of the day. You could not identify their role by their dress. Baptism was the Sacrament which made them equal to other Christians. They formed the discipleship or community of equals. They were not interested in hierarchy or their status among other Christians* (Gideon Goosen, 2017).[63]

People of God

The Catechism of the Catholic Church (CCC, para. 781) refers to disciples as the People of God who possess a covenant with God 'ratified in Christ.' This 'new temple in the Lord' comprises 'Jews and Gentiles' who are called to be one, 'not according to the flesh, but in the Spirit.' It is a community of disciples that is united by faith in Christ and confirmed through Baptism. As disciples of Jesus Christ 'the one whom the Father anointed with the Holy Spirit and established as priest, prophet and king; the whole People of God participate in these three offices of Christ' (CCC, para. 783).

Participation in the priestly, prophetic and kingly offices of Christ respects the unique situation and gifts of each person and community while also recognising the 'responsibilities for mission and service that flow from them' (CCC, para. 783). All the baptised are called to be priestly people who reach out in mercy to all, particularly the most deprived, the most distant, and the lost. As an agent of the universal prophet, those who follow Christ draw from his Spirit and are

---

63 From Church Reforms and the Laity by Gideon Goosen. Mission and Spirituality News – 5 June, 2017. Gideon Goosen is a theologian and member of the Australian, European and North American Catholic Theological Associations.

called to be prophets to the world. As sharers in the kingship of Christ, their 'good shepherd' leadership is guided by the power of the Holy Spirit who dwells fully in him and whom he breathes into his disciples (CCC, paras. 784-786).

Discipleship metaphors

The significance of the relationship between Christ and his followers is expressed in the Dogmatic Constitution of the Church (LG, para. 31) and given additional emphasis in the Decree on the Apostolate of the Laity (AA, para. 10). It received further reinforcement by Pope John Paul II at the beginning of his pontificate (CL, para. 32) and continues to be associated with the clear intention of bringing grace and dignity to the baptised along with the challenges of freedom and responsibility to live the Christian life.

The mission of the Church becomes clearer when one considers the variety of functions and the richness of gifts which Christ confers on it through the Holy Spirit. These functions and gifts are summed up in the Priestly, Prophetic and Kingly ministry of the Church. These are the three ministries of the one mission of the Church (Australian Episcopal Conference, 1970, para. 9).

As priest

The priestly mission of the Disciples of Christ involves living, sharing and celebrating life in ways appropriate to situations and circumstances. These experiences are not something unique or particular, but rather entail the totality of living. They stem from an awareness of the Spirit and a response to the life of the Gospel in the everyday experiences of life. "All of these become spiritual sacrifices acceptable to God through Jesus Christ. This 'priestly' activity finds its fulfilment in the celebration of the Eucharist and serves as a spiritual consecration of the world itself to God" (CL, para. 14).

The Church is a priestly people. Jesus Christ makes it share in his priesthood so that all baptised people constitute a 'line of kings and priests' to serve his God and Father. Though they differ from one another in essence and not only in degree, the common priesthood of the faithful and the ministerial or hierarchical priesthood are nonetheless interrelated. Each of them in its own special way is a participation in the one priesthood of Christ (Australian Episcopal Conference, 1970, para. 87).

As prophet

The characteristic of sharing in Christ's mission through prophecy is found in witness and service (CCC, para. 785). This is a responsibility of listening to God, responding to the call, engaging a tradition and aligning it within a contemporary Christian culture that is potentially under threat (Coleridge, 2017). The voice and actions of the prophet remind the community that their society is God centred; a counter culture, one that stands apart from other communities. Trust and hope are hallmarks of prophecy, with story and interpretation the instruments in binding and reminding a community that their commitment lay in relating to God who journeyed with them.

He is Prophet, Priest and King not only for those who follow him but for all the peoples of the earth. The Father offers him as the Way, the Truth and the Life to all men and women, to all families and communities, to all nations and to all generations (EO, para. 8).

As king

The characteristic of sharing in Christ's mission through kingship at first glance presents as unusual. However, when kingship is equated with leadership, and leadership is seen as living the kingdom vision of Christ, the concept is more accessible. This notion of kingship is exemplified in the question of Pilate to Jesus "Are you the King of Jews?" (John 18:33), and the response "My kingdom is not from this world" (John 18:36). The leadership of Jesus was leadership in awakening the kingdom of God and leading in ways that manifested this vision. The invitation to share in the royal or kingly office of Christ involves leadership in light of the Gospel vision and the unification of the kingdom in history (CL, para. 14).[64]

King is another name for the father or grandfather ... the strong and stable energy that can hold together chaos, fear and doubt to an amazing degree just as the queen does in the feminine form ... the king or the father is somehow the very oneness of God which holds together our disparate, divided or inimical parts (Richard Rohr, 2012, CD).

The vocation of the Christian in sharing in the priestly, prophetic and kingly roles of Christ is lived out in the multiplicity of callings and circumstances that constitute personal, family, social and working life. Christians are called to the 'sanctification of the world from within, like leaven, in the Spirit of the

---

[64] *The Dogmatic Constitution on the Church* (1964) and *The Catechism of the Catholic Church* (1994) use the terms *kingly* and *royal* to promote the same concept.

Gospel, by fulfilling their own particular duties' (LG, para. 31). This mission is primarily designed to manifest Christ's message by words and deeds and to communicate his grace to the world (see AA, para. 6). It entails a progressive and deepening appreciation of the Spirit and the challenge to align with this Spirit already present in self, others and creation (Figure 5).

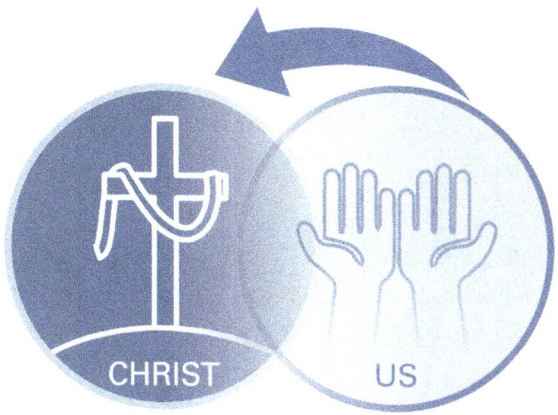

Figure 5. Alignment with the person and message of Christ

Missionary discipleship

Ecclesia in Oceania (2001) confirmed the significance of testimony to Christian life through word and works. The invitation was to mission, a process of engagement that called for a new understanding of the concept and a new means for its activation.

> *The present generation of Christians is called and sent now to accomplish a new evangelisation among the peoples of Oceania, a fresh proclamation of the enduring truth evoked by the symbol of the Southern Cross. This call to mission poses great challenges, but it also opens new horizons, full of hope and even a sense of adventure (EO, para. 8).*

A new myth for mission

Mission today is evidenced in a new myth;[65] one that recognises and engages the Spirit of God already present and active in the world. Anthony Gittins CSSp summarises this phenomenon as "all people are called to be saved, this is not a salvation contingent upon 'a missionary with water;' and the Church is not the

---

[65] Myth in this context refers to a break from the traditional legendary stories that invited an imagination of missionaries being sent to bring the faith to foreign lands with outcomes measured in Baptisms, Church structures or other manifestations of the traditional faith.

ark of salvation alone on the sea but a sign, a signpost and a beacon which some may discover and some may not" (1994, p. 150). In this light, mission is more akin to an inside out approach which seeks to become awake and celebrate God's presence in contrast to an outside in orientation where the presumption entails bringing God into a community thought to be deficient of the spiritual.

> *Mission, indeed, does not belong to us, but is done as we participate in the very mission of God. It is not simply about the expansion of Church, but about the transformation of the world, hoping for the day when God will establish God's Reign within the whole of creation* (Stephen Bevans, 2012).

The proposition of Stephen Bevans SVD is that mission comes first. The active, dynamic and life of the Spirit of God in the world has a following and in some instances this is the Church. This mission is first that of God's mission through the Spirit, in Christ. From a Christian perspective it is a complex concept, one that develops in a variety of ways and is centred on discipleship and operationalised through at least three principles. The first is that of engagement and the generation of knowledge from being present to the experience of the current reality; the second involves the development of understanding and the alignment of purpose that resonates with the aspirations of the community in light of the Gospel; and the third is that of empowering the community in ways that provide for advancement of purpose and mutual transformation through the process (Figure 6).

Figure 6. Mission expression through discipleship

All within the Church are called to share and continue the mission of God in the world. It is an invitation to understand, experience and be open to mutual liberation in accord with the Gospel. This implies that the Church does not exist to expand or perpetuate itself. Rather, it acts not so much as an answer, but a response to God's call to continue God's loving, redeeming, healing, reconciling, liberating, forgiving, and challenging mission. Jesus called this outcome the Kingdom of God and envisioned it as a community of those who were forgiven and forgiving, a community which includes everyone, those who recognise and rejoice in the abundance of God's grace and presence (Bevans, 2009, p. 5). In this light all people are invited to evangelise, "all are missionary disciples" (EG, para. 120), and all are challenged to operate in ways that reveal oneness with what already exists and with what might be in terms of a Kingdom view of life and living.

The notion of the new evangelisation was first raised by Pope John Paul II in Haiti on the occasion of the 500th anniversary of the first evangelisation of Latin America. It implied that countries and societies that were once evangelised had lost the vigour of faith needed to receive the message in a fresh and vital way in order to win them back to Christ (Julian Porteous, 2008, p. 11).

Archbishop Porteous makes the point that missionary discipleship is a twofold experience; a personal encounter, and a response that flows out of and grows with the experience of love. The experience is centred on Christ and an attitude "I have met Jesus Christ and nothing else matters" (Porteous, 2018). The task is to 'remain in my word' (John 8:31) and to take up this engagement which gives both life and entails the experience of the cross (Luke 14:27). This is the challenge of fullness through discipleship and openness to where the Spirit of the Rabbi Jesus might lead. This is discipleship that is explicitly intentional, saying yes while also knowing, experiencing and committing to its challenges.

Intention ... is something you plunge into. When you activate it, you'll begin to feel purpose in your life, and you'll be guided by your infinite self. ... A force that is everywhere. There's no place that you can go where it isn't. It can't be divided and is present in everything you see or touch. ... It sets in motion your non-physical aspects, including your emotions, thoughts and dispositions. In this instance, intention is infinite potential activating your physical and non-physical appearance on earth (Wayne Dyer, 2004, p. 8-9).

The significance of intentional discipleship is that it begins with 'eyes wide open' and engages the challenge of 'can you drink the cup'?[66] The experience balances a spirituality of descent[67] with the promise of 'life to the full,' (John 10:10), finding the pearl of great price (Matthew 13:45-46), and encountering the treasure hidden in a field which precipitates selling all and buying that space (Matthew 13:44). In this light, Pope Francis asks "What are you waiting for?" (EG, para. 120).

Life grows by being given away and it weakens in isolation and comfort. Indeed, those who enjoy life most are those who leave the security on the shore and become excited by the mission of communicating life to others (EG, para. 10). ... *On the lips of the catechists, the first proclamation must ring out over and over: Jesus Christ loves you; he gave his life to save you; and now he is living at your side every day to enlighten, strengthen and free you* (EG, para.164).

Discipleship in the Catholic school

The Spirit of Christ in the Catholic school reveals the dynamic and energising power of God which operates in and through all. Just as on the occasion of the first Pentecost, it is an experience of fullness which "was unlike anything they had ever experienced before" (Acts 2:2-4). It is this same Spirit that brings grace, God's love, to all human activity and leads to liberation and transformation.

The means by which the living stones give expression to the vision of the cornerstone invite a new form of evangelisation (EN, para. 14; AGD, para. 18; CSTTM, para. 2). No longer is the Good News shared through osmosis (Coleridge, 2008; O'Loughlin, 2007) but seen in innovative and co-creative ways that address the signs of the times as part of the living tradition of the Church. At the heart of sharing this Good News is a Gospel imagination which shapes and guides the totality of curriculum and culture. Central to this imagination and engagement is the work of the Spirit. It is from this Spirit that the Catholic school draws its inspiration and manifests this in its relationships, curriculum, religious life, processes, systems and structures.

---

66 Taking the communion cup as the image and even drinking coffee, tea, or wine with friends, Henri Nouwen likens the cup to our life, with all the sorrows and joys we experience and guides us to "drink to the bottom," fulfilling the mission God has called us to.
67 The path of descent is discussed by Richard Rohr as the process of admitting that power and authority rest with God, not self, and that spirituality centred in God is a process of gradual acceptance and surrender; pursuing a path of descent otherwise dominated by the ascent of the ego.

> *The Gospel offers us the chance to live on a higher plain, but with no less intensity: life grows by being given away, and it weakens in isolation and comfort … when the Church summons Christians to take up the task of evangelisation, she is simply pointing to the source of authentic fulfilment. True faith in the incarnate Son of God is inseparable from self-giving, from membership in the community, from service, from reconciliation with others. The Son of God, by becoming flesh, summoned us to the revolution of tenderness* (EG, para. 88).

Christian discipleship is the response that an individual makes to the challenge and invitation of the Gospel. It is more than a concept, a theoretical view on how life can be lived. It has to do with action and living in relationship "not only with God, but also with the presence of the Spirit in others and the world" (Groome, 1998, p. 30). It begins with the presumptions of good people doing good things and seeks to engage, name, celebrate and enact this Spirit with gratitude, relationship and intentionality. "Ministry as Discipleship embraces everything we are, think and do in relation to the triune God who is present in and yet transcends all that is" (McBrien, 1988, p. 79).

> *Authentic contemporary spirituality is therefore not about something additional or even something new. It is not meant to take us out of anywhere, but should give depth, meaning and resonance to the ordinary in daily life* (Helga Neidhart RSC, 1997, p. 20).

Discipleship within the Catholic school is becoming awake to the work of the Spirit within the context of one's responsibilities, relationships, and community. It reaches into religious education, the wider curriculum, the religious dimension of the school, culture and community and has implications in all manner of places and relationships (Figure 7). In practical terms it is "What faith looks like in everyday attitudes and behaviours" (Dreyer, 1996, p. 13). It is a focus on God and a conversion to a particular way of living. To be a disciple within the community of the school is to pursue a way, a pilgrimage, and a journey with Jesus Christ. It is an invitation to a vision where the ordinary events of life are filled with divine energy and grace. In this regard disciples "are called to theologise grassroots experience … challenged to create a new spirituality for a new age, a new awareness of ourselves as co-creators with our Creator and as ministers in the work of Christ" (Foley & Schmaltz, 1987, p. 6).

Figure 7. Spirituality and the Catholic school

INTEGRATION

Executive Summary

Walking his way: A spirituality of engagement incorporates appreciating and responding personally and professionally to the mission of God in the Catholic school. It is centred on the person and message of Christ and involves becoming awake to the presence of the Divine through spirituality and spiritual practices. Encounters with the Spirit are manifested through discipleship which holds blessing and challenge, opportunity and commitment. A spirituality of engagement invites a way of life and living across the spectrum of mission activities within a community informed by, attentive to, and responsive to a living faith.

Reflection: "Is that Jesus?"

The official opening ceremony brought to a climax much planning, fundraising and the construction of greatly needed school facilities. There was an air of excitement about the gathering which, for purposes of organisation, was held in the parish Church. Students, parents, supporters, teachers and support staff were all in attendance. As well, there were numerous visitors from the Catholic Education Office and some government officials. Also present were the Parish Priest, the Bishop and a small group of attendants to assist with the ceremony. For the very young children, the occasion was somewhat overwhelming. As the procession entered the Church, led by the altar servers, followed by readers, the Parish Priest and ultimately the Bishop, the young heads began to turn and observe. A level of astonishment, commentary and questioning followed. Seeing the grandeur of the Bishop's crosier and mitre, one young student asked expectantly. "Is that Jesus?" The friend next to him, turned around, and replied, after a longer, more inquiring gaze; "I think so."

The exchange between the two young students may not have been heard by many but was significant. It reminds us that young people, families, colleagues, visitors - all of us - make observations about the people and the activities that constitute life. Impressions are given through the multiplicity of interactions, verbal and non-verbal language, and the continuous stream of behaviours and symbols that constitute life in community. In its broadest extent, this is what evangelisation involves: the messages that are given about what is central in the life of the individual, group and community. They reflect the nature of what inspires, what animates, what is important.

Questions

1. **Head:** How effective is the term missionary disciple as a means of describing intentional professional practice?
2. **Heart:** Have you experienced in your own life any change in your spirituality?
3. **Hand:** Can you observe any unique patterns in behaviours that flow out of your spirituality?

Activities

Theme: Where are you looking?

Goal: Being attentive to the Mystery of God

Task: Consider the following questions and then enter into some personal reflection with a colleague.

- Where is your attentiveness directed in the day-to-day?
- If you look 'inside' what do you see?
- What is it that keeps you focused on your 'true north'?
- How does self-awareness support your relationships?

Theme: Why is it so?

Goal: Becoming awake to the work of the Spirit

Task: Reflect upon a successful ministry experience and explore potential factors that underpinned the outcomes. The following guidelines may assist with the reflection.

- *What happened?* Describe the experience.
- *When and where?* Expand the context.
- *Why did it work?* What factors contributed to the success of the experience?

Theme: Exploring similarities and difference

Goal: Clarifying concepts: Mission, Life, Culture and Identity of the Catholic school

Task: Terms and concepts within Catholic schools are sometimes used interchangeably. Consider the following statements and discuss with a colleague the sameness and difference of the following.

- *The Mission* of my Catholic school seeks to…
- *The Life* of my school involves…
- *The Culture* of my school entails…
- *The Identity* of my Catholic school refers to…

Activities

Theme: Emmaus walk

Goal: Becoming aware of the sacred

Task: Team up with a colleague and select an outside location, ideally within an environment of interest, in which to walk and observe. The following 'parameters' might apply to the journey.

- Resist discussion on issues and situations;
- Comment only on what is observed as indicative of the Divine;
- Be present to the now of the experience;
- Be patient and wait upon the inspiration.

CHAPTER THREE
Telling his truth: The prophetic mission of the Catholic School

Chapter Outline

CHAPTER THREE	70
TELLING HIS TRUTH: THE PROPHETIC MISSION OF THE CATHOLIC SCHOOL	70
INTRODUCTION	70
Reflection	70
At a glance	70
Focusing story: "Go back and tell John"	71
From your experience	71
THEMES AND MAIN IDEAS	71
Humble beginnings to established service	71
In the beginning - denominational schools	72
A century of Religious	74
Post-conciliar era	75
Beyond the crossroads	78
International perspectives	79
The Australian context	80
A distinctive philosophy	84
Agency of Church	84
Learning as liberation	86
Aims, models and principles	87
Signposts from Vatican II	88
Post-conciliar emphases	90
Constants in context	94
Mission alignment	96
Christian anthropology	96
Engagement typology	97
Constants and characteristics	100
Purpose, goals and the 'elevator pitch'	102
INTEGRATION	104
Executive Summary	104
Reflection: "You are that tree"	104
Questions	105
Activities	105

CHAPTER THREE
Telling his truth: The prophetic mission of the Catholic School

INTRODUCTION

Reflection

"While the people pressed upon him to hear the word of God, he was standing by the lake of Gennesaret. And he saw two boats by the lake; but the fishermen had gone out of them and were washing their nets. Getting into one of the boats which was Simon's, he asked him to put out a little from the land. And he sat down and taught the people from the boat" (Luke 5:1-3).

At a glance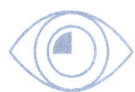

Telling his truth explores the invitation of Christ to view and live in the world in a special way. This is an anthropological view which shapes the mission of the Catholic school within a new social context and by a community with a diverse profile.

The chapter presents the Catholic school as integral to Church mission, possessive of distinctive characteristics and aligned with the theological and educational insights of Vatican II. The provision has grown from humble beginnings to an established service where relationships are complex and where community engagement is welcomed. As a place of mutual transformation, it engages a new context through the education of the whole person towards a civilisation of love in the spirit of human solidarity.[68] Drawing from a continuing stream of research and Church exhortations, constants in mission reveal its ecclesial foundations, distinctive anthropology, community engagement, and, as a place of formation for its overall community.

---

68 The most recent Congregation for Catholic Education document, 2017, makes reference to the goal of educating to fraternal humanism in building a civilisation of love.

Focusing story: "Go back and tell John"

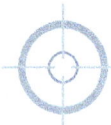

Sacred scripture gives an account of the imprisonment of John the Baptist, his growing interest in the ministry of Jesus and the effects this is having on the people of Galilee. John becomes so curious that he asks some of his followers to go to Jesus and ask whether he is the Messiah or is another to come. The disciples ask the question in due course with the response of Christ being "Go back and tell John what you are hearing and seeing: the blind can see, the lame can walk, those who suffer from dreaded skin diseases are made clean, the deaf hear, the dead are brought back to life, and the Good News is preached to the poor. How happy are those who have no doubts about me" (Matthew 11:4). It is in these few words that a perspective on the living ministry of Christ is offered; a ministry that complements visionary preaching with practical engagement that gives life and wholeness.

From your experience

1. What characterises the prophetic mission of your Catholic school?
2. How transparent is the alignment of mission with school practice?
3. Is your school a learning community in dialogue with community?

THEMES AND MAIN IDEAS

Humble beginnings to established service

The Catholic school in Australia is described as a "pearl of great price that permits young men and women to discern a purpose in life, with the person of Jesus and his message as a beacon of hope" (Canavan, 1999, p. 2). It was founded upon the generosity of lay people (the first hundred years), an era 'of giants'[69] that revealed the enormous contribution of Clergy, Religious Sisters and Brothers (the second hundred years), and today is served by dedicated and competent lay educators (Benjamin, 1999), who seek to continue an authentic service in dialogue with a wider community.

---

[69] Commentary on the present status of Catholic schools in Australia uses the term of 'standing on the shoulders of giants' which refers to the breadth and depth of contribution by multiple Religious Institutes across the period of 1870 to 1970 but not confined to such.

In the beginning – denominational schools

Ross Thomas in the milestone analysis of Catholic schools in Queensland, *Project Catholic School*, speaks of Catholic schools as the 'great survivors of Australian education'. He advances that the story of Catholic schools is truly colourful, one that merges readily "into the equally colourful backdrop of the history of colonies and the nation." It is a story in three parts across three centuries.

The arrival of the first fleet in 1788 and the establishment of a penal outpost of the British Empire saw the commencement of settlement and the beginnings of the Catholic faith in Australia. As about one quarter of the prisoner exiles were of Irish origin, the Catholic population that constituted the early colony of New South Wales commenced in misery and degradation. These first Catholics were convicts and were looked on with considerable suspicion. They came from a country that had withstood British domination and were lacking the sophistication thought to be associated with British political and social conventions. These first arrivals were largely peasants, some speaking only Gaelic. They were said to have only nominal faith, although the majority did identify as Catholic (Briody, Ruddiman & Doherty, 2003).

Catholic identity within the new colony can be seen in the context of the eighteenth-century penal laws that impoverished and destroyed social structures. In response, the Irish "Turned to the Catholic religion as the sole focus of their national spirit" (Campion, 1987, p. 3). However, this was still considered 'relatively weak, and its practice confined and erratic.' It was not until 1820 when two priests arrived in Sydney, Joseph Thierry and Philip Connolly, that the faith gained particular institutional and pastoral support. Other priests followed and, some fifteen years later, the first Bishop was appointed, a Benedictine, John Bede Polding (1794–1877).

Education was seen as a practical means for civilising the population and reducing crime and disorder. It was initially provided through the Anglican Church but was later changed to allow for religious pluralism through the 1836 *Church and School Act* that permitted "A rough and ready equality among the main denominations" (Campion, 1987, p. 35). In the wake of this Act some government funding of schools was permitted and the previously established Catholic schools at Parramatta and Sydney received financial support. This was the start of the denominational schools' period which was to continue for decades.

The Church's attitude to Catholic schools in the relatively young colony was that schools were integral to the Church's mission and the Church was reluctant to surrender its authority in education to either the state or anyone else (Wilkinson, 2018). However, the establishment of a separate system was said to be daunting as the Bishops appreciated that many Catholic parents did not necessarily support the role of Catholic education as integral to the establishment of the Catholic faith.

> *The essence of Catholic education for the Bishops was that it must take place in, and be infused by, a religious atmosphere which acts on the child's whole character of mind and heart. It was not just the direct teaching of Catholic doctrine, but above all the interpenetration of a vital Catholic atmosphere in the school, its infusion with a Catholic life, and a spirit of prayer* (Peter Wilkinson, 2018).

The experience of the *Church and School Act* proved to possess inefficiencies and became increasingly expensive (Briody, Ruddiman & Doherty, 2003). Moreover, as the population increased the press for a more general system of education was considered but the resistance from authorities in London was considerable. The resistance also from the Church was significant, particularly with the growth in the Australian Church hierarchy. However, with the 1850 *Australian Colonies Government Act* authorising the colonies to make their own Constitutions, the debate around educational provision intensified. Enacted by the British Parliament, the Act enabled the creation of new Australian colonies with a similar form of government to New South Wales.

> *The denominations saw state funding for education as an antidote to moral degeneration, the common Christianity party highlighted the wastage of resources in the denominational system, while the liberals and secularists, imbued by sentiments then sweeping Western Europe were engaged with a vision of a new Australia created by the agencies of an enlightened national education* (Pat Briody, Wendy Ruddiman & John Doherty, 2003, p. 5).

The financial support to denominational schools was not to last and in the 1870s this state aid was removed and replaced by free, secular and compulsory education across the states. Thereafter, the survival and development of Catholic schools became a function of three factors: the energy of clergy who made parishes the centre of Catholic life and spearheaded the establishment and maintenance of Catholic schools; the work of Religious Brothers and Sisters who staffed these schools, often enduring heroic poverty; and the cooperation and self-sacrifice of the Catholic laity who offered community support and exercised their right of choice in electing Catholic schooling for their children (Briody, Ruddiman & Doherty, 2003).

> *Notwithstanding the obvious and immediate obstacles placed in their way, the clergy set about the task of developing a 'system' of Catholic education that would serve to pass on the 'true' vision of humankind. Spearheaded by Archbishop Vaughan[70] the Bishops elected to increase the number of Catholic schools. The construction of buildings and the recruitment of teachers soon absorbed much of the energy of the clergy and served to indicate, for the century ahead, the direction that the endeavours the parish priest would inevitably take* (Ross Thomas, 1979, p. i).

A century of Religious

The conclusion of Ross Thomas was that the period that followed was one of the most important in the history of Catholic schools in Australia. Building programmes were accelerated and the replacement of lay teachers by members of Religious Orders gathered momentum. The response by Religious Institutes, internationally and nationally, was extraordinary, so much so that by the commencement of the First World War, parish primary schools were staffed substantially by Religious.

The Catholic community between the Great Wars was connected and uniform through liturgical, social and ritual practices. Movements such as the Young Christian Workers, National Catholic Girls, Holy Name and Sacred Heart Sodalities, Catholic Women's League, Children of Mary and Holy Angels all created a community that was tied together in social and religious beliefs. Social life for Catholics was focused around the Church, with Catholic balls, football clubs and tennis groups being prominent. Catholic religious values and ways of faith practice were similarly strong and present in the home.

The Catholic school prior to Vatican II provided a key role in socialising young Catholics in Catholic religious values supported in the home and reinforced by the institutional Church. The context was one of emancipating Catholics to assume responsible social roles within a social milieu that was perceived to be potentially hostile, sectarian, and bigoted. The situation precipitated substantial enrolment growth within Catholic schools[71] but with the numbers of Catholics increasing, the Catholic schools could not keep pace with the demands being placed on them. The Goulburn strike of 1962[72] reinforced the financial pressures on Catholic schools particularly in a context of increasing expectations of education as a key, progressive, innovative, and costly service to the community.

---

70 Roger William Bede Vaughan (9 January 1834 – 18 August 1883) was an English Benedictine monk of Downside Abbey and the second Roman Catholic Archbishop of Sydney in Australia from 1877 to 1883.
71 Ross Thomas comments that 80 per cent of school aged Catholics were enrolled in Catholic schools.
72 On Friday July 13, 1962 six Catholic schools in the diocese of Goulburn closed and instructed their pupils to enrol the following Monday in the government school system.

Within a relatively short period, the national government provided alleviation of some of the building needs of Catholic schools in terms of Science and Library facilities. As well, the financial burdens on Catholic families and parishes began to be addressed through the establishment of the Schools Commission in the wake of the Karmel Report. It was this inquiry that added weight to the needs of Catholic schools, particularly in the smaller and disadvantaged Parishes. Further support to schools came with the establishment of Catholic Education Offices who provided assistance in areas such as resource distribution, policy formulation, staffing and educational services support.

On 12 December 1972 the newly elected Whitlam government appointed an Interim Committee for the Australian Schools Commission. Chaired by Peter Henry Karmel, the Committee was to examine the position of government and non-government primary and secondary schools throughout Australia and to make recommendations on the financial needs of those schools, and the measures to assist in meeting them. The report identified many inequities in the funding system, which for the first time led to the federal government providing funding to state schools (Australian Government Department of Education, Employment and Workplace Relations, 2012).

Post-conciliar era

The third phase of Catholic schooling in Australia, the post 1970s era, evidenced a period of renewal in keeping with a host of ecclesial, pastoral, organisational, financial and administrative adjustments. Within this immediate post-conciliar era, two complementary projects characterised new directions. The first, *Project Catholic School* (McLay, Coghlan, Corkeron & Druery, 1979),[73] provided a blueprint for the administration of Catholic schools in Queensland;[74] and the second, *A Tree by the Waterside* (McLay, Druery, Murphy, & Shaw, 1982) expanded on the vision of Christ as the foundation for its life and culture.

The identity of institutions generally, and the identity of Catholic institutions, in particular, must be thought of as something caught in a dialectic of continuity and discontinuity - constantly growing, constantly changing, and being engaged with, and challenged by, variable circumstances - whilst at the same time, capable of recognising self as an uninterrupted narrative of meaning (David Ranson, 2008, p. 85).

---

[73] The national conference in Armidale on the organisation and administration of Catholic education in Australia, Tannock (1975) provided a stimulus for the research.
[74] Findings shared within a national context through the National Catholic Education Commission.

The blueprint for Catholic school administration, *Project Catholic School*, stemmed from a context of increasing Catholic enrolments and the motivation to improve the quality of service at multiple levels within the Church. Outcomes from the four-hundred-page report narrated responsibilities within school, parish and diocese; with state and national entities providing the necessary interface with respective governments. Typically, organisational systems addressed development needs and accountability requirements and incorporated a variety of systems through which the learning goals and administrative experiences of the school could be developed.

The provision of Catholic schools within Australia is one of governance by the Episcopacy and Religious Institute leaders, and administration by Catholic Education Offices and Religious Institute service teams. Cardinal Pell (2007) makes reference to the emergence of these 'education bureaucracies' and states that they are a new phenomenon with the goal of contributing to the evangelising mission of the Church. At the same time, these 'offices' are regarded as comprising "indispensable leaders and allies of the Bishops and Superiors of Religious Institutes in relation to reform, standards, curriculum and religious education" (Pell, p. 840).

The *A Tree by the Waterside* initiative also looked to the future of Catholic schools through processes that ensured continuity of the tradition. Reminiscent of the principles and processes of Vatican II, the applied research explored new ways of advancing mission and the goal 'to keep on bearing fruit' (McLay, Druery, Murphy, & Shaw, 1982, p. 5). Central to the process was the expansion of the traditional model of Catholic schooling as one of a family, to one that was more engaged with community and more interdependent in its relationships. The Catholic school was called to be both an educational community and a model community; a place where diversity is embraced and where processes of conversation facilitated inclusion in light of Christ and the Gospel.

> *We have many life-giving roots, but our tap root is Christ. We belong to a community, a church, that has for twenty centuries tried to live a certain way of life as an attempt to respond to the call and vision of Jesus Christ, the Son of God. Basic to that vision is a call to teach the Good News, to help one another grow in the truth and love that will alone create a new earth in its full human and spiritual development. This call is the tradition against which we must ultimately test our contemporary understanding and practice* (Anne McLay, Alan Druery, Molly Murphy, Francine Shaw, 1982, p. 5).

The process of enhancing Catholic schools continued in resourcing and organisational terms across the latter decades of the twentieth century and came to a high point with the change of government in 2007. Speaking at a public education forum, the then Commonwealth Education Minister, Julia Gillard, foreshadowed an education revolution and reinforced national principles that would "make sure that every child in every school receives an excellent education regardless of their background or the ethos or location of their school" (Gillard, 2009). These principles were to be manifested in equity and excellence, the articulation of national goals and the advancement of policy with practical implications in the development of quality teaching, facilities and curriculum reform, together with the strengthening of the workforce and processes of accountability.

The National Goals for Schooling hold a central place within the educational revolution agenda for twenty-first century learners. The context for education is seen as the building of a "democratic, equitable and just society" (Ministerial Council on Education, Employment, Training and Youth Affairs, MCEETYA, 2008, p. 4) with the three associated national goals of students becoming: successful learners, confident and creative individuals, and active and informed citizens. Within such a framework, schools of the twenty-first century will promote "the intellectual, physical, social, emotional, moral, spiritual and aesthetic development and wellbeing of young Australians" (MCEETYA, 2008, p. 4).

The raft of initiatives that flowed out of the national principles and goals were geared towards transforming learning and teaching, addressing disadvantaged schools, and increasing transparency and accountability. The changes are directed to all educational jurisdictions and every school in the spirit of building a "new national effort ... another big step to better Australian schools" (Gillard, 2008). Notwithstanding these unprecedented changes, initiatives continue from the review of resourcing by David Gonski (2018). The Guardian newspaper (July, 2018), for instance, reports a continuing debate around funding equity, new indicators of school performance, training of teachers in literacy, closing the gap for Indigenous and non-Indigenous Australians, and processes of review in literacy and numeracy. It is within this framework of government expectation and support that Catholic schools are challenged to respond in ways that are authentic. The response incorporates identifying what is important within a changed and changing profile and interpreting this through the lens of mission.

The Bishops of Australia continue to examine the culture within which Catholic schools operate and the interaction of this with overall mission. The Queensland Bishops' Project, *Catholic Schools for the 21st Century* (2001), and the New South

Wales (NSW) and Australian Capital Territory (ACT) Bishops' Pastoral Letter, *Catholic Schools at a Crossroads* (2007), for instance, seek to position Catholic schools as continuing the tradition while being responsive to the circumstances and needs of the time.

Within the Queensland context, the Bishops advance that Catholic schools "will have a strong Catholic identity and give witness to Christian values; be open and accessible to those who seek its values; have a holistic curriculum; and be staffed by qualified, competent people who give witness to Gospel values" (Queensland Bishops' Project, 2001). At the same time, the Catholic school is argued to be recognised as an education and worshipping community through "vigorously participating as an ecclesial entity in implementing the Church's mission of evangelisation." The school is described as a 'face and place of Church' in circumstances where the vast majority of students and families (61% to 80%) rarely, if ever, attend Church beyond the confines of the Catholic school (ACER, 2009).

The position statement from the Bishops of NSW and the ACT (2007), *Catholic Schools at a Crossroads*, gives significance to the cultural identity of the Catholic school while drawing attention to the changes in enrolment patterns and the educational and cultural context within which the Catholic school ministers. The statement offers a detailed expression of this new context and provides a challenge for Catholic schools to be responsive without compromising tradition. This challenge entails Catholic schools being centres of the new evangelisation and enabling students to achieve high levels of 'Catholic religious literacy' within an identity that is centred in Christ and in the Church's continuing attentiveness to tradition through life in the Spirit.

> *We are not government organisations, we are not the funded sector, we are not (or should not be) big businesses making strategic decisions about whom we engage with and what we do based solely on market principles. We are faith-based mission-driven organisations. Our work is always and everywhere to uphold the human dignity of each person, to believe 'in the revolutionary nature of love and forgiveness' and to remain faithful to those who are, in fact, evidence of failure of the market economy (EG, para. 288).*

Beyond the crossroads

The experience of continuous change within Catholic schools of Australia was articulated by the Bishops of New South Wales and the Australian Capital Territory as constituting a crossroads (2007, p. 3). That is, a situation had arisen where demonstrable changes were apparent and new pathways needed to be considered. The choice of 'crossroads' as an image highlighted a sense of journey and the resultant need to make decisions about direction setting. Other commentators (D'Orsa & D'Orsa, 2010, p. 7) describe the situation as more critical and advance the more confronting image of 'frontier' to illustrate the contemporary reality. The argument is made that the concept of 'frontier' depicts aspects of the 'unknown' with the associated need for 'map-making' and 'bridge-building' in an environment of challenge.

The institutions and the world we live in are at a crossroads. This historical moment is redefining what it means to be in relationship with each other on a local, regional and global level. As the Internet, social media and other technologies continue to evolve; society also is redefining traditional relationships, connectivity, institutions and culture. In the process, we are being opened to the entire world on a daily basis. Each day the news and life questions are intertwined between local and global connections. While each nation tries to maintain its unique culture, the world is becoming more interconnected (Mark Clarke, 2014, p. 3).

International perspectives

The inaugural *International Handbook of Catholic Education* (Grace & O'Keefe, 2007) confirms a new context for Catholic schools and specifies a similar set of challenges for Catholic schools across 35 societies. While there exists predictable variation in priority and interpretation across cultures, the challenges reveal a context characterised by secularisation and a response needing to address globalisation, new political situations, Church and State partnerships, a preferential option for the poor and the economics of Catholic schooling. Moreover, within the Catholic school itself, the continuing need to hear the voices of students, to highlight the particular rights of girls in certain spheres of the world, and to give primacy to faith, morality and formation illustrate powerful themes for review and renewal (Table 1).

Table 1. International challenges for Catholic Education

CHALLENGE	INTERPRETATION
Secularisation	The denial of the validity of the sacred and of its associated culture
Globalisation	The extension of capitalist values in every part of the world
Political Contexts	Church–State relations on the provision of Catholic schooling

CHALLENGE	INTERPRETATION
Preferential Option for the Poor	A radical commitment to the service of the poor (comprehensively defined)
The Voice of Students	Enhancing the role of students as active participants in the life of the school
Faith Formation	Preservation of Catholic identity through the continued spiritual development of the next generation of staff
Catholic Schooling for Girls	Commitment to the development of girls in a global society
School Leadership	The challenges of recruitment, formation and retention of Catholic school leaders and teachers
Moral and Social Formation	Addressing a culture preoccupied with individualistic personal 'success,' a cult of 'celebrity' with commodity worship, and an explicit and sexualised media and entertainment culture

The Australian context

While the pattern of influences on Catholic schools internationally are significant, Catholic schools in Australia face their own particular demands. A benchmark study conducted under the auspices of the Australian Catholic Bishops' Conference (Holohan, 1999) revealed a growing set of challenges, specifically in terms of Religious Education. Issues of curriculum relevance, developmental differences, variable faith situations, financial resourcing, enculturation, and the variable nature of student learning experiences, all suggested that Catholic schools were being challenged to be more responsive as the new millennium dawned. Key to the process was the integration of Christian witness and ministry of the Word across the multiple environments in which faith finds expression. The research confirmed the 'seeds of the Gospel' (Holohan, 1999, p. 58) already present and identified the significance of educators, particularly religious educators, within cultures and places where change is significant and formation a priority (Holohan, 2009).

> *Teachers of religion, therefore, must be men and women endowed with many gifts, both natural and supernatural, who are also capable of giving witness to these gifts; they must have a thorough cultural, professional, and pedagogical training, and they must be capable of genuine dialogue* (Congregation for Catholic Education, 1988, para. 96).

The profile of the Catholic school in Australia, defined in terms of the students and families it serves, those who provide the service, the expectations of its wider community and the profession of education has changed. While not exhaustive nor reflective of particular schools, systems of schools, or State and Territory patterns, national trends illustrate the situation of Catholic schools being at a crossroads and the concept of a new frontier for mission inviting creative, collaborative and authentic responses.

Schools and enrolments

Catholic schools around the world number 216,000 and educate 61 million students.[75] Within Australia there are 9,414 schools (Government - 6,634, Catholic - 1,738, and Independent - 1,042) educating approximately 3.8 million students.[76] Overall, the share of national student enrolments at the affiliation level reveals 65.4 per cent in Government schools; 20.2 per cent in Catholic schools; and 14.4 per cent in Independent schools. Across 2015 - 2016, the number of students enrolled in Government schools rose by 1.6 per cent while in the non-government sector, students enrolled in Catholic schools showed a slight increase (0.2 per cent) and students in Independent schools increased by 1.3 per cent.

Student profile

Growth in school numbers continues to match an increasing population as evidenced in Government, Catholic and Independent provision. However, within this growth there has been a shift in the nature of the profile. Students with disabilities moved from 4 per cent in 2011 to 4.5 per cent in 2015, and Indigenous students from 2.2 per cent to 2.7 per cent across the same period. In contrast, full-fee paying students and boarding students decreased to .2 per cent and .8 per cent respectively. The National Catholic Education Commission (NCEC) Report of 2015 reveals that 69 per cent of students are Catholic and that 31 per cent other than Catholic. The percentage of other than Catholic in secondary schools is 33 per cent compared with 29 per cent in primary schools.

Socio-economic status

The conclusions of Susan Pascoe (2007) and Brian Croke (2007), together with commentary from Archbishop Anthony Fisher (2006) indicates that the socio-economic position of students in Catholic schools has changed. Within a tradition of providing a preferential option for the poor and primarily catering for students from Catholic families, the profile is now such that "Poorer Catholic

---

[75] Numbers cited by Archbishop Zani, Secretary of the Congregation of Catholic Education, in an address to a national forum of Catholic school leaders in Sydney, Australia, March 6, 2018.
[76] Figures drawn from the Australian Bureau of Statistics, Census Data 2016.

children are increasingly attending State schools; wealthier Catholic children are increasingly attending non-Catholic private schools; and middle income other than Catholic children are increasingly attending Catholic schools" (Fisher, 2006, p. 4). More recent research in 2016 by the Independent Schools Council of Australia on the total non-government sector reports that in 2014 the majority of non-government schools (Catholic systemic and Independent) were in the middle socio-economic range.

Religion and spirituality

An international study (Search Institute, 2008) conducted with young people (7000 youth between 12 and 25 years old across 17 countries and 6 continents), illustrated substantial shifts and national variation in commitment to religion and spirituality. On an optimistic note, the majority of youth (93 per cent internationally) reflected a spiritual dimension to life; and, while religion and spirituality were regarded as different, they were viewed positively. Religion was seen as more rule based, whereas spirituality was perceived as encompassing the 'heart.' With respect to international comparisons, Australia ranked highest as the country declaring an absence of spirituality among youth (47 per cent compared to the group mean of 24 per cent).

The research of Mason, Singleton and Webber (2008) into the attitudes of Generation Y (people born, 1977-1995) confirmed the level of disinterest in faith and spirituality among young Australians. Significant among the findings was a general low level of interest and involvement in religion and/or spirituality (17 per cent), with 51 per cent of respondents declaring a belief in God, 32 per cent being unsure and 17 per cent indicating non-belief. Overall, while some importance was given to Church and school influences on faith and spiritual development, the research revealed comparatively low levels of this influence: from family (44 per cent); friends (15 per cent); religious organisations (14 per cent); school (6 per cent); and youth organisations (4 per cent).

Parent priorities

A survey of over 5000 Catholic, State and Independent school parents (Sultmann, Rasmussen and Thurgood, 2003) yielded consistent priorities in school selection. Choice centred on care, quality of teaching, school discipline, parental consultation, moral development, and vision and values. For the group of parents who elected Catholic schooling; expected criteria for their choice scored comparatively low. For example, in response to the question 'What is absolutely essential?' less than half the sample gave significance to faith development (46 per cent), pastoral care and concern (47 per cent), and religious education (39 per cent). These priorities were reinforced in the report of Kennedy, Mulholland and Dorman (2010, p. iv) which confirmed an overall preference by parents for "positive relationships within safe, caring, concerned school communities."

Parent motivations for Catholic schooling are now argued to be based on values and discipline McKay (2018). While Catholic and Christian populations are comparatively in decline, confidence exists in faith-based schools to nurture values and provide a safe environment for students. McKay argues that a 'quiet revolution' within and without the Church is becoming noticeable and this is maintaining enrolment interest. Factors of significance include a more informed concept of God, whose essence is a loving Spirit; the need for community to enable the expression of love; the orientation of young people to spirituality as distinct from institutional religion; the essence of religion in offering a meaning system for life; and, the realisation that all of the human family is connected and that aspects of respect, kindness and compassion provide a common ground for harmony and development.

Religious affiliation of staff

Staff in Australian Catholic schools numbered approximately 91,000 in 2016[77] with the vast majority being lay staff. The NCEC report of 2016 states that of these, 80 per cent of primary school teachers and 61 per cent of secondary school teachers identify as Catholic. Moreover, the report adds that 25 per cent of Catholic school staff are engaged in regular worship and parish leadership activities, and hence the reality is that "For most staff, the Catholic school is their only regular experience of Catholicism" (NCEC, 2017a, p. 11).

A summation of the profile of the contemporary Catholic school is that it is no longer predominantly Catholic; focused primarily on the poor; staffed by Religious; supported through family catechesis; small and under-resourced; principally tied to Parish; largely independent in accountability; and without system advocacy and support. This once organisationally simple, independent, homogeneous faith based endeavour within a largely mono-cultural community has transitioned into a complex, interdependent, multi-faith and multicultural community. The challenge of this new profile is to engage with its immediate and wider community, operate in harmony with its mission, and nurture informed, committed, professional and engaged personnel within and for a distinctive philosophy.

---

77 National Catholic Education Commission, Catholic Schools in Australia 2016.

A distinctive philosophy

Agency of Church

The distinctiveness of Catholic schooling is aligned to the distinctive characteristics of Catholicism itself (Groome, 1996). Five perspectives to the school that signify uniqueness to Catholicism include: a positive anthropology of the person, the sacramentality of life, a communal emphasis, a commitment to tradition as a source of its story and vision, and an appreciation of rationality and learning. In addition, three other 'cardinal' characteristics are nominated as defining Catholic education; commitment to individual personhood, social justice, and inclusion.

Positive anthropology

At the core of Catholicism and Catholic education is a shared understanding of the human person as made in the image and likeness of God. The practical aspects of this philosophy are that people function within God's grace and make a positive contribution towards personal and communal welfare. The practical implications are evident in the attitude of educators towards students (honouring uniqueness, acknowledging dignity, developing gifts, and observing rights) and supporting students to recognise that they can contribute meaningfully to their life and world.

Sacramentality

The principle of sacramentality is a belief that God's presence and grace are manifested through the ordinary events of life (Groome, 1996, p. 112). The seven sacraments of the Church represent these high points of everyday experiences, ritualising their power and significance. The impact of this sacramental consciousness is that the entire curriculum can be permeated with it. No longer is it important to seek ways of making curriculum areas more 'religious.' Rather, the challenge is to look at each area to see the manifestation of God in the unfolding of knowledge, the witness of people, and in the processes through which learning and teaching occur.

Community

The focus on community is found in the traditional connections with parish and the Local Church of the Arch/diocese and the universal Church, a broader commitment to the common good, and the challenges of social justice at all levels. The Catholic school by virtue of its own community of students, families and staff, becomes an embryonic Christian faith community and shares in the responsibilities that all Christian communities have towards their members.

Care, inclusion and the formation of right relationships are fostered among all participants. A pedagogy that is grounded in relationships and marked by participation, conversation and cooperation is promoted (Groome, 1996, p. 116).

Catholicism

The story of Jesus, the message of his revelation and the values that he taught and lived are at the heart of the Catholic school. This is a story with an accompanying tradition, a history of interpretation represented in creeds, dogmas, doctrines, rituals, theologies, symbols, spirituality, language and gestures. It is a story that is evidenced in the personal, interpersonal, professional and communal domains that define life within the Catholic school. It is a tradition that illumines knowledge, events and circumstances in the light of faith and the mystery of God's love and revelation.

Rationality and learning

The capacity for insightful and reasoned thinking incorporates the notion of 'faith seeking understanding.' It is the conviction that faith goes 'hand in glove' with understanding and that reason and revelation, need and enhance each other. In this view, reason is regarded as a God-given gift to be used for discernment and to support growth in faith as part of human development. The implication is that students are encouraged to pursue independence in thinking, development of right judgment and moral responsibility. The task entails 'helping people to think with imagination and perception, to discern the ultimate in the immediate, and to be critically conscious about society (Groome, 1996, p. 121).

Implications: cardinal characteristics

The alignment of the identity of the Catholic school with the identity of the Church is argued by Groome (1996) to possess three implications. First, that knowledge is not divorced from 'being.' That is, the student is supported to integrate knowledge with the goal of being a whole person, an expression of God, a fully alive person. The second is educating towards a sense of justice whereby people see themselves in relationship to God and neighbour and thus develop a commitment to those who experience and possess less. It is a commitment to equality, based on dignity and the fostering of human rights for all. A third implication is for Catholic schools to be inclusive in the way that Catholicism attempts to be. This is a call to hospitality and welcome, a manifestation of unity in God's whole family, and the challenge of the Catholic school to be liberating for the individual and community.

Learning as liberation

Education as a liberating life-giving process for all is developed in the work of Paulo Freire. *Pedagogy of the Oppressed* (1970) characterises education as a process of the teacher and learner engaging in dialogue for mutual advantage. No longer is the learner to be viewed as a passive recipient whose education entails 'banking knowledge' but rather someone who is creative and proactive with the teacher who acts as facilitator and guide. In this light, educational processes move from being a 'gift' to the recipient to becoming an instrument of engagement and liberation for all. Central to the process of mutual liberation is the significance of dialogue. This is more than mere communication as dialogue is underpinned by dignity and humility and "an intense faith in humankind, faith in their power to make and re-make, to create and re-create, faith in their vocation to be fully human" (p. 71). This is not the response of solely talking about (verbalism), or acting out (activism), perspectives on education, but the engagement of both through praxis (action and reflection) in ways that empower the learner, teacher and the community.

The Catholic School on the Threshold of the Third Millennium depicts Catholic schools as making an active contribution to the liberation of individuals and communities. The continuing challenge, in fact demand, is for 'new contents, new capabilities and new educational models' (CSTTM, para. 2). This challenge comes not only as a reminder of the essential features for the Catholic school, but also points to identifying new means for generating meaning in service of a contemporary society and culture. Similar to the perspectives offered by Groome (1996), *The Catholic School on the Threshold of the Third Millennium* reminds educators of the significance of engaging the signs of the times, and the importance of aligning the teaching and learning process with the mission of the school within the life of the Church.

Central to learning are aspects of Pedagogy, Content and Knowledge (PCK). Also apparent in contemporary Catholic schools is the emergence of Information and Communication Technologies (ICT) which serve as a mechanism for enhancing opportunities to address accelerating changes in knowledge and processes of knowledge acquisition. While the focus of schooling is learning, it is learning informed and committed to a social and cultural order where the goals concentrate on the development of the person in relationship with the community and through rich and diverse pedagogies. This is holistic teaching, facilitating authentic human growth where meaning, knowledge, skills and service nurture development and find meaningful outcomes in self, others, community and creation (Figure 8).

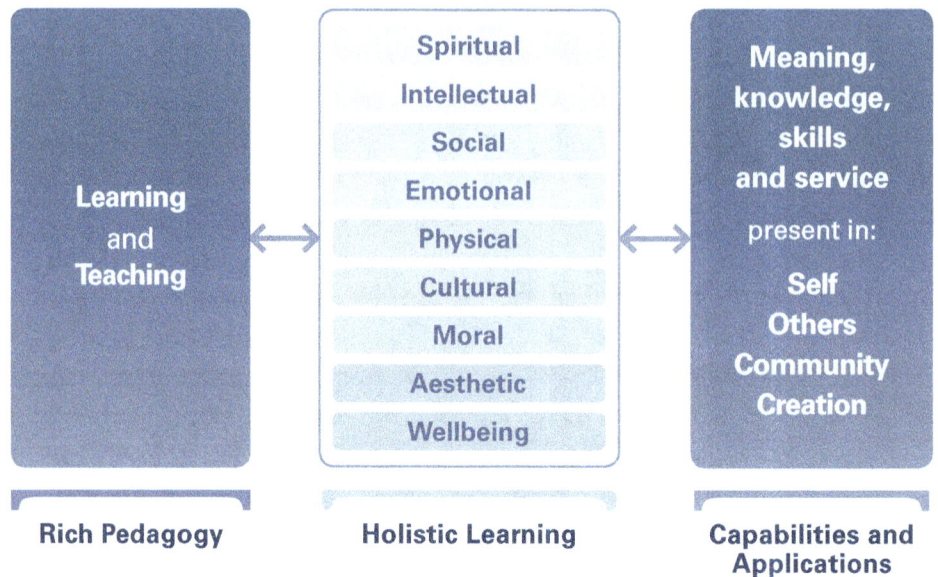

Figure 8. Facilitating authentic human growth

Aims, models and principles

Education within the Catholic school entails facilitating authentic human growth informed by a Catholic Christian view of what it means to be fully human. Within this purpose, a sub-set of aims provide for a deeper appreciation of the process and act as overall beacons to name, shape and renew services and processes. However, impacted by variable religious, social, political, and cultural contexts within which Catholic schools minister, the expression of services varies and is characterised by different models in service delivery. Notwithstanding this diversity, the exhortations from Church teaching and the lived experience within Arch/dioceses and Religious Institutes have given rise to particular and consistent principles that have underpinned the nature and purpose of Catholic schools.

The comprehensive research of McLaughlin (2000) on the purpose of Catholic schools identified a core set of aims summarised as the facilitation of holistic human development; attentiveness to the developmental stages and individual differences of the learner; recognition of the dignity of the learner and teacher; and, the educative process as incorporating a personal and community dimension. These foundational aims, when pursued across varying social and cultural contexts are evident in differing models of provision, paths, which enable particular directions with a common destination in mind (D'Orsa & D'Orsa, 1997). These paths are nominated by Treston (1997) as 'traditional,' by virtue of Catholic religious character; 'evangelising,' which includes outreach through

Catholic ethos; 'secular,' in culture, although externals may appear Catholic; 'ecumenical,' in Christian practice and symbols; and 'public sector,' in terms of integration into a public system.

Models of Catholic schooling while seemingly different at the level of service orientation, can also be observed in terms of their foundational principles. These are the fundamental philosophical values that provide the motivation for establishing Catholic schools and guide their service and relationships in the broadest of terms. They are the common set of understandings that typically apply to all Catholic schools; principles that have shaped the mission of Catholic school and continue to be refined and applied on the basis of Magisterial teaching and service experience. While not exhaustive or finalised, the principles of personal dignity; Church and school relationships; education as a human service; and community relationships are identified as significant (Figure 9).

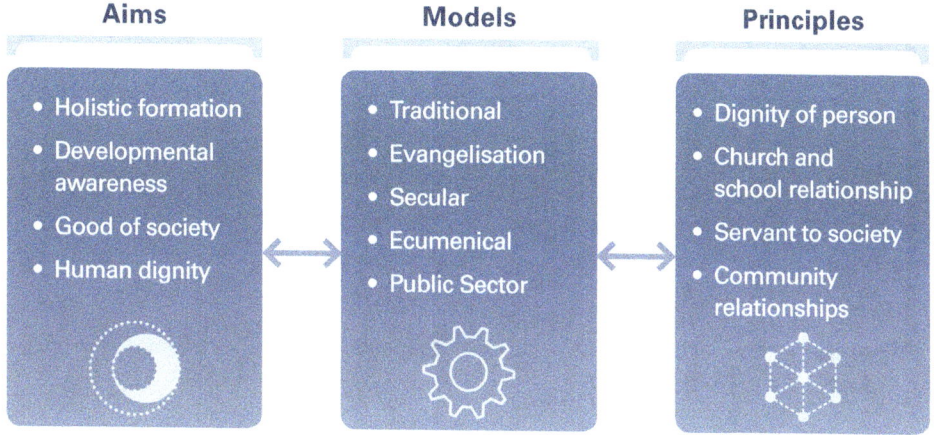

Figure 9. Aims, models and principles of Catholic schools

Signposts from Vatican II

Dermot Lane (2015) introduces a commentary on Catholic Education in light of Vatican II by stating that it is by nature an 'aerial view,' one that endeavours to offer seminal ideas and large patterns of directions (paradigm shifts) evident in Vatican II documents. It is a collective overview as distinct from a discussion of individual documents. Notwithstanding the value of individual statements, his 'shorthand summary' extracts the structural shifts and generic change principles (signposts) which are said to have 'a direct bearing on Catholic Education' (Lane, 2015, p. 19). Summarised in Table 2, these shifts underpinned the development of the final document of the Council, *Declaration on Christian Education*, and established a foundational pattern for subsequent documents over fifty years (Table 3).

The Declaration on Christian Education invites Catholic educators into a new reflection of what might be a future sustained by the richness of the past and yet responsive to the needs of the present. The structural shifts recorded in Table 2 demonstrate engagement by the Church with its own and wider community through an appreciation of the faith story and by means of dialogue. The associated principles then give significance to the practical aspects of this dialogue and the accompanying challenges with language, being informed through formation and identifying the intimate relationship regarding the integration of faith, life and culture.

Table 2. Structural shifts and principles underpinning Vatican II

STRUCTURAL SHIFTS – a move to
❖ A relationship of openness to the modern world
❖ A relationship manifested in dialogue and mutuality
❖ A new dialogue with other Christian Churches
❖ Appreciation of truth and grace in the world and other religions
❖ Personal and dialogical understanding of revelation
❖ An appreciation of historical consciousness as key to understanding the human
❖ An experience of inductive, historical and experiential knowledge as relevant to revelation, faith and theology
❖ Reading the signs of the times as informing the presentation of the Gospel today
❖ A new awareness of anthropology as central to the proclamation of the Gospel
PRINCIPLES – a recognition about
❖ Presenting the 'deposit of faith' in new and creative ways
❖ A view of evangelisation as the adaptation of the faith to the concepts and language of people
❖ The intimate relationship between faith and culture
❖ An enhanced recognition of the hierarchy of truths in the Christian faith

The particular and immediate implications for the Catholic school arising from the deliberations of Vatican II are contained within the *Declaration on Christian Education*. The challenges give precedence to education that is holistic, informed by the Gospel and in partnership with parents. The document offers an unambiguous purpose with emphases from the tradition and applications that can be respectful of social and cultural influences while not compromising a living faith in the life of the school. Significant to the focus is the centrality of Christ and the meaning that this offers in the pursuit of all manner of aims, relationships and processes (Table 3).

Table 3. A summary of 'calls' to Christian Education from Vatican II

CHRISTIAN EDUCATION – The call to
❖ A holistic praxis engaging the whole of life and a 'heavenly' calling
❖ Formation of the human person in pursuit of one's ultimate end and the good of society
❖ Being informed by advances in Psychology and the Arts, the science of teaching and seeking to promote the physical, moral and intellectual development of the person in service of freedom and the common good
❖ A similar standard of renewal in formation equivalent to that for secular subject formation
❖ Pursue goals of supporting the maturity of the individual as a child of God; being conscious of the gift of faith; learning how to worship God; and, understanding Christ as redeemer
❖ Recognise parents as the primary educators and to foster the knowledge and worship of God and love of neighbour
❖ Support parents in their freedom to choose the school/s for their children
❖ Become animated by the Gospel Spirit of freedom and love; to be open to the contemporary world; to be receptive of students other than Catholic; and caring for those who are poor
❖ Promote harmony between faith and science as well as a convergence between faith and reason
❖ Link non-Catholic universities through centres under Catholic auspices

Post-conciliar emphases

Within the post-conciliar period of Vatican II, a flow of documents from the Magisterium have continued to shape the mission of Catholic schooling worldwide. The progressive publication of this literature has served to extend the Council's vision for the Catholic school by situating each statement within a particular and post-modern context. Notably, the title offered to each exhortation, together with its overall thematic emphases, record the significance of directions in relation to the challenges and opportunities of context.

The Catholic School was the first of the post-conciliar documents on Catholic Education from the Magisterium. It advanced the thinking of the *Declaration on Catholic Education* and reinforced the fundamental philosophy underpinning the Catholic school. That is, "Jesus Christ is the foundation of the whole educational enterprise" (1977, para. 33). More specifically, within the totality of its life, in the ordinary and not-so-ordinary happenings, the pervasiveness of Christ is experienced. "His revelation gives new meaning to life and helps humankind[78] to direct thought, action and will according to the Gospel, making the beatitudes the norm of life" (para. 33). In this light, the Catholic school is challenged to review its entire programme according to the vision from which it draws its inspiration and on whom it depends.

Its task is fundamentally a synthesis of culture and faith, and a synthesis of faith and life: the first is reached by integrating all the different aspects of human knowledge through the subjects taught, in the light of the Gospel; the second in the growth of the virtues characteristic of the Christian (Congregation for Catholic Education, 1977, para. 37).

The second post-conciliar statement, *Lay Catholics* in Schools in: *Witnesses to Faith* (1982), addressed the vocational crisis and the growing limitations of Religious Congregations in establishing, staffing and managing Catholic schools. Historically, the presence and generosity of religious Priests, Brothers and Sisters had been part of a tripartite team of parents, clergy and religious who had collaborated to build, advance and sustain Catholic schools for more than a century. The statement was illustrative of a new reality that suggested Catholic schools not only look to those being served but equally to the community of people engaged in service. Sustainability and authenticity were viewed as intimately connected to the calling of lay people to fulfil a baptismal vocation within the mission, life and culture of the Catholic school.

Therefore, the educational community of a school is itself a school. It teaches one how to be a member of the wider social communities; and when the educational community is at the same time a Christian community - and this is what the educational community of a Catholic school must always be striving toward - then it offers a great opportunity for the teachers to provide the students with a living example of what it means to be a member of that great community which is the Church ... (para. 22)

---

[78] Insertion of 'humankind' is offered to give an inclusive expression to the concept, and the removal of 'his' prior to the original quotation of 'his thought' is in keeping with this principle, as is the removal of 'his' with respect to 'making the beatitudes his norm of life.'

... the presence of lay Catholics in these schools is the only way in which the Church is present. This is a concrete example of what was said above: that the Church can only reach out to certain situations or institutions through the laity (Congregation for Catholic Education, 1982, para. 18).

The subsequent document of the Congregation, *The Religious Dimension of Education in the Catholic School* (1988), recognised not only the new reality of staff, but the focus of this community in terms of mission. The statement argues that what makes the Catholic school distinctive is the religious dimension expressed in its educational climate, the personal development of each student, the relationship established between culture and the Gospel, and the illumination of all knowledge with the light of faith. The document recognised the scholarship that accompanies methods, programmes, and structures, each and all of which contribute to the quality of the Catholic school's educational endeavour. In this way, the Catholic school is challenged to fulfil its educational goals by blending human culture with the message of salvation into a coordinated programme, one that allows the Gospel to permeate, in the manner of leaven, all of the systems that constitute sound educational practice.

Its aim, methods and characteristics are the same as those of every other school. On the other hand, it is a "Christian community," whose educational goals are rooted in Christ and his Gospel (Congregation for Catholic Education, 1988, para. 84).

The Catholic School on the Threshold of the Third Millennium (1998) took renewal to a new level whereby the Catholic school is challenged to bring forward new content, capabilities and models besides those followed traditionally. Catholic schools are nominated as places of the new evangelisation within which a lively dialogue allows for enculturation and formation of people with differing religious and social backgrounds. The vision of Vatican II becomes realised with the explicit call to the school to renew itself (aggiornamento) and to engage its tradition (resourcement) while promoting connection and outreach with the community it serves. In this light the "Catholic school sets out to be a school for the human person and of human persons" (para. 9).

(The Catholic school) ... fulfils a service of public usefulness and, although clearly and decidedly configured in the perspective of the Catholic faith, is not reserved to Catholics only, but is open to all those who appreciate and share its qualified educational project (Congregation for Catholic Education, 1998, para. 16).

Educating Together in Catholic Schools: A Shared Mission Between Consecrated Persons and the Lay Faithful (2007) continued the emphasis of the Council to engage the 'signs of the times' through a deeper level of response by those who serve. Building on a theology of Trinity, a focus is given to communion, first with Christ and then among all who comprise the community of the school. Based on the assumption that the school is an ecclesial community, the document highlights the school as a 'home and school of communion,' a place of formation for the individual and the community of persons who comprise it. The implication is that all within the school community are called to be conscious of the privilege and responsibility, their communion in mission and dialogue within the school and the world. The invitation is to a "personal vocation in the Church, and not simply as the exercise of a profession" (para. 6).

> *Education contains a central challenge for the future: to allow various cultural expressions to co-exist and to promote dialogue so as to foster a peaceful society ... (Introduction) ... The communion lived by the educators of the Catholic school contributes to making the entire educational sphere a place of communion open to external reality and not just closed in on itself* (Congregation for Catholic Education, 2007, para. 43).

Educating to Intercultural Dialogue in Catholic Schools: Living in Harmony for a Civilisation of Love (2013) brings to a high point the challenges of a new cultural context and the breadth and depth of engagement by Catholic schools. The plurality of cultures is identified, approaches to pluralism are offered and foundations for an intercultural dialogue are forged. Significantly, foundations in theology and anthropology are introduced and the educational community is imaged as an experience of intercultural dialogue. The nature and importance of formation for teachers and administrators is reinforced and processes of integration, guided interaction and the recognition of others, are emphasised. The school is viewed as a learning community where all are called and challenged to educate for and within a civilisation of love.

> *With the gradual development of their ecclesial vocation, lay people become increasingly more aware of their participation in the educational mission of the Church. At the same time, they are also driven to carry out an active role in the spiritual animation of the community that they build together with the consecrated persons. Communion and mutuality in the Church are never one-way streets. If, in fact, in the past it was mostly priests and religious who spiritually nourished and directed the lay faithful, now it is often the lay faithful themselves (who)*

> *can and should help priests and religious in the course of their spiritual and pastoral journey* (Congregation for Catholic Education, 2013, para. 32).

The most recent exhortation of the Congregation for Catholic Education, *Educating to Fraternal Humanism: Building a Civilization of Love 50 Years after Populorum Progressio* (2017) draws from foundations in faith grounded in the signs of the times. The call is to educate through a culture of dialogue. The document advances vision and mission through the goal of building a civilisation of love through an understanding of what it means to be fully human. It incorporates the theological and anthropological foundations of Vatican II; reflects the practical implications of *Laudato Si and Gaudium et Spes*; and aligns and integrates the volume of literature on the Catholic school in the post-conciliar years. The document offers signposts for Catholic schooling in the twenty-first century; directions based on a paradigm of peace, justice and solidarity that is fundamentally grounded within an era of globalisation.

> *The nature of education lies precisely in being able to lay the foundations for peaceful dialogue and allow the encounter between differences with the primary objective of building a better world. It is, first and foremost, an educational process where the search for a peaceful and enriching coexistence is rooted in the broader concept of the human being - in his or her psychological, cultural and spiritual aspects - free from any form of egocentrism and ethnocentrism, but rather in accordance with a notion of integral and transcendent development both of the person and of society* (Congregation for Catholic Education, 2017, para. 15).

Constants in context

The literature from the Congregation for Catholic Education has provided continuing and timely reflections on the nature and mission of the Catholic school. One question of interest from the overall collection of documents is the extent to which mission characteristics can be identified and clustered so as to inform current and future practice. That is, to what extent is the magnificent and voluminous literature able to be summarised in a way that the distillation of concepts allows for greater clarity and precision in mission aspiration and delivery.

A series of Leximancer analyses, digital data mining processes of narrative text (Leximancer Manual, 2017) are reported by Hall, Sultmann and Townend (2018) on the eight individual and overall collection of Magisterial documents of the conciliar and post-conciliar era. The themes and summary discussion points for each document are shown in Table 4 with the dates of each release identifying the document discussed previously.

Table 4. Themes and concepts of the conciliar and post-conciliar period

⟵ YEAR ⟶

	1965	1977	1982	1988	1998	2007	2013	2017
Themes	Schools	School	Human	Human	School	School	Dialogue	Fraternal
	Education	Life	Lay	School	Religious	Persons	Human	Dialogue
	Life	Society	Education	Students	Community	World	Schools	Society
	Sacred	World	World	Love	Public	Formation	People	Principles
	Students	Social	Christ	World	Countries	Open	Love	Challenges
Concepts	Collaboration with community	Inclusion	Vital role of laity	Equality of humans	Equality of humans	School is immersed in greater world community	In the global context	Collaboration
	Catholic school alone is not solely responsible for education	Education and wisdom	Community connection	Knowledge seeking	Collaboration and vocation	Formation of spirituality in global context	Inclusion	Respect of perspective and religious pluralism
		Mission	Vocation	Daily communion	Multiculturalism and community	Mission	Respect	World community
			Mission		Mission		Collaboration	

The findings from the individual document analyses are suggested to offer discussion starting points for Catholic school mission in relation to particular themes and challenges. With due recognition of multiple interests and priorities, school communities are invited to utilise the themes as a basis for mission dialogue. In terms of the collective document analysis, the goal is to explore the insights that have characterised Catholic school mission for over half a century.

The analysis of the collective documents revealed four continuing constants proposed as: Mission alignment (Catholic school as integral to the life and mission of Church); Christian anthropology (Catholic school philosophy on what it means to be fully human); Engagement typology (Catholic school mission in service of the community); and, Catholic school as a formative place (Catholic school mission, life and culture supported by formation and the insights of the new evangelisation). Drawing from the report, a summary position is offered on each of the mission constants and four paradigms; Faith, Learning, Community and Formation are proposed as constituting the significant, pervasive and continuing aspects of Catholic school mission.

Mission alignment

Mission is no longer defined by being sent to serve or even to view service as the first response within community. Rather, mission is characterised by being present, observing and advocating for that which is already evolving, life-giving and life-enabling. It is a process of being aware, encountering the Spirit of Christ already present, already supportive and already informing. This realisation about mission is underpinned by a respectful valuing of people and appropriate engagement and discernment which is mutually transformative. The engagement takes no process for granted and seeks to operate and identify with those who are in most need, those at the margins.

Jesus began to preach the Good News in the "Galilee of the Gentiles," a crossroads for people of different races, cultures and religions. In some ways this context is similar to today's world. The profound changes that have led to the ever-spreading multicultural societies requires those who work in schools and universities to become involved in the educational programmes of exchange and dialogue, with a bold and innovative fidelity able to bring together the Catholic identity to meet the different "souls" existing in a multicultural society (Pope Francis, 2014).

Christian anthropology

Education, drawn from the Latin *educare*, meaning 'to lead out of or lead forward,' is foundational to human community and continuity. Education begins with a view of what it is to be human and what it is that humans are being led forward to.

What it means to be human, establishing one's basic anthropology, is at the heart of all educational endeavour. *Laudato* Si invites consideration of a small but inter-related set of anthropological principles. First, pride of place is to be given to the primacy of relationship; relationality before individuality and the fostering of kinship within the human and natural world. Second, the centrality of dialogue as the means for understanding and building relationship in a common home involves "fruitful dialogue on the relationship of religion and science, between ecology and spirituality, between politics and economics, as well as a dialogue among religions and equally among the various sciences"

(Lane, 2015, p. 64). Third, a revitalised anthropology assumes embodiment. That is to say, "human consciousness, interiority, subjectivity are only available as embodied (Lane, 2015, p. 66). Two further principles: language, and a movement away from anthropocentricism; reiterate language as enabling communication and relationship, and the shift from anthropocentrism as a movement from the ego as central to an appreciation of oneself in relationship.

Catholic school anthropology is based on a model and a vision for people in community. Jesus is the perennial model and his view of the kingdom, marked by right relationships of justice, peace, liberation and compassion, provides the basis for what it is to be authentically human. Through their professional practices and personal and communitarian witness, Catholic educators not only give expression to these fundamentals, but also see them as outcomes for their students. "The Catholic school is committed thus to the development of the whole person, since in Christ, the perfect human, all human values find their fulfilment and unity" (TCS, 1977, para. 32). In this way, the essence or mission of Catholic education is the facilitation of holistic development (personally and collectively) centred in Christ.

Engagement typology

Catholic schools function in a diverse and multiple contexts and are challenged to adjust in ways that are authentic to Gospel living. Where the culture of Catholic schools have become 'increasingly secularised, de-traditionalised and more recently also pluralised' (Pollefeyt & Bouwens, 2010, p. 199), the challenge of a new reality is argued to require "Bridging the gap time and again and of communicating the Catholic faith to youngsters who grow up in contemporary culture" (Pollefeyt & Bouwens, 2010, p. 199).

The *Enhancing Catholic Schools Identity Project* (ECSIP) has established itself as a strategy for engaging community in respectful dialogue. The essence of the project "draws from the resources of Theology, Sociology and Religious Education to develop survey instruments which can be used to profile students as a basis for designing and delivering an effective religious education programme" (Sharkey, 2018). Where the project has been applied, there exists evidence of re-contextualisation in terms of "Approaches to Scripture, prayer, sacred spaces and rituals" with goals of making Religious Education "more explicit, more dialogical and more connected to the current context" (Larkins & Watherill, 2018).

The application of ECSIP survey instruments reveals variable expressions of Catholic institutional identity and the levels of Catholicity present (Gowdie, 2017, p.141). The instruments address the **belief systems of people** who constitute the Catholic school (*the Post-Critical Belief Scale*); a typology which situates a **school's Catholic identity** from traditional to more contemporary forms (*the Melbourne Scale*); and the presentation of **pedagogical options** in a pluralistic context (*the Victoria Scale*). While the *Post-Critical Belief and Melbourne Scales* reveal valuable insights, *the Victoria Scale* pursues Catholic school identity from the perspective of how it might engage its community.

The Victoria Scale consists of two dimensions: the vertical (*Christian Identity*) "The measure in which its members live out of a generally shared, Catholic inspiration; and the horizontal (*Solidarity with People*) - the measure of openness to and receptivity of other life visions and life attitudes" (Pollefeyt & Bouwens, 2010, p. 205). The depiction of the two dimensions produces an 'identity square' with four "Typical strategies that schools can adopt to give shape to their pedagogical responsibility" (p. 205). The descriptions of the particular typologies are conversationally summarised as: colourful - *what works*; monologue - *we do it our way*; colourless - *nothing emphasised*; and dialogue - *in and through relationship*. The dialogue school is the strategy that recognises the plurality of beliefs within the community while holding to the Catholic message which sets the tone for this dialogue (Figure 10).

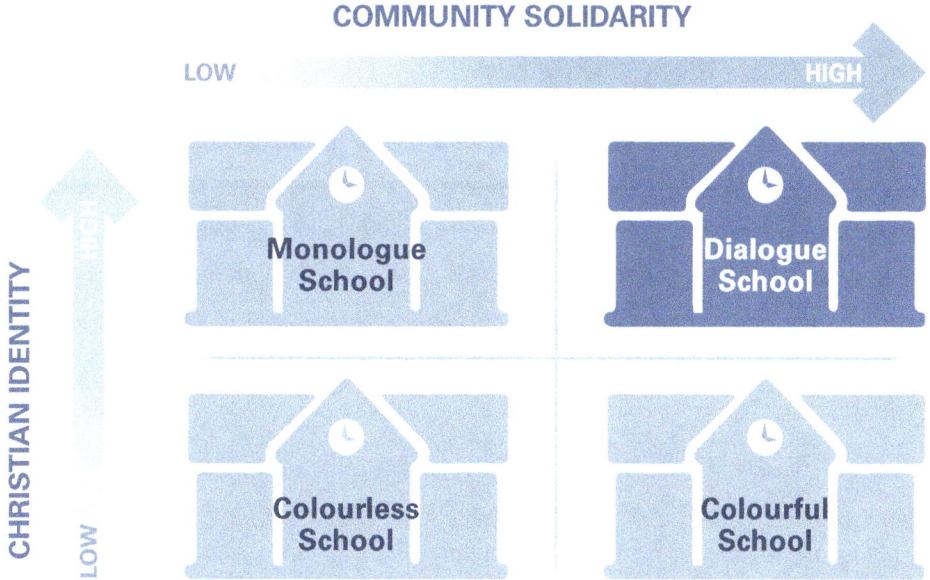

Figure 10. A typology of Catholic school mission

Formation for mission in the Catholic school is encouraged (ETCS, para. 6) and is advocated as a form of 'doing' theology, 'grassroots theology,' as educators "make sense of their experience, individual and collective, from the perspective of faith" (D'Orsa & D'Orsa, 2010, p. 4–5). Formation in this context is an opportunity for imagination, where the 'beginner's mind'[79] can be developed through engagement with the Mystery.

Schools can and must be a catalyst, it must be a place of encounter and convergence of the entire educating community, with the sole objective of training and helping to develop mature people who are simple, competent and honest, who know how to love with fidelity, who can live life as a response to God's call, and their future profession as a service to society (EID, para. 18).

The Catholic school is called to draw upon its traditions and recognise the complexity and needs of the current social reality, while proclaiming the fundamental imperative to focus on Christ and the Gospel. Within this context Pope John Paul II introduced the concept of a new evangelisation, a means for interpreting the Gospel with new vigour and ardour, recognising the status of humanity, the culture of our times and analysing human needs. It implied that countries and societies that were once evangelised had lost the vigour of faith needed to receive the message in a fresh and vital way in order to win them back to Christ (Porteous, 2008, p. 11).

For this, an educator is in need of permanent formation. It is necessary to invest so that teachers and supervisors may maintain a high level of professionalism and also maintain their faith and the strength of their spiritual impetus. And in this permanent formation too I would suggest a need for retreats and spiritual exercises for educators. It is a beautiful thing to offer courses on the subject, but it is also necessary to offer spiritual exercises and retreats focused on prayer! For consistency requires effort but most of all it is a gift and a grace. We must ask for it! (Pope Francis, 2014).

Not to be dissuaded by the challenges of the new evangelisation, (Porteous, 2008) refers to the evangelists of the early Church; Origen, John Chrysostom, Gregory Nazianzus, Ambrose, Augustine and Leo the Great, who are said to have been successful in a challenging context. Two consistent themes associated with these Patristic teachers are their familiarity with the central figure of Jesus, and their depth of conviction arising from a conversion of the heart, *metanoia*, through meaningful encounters. In other words, the traditions and processes of evangelisation remain the same for the first Church and the Catholic school today. It is the Spirit at work in and through the human experience with the model and message of Christ as foundational. An illustration

---

79 A term used by Richard Rohr to indicate the early stage of faith inquiry.

of this human experience within a context not necessarily thought to be religious is offered by a newly ordained priest in the following recollection.[80]

> *Walter Camp lived at Floraville on the Leichhardt, near Burketown. There were no Catholics there. He was delightful company and I regularly called in. I think it was the last time I saw him alive that we shared a reflection. Standing at his gate, I asked myself and commented to Walter - "did I come to evangelise you Walter or to simply enjoy your company?" I then said to him, "I admit Walter that it was to enjoy your company." Walter replied, "and in so doing you evangelised me powerfully my friend."*

The challenge of sharing perspectives on mission involves identifying language, processes, opportunities, events, situations and symbols that speak to a contemporary world. In short, it is sharing meaning so as to advance "the reality of belonging to a community of people who really believe without fear and who really care and support one another" (Hodgens, 2008, p. 54). It is sharing a Gospel imagination in the total fabric of life. It is premised on openness, with dialogue as a practice, and where personal and communal reflection nurture life within the Spirit.

Key to the new evangelisation in the Catholic school is an appreciation of mission. It is a challenge that borrows from the tradition as distinct to giving way to relativism, which, in the colourful words of Archbishop Anthony Fisher, incorporates "eclectic mixes of religion lite, DaVinci Code Catholicism, fundamentalist secularism" (Fisher, 2006, p. 9). Clearly, the call is to 'full-cream' activity where the Catholic school is a center for the new evangelisation which engages culture and starts with the 'story' of the individual, the school and the Church that preaches Christ. It entails "proclaiming the Gospel anew, nurturing 'seeds of faith' in a context of freedom and yet being 'up front' about educational and catechetical goals" (NSW and ACT Bishops 2007, p. 12-13). Such a position signals witness, formation of the heart and service.

Constants and characteristics

The constants of Catholic school mission from the analysis of the collective Magisterium documents (Hall, Sultmann & Townend (2018) were consistent with the identity themes for Church and school, (Groome, 1996), the conclusions from mission research (McLaughlin, 2000; Miller, 2010; Sultmann, 2011; Sultmann & Brown, 2011; 2013) and the analytical commentaries by Cardinal Versaldi (2017) and Archbishop Zani (2018). A summary of the constants and

---

[80] The story of evangelisation was recounted by the late Reverend John Butcher when sharing perspectives at a Diocesan Synod.

characteristic elements integral to Catholic school mission synthesised from the research is shown in Table 5.

Table 5. Constants and characteristics of Catholic school mission

CONSTANTS	CHARACTERISTIC ELEMENTS
FAITH Faith in a Catholic school is	❖ Founded on the person and message of Christ ❖ Attentive to Church Tradition ❖ Personal and communal in nature ❖ Supported by an ecclesial community ❖ Inclusive and outreaching, especially to the poor and marginalised ❖ Expressed through spirituality ❖ Conscious and committed to a shared mission ❖ Reflected in joy and hope within personal and communal life
LEARNING Learning in a Catholic school is	❖ Based on a Catholic anthropology of the person ❖ Consistent in its purpose, goals, programmes and processes ❖ Facilitated through quality professional practice and relationships ❖ Prophetic and liberating ❖ Grounded in a relevant and responsive pedagogy ❖ informed by religious climate, processes, systems and structures ❖ Responsive to the needs of the person, community and creation
COMMUNITY Community in a Catholic school is	❖ A community united in Spirit ❖ An ecclesial servant community ❖ A learning community ❖ Possessive of shared beliefs and values ❖ Connected to Parish, Local (Arch/Diocese) and Universal Church ❖ Respectful dialogue with context and culture ❖ A home and school of communion ❖ Renewing itself for service within the world
FORMATION Formation in a Catholic school is	❖ Evidenced in the integration of faith, life and culture ❖ Integral to identity and mission ❖ In dialogue and connection with 'story' ❖ Seen in transformation processes of the 'head, heart and hand' ❖ Advanced through personal readiness and commitment ❖ Progressive and developmental in nature ❖ Observed in witness, religious literacy and faith practice

The four pervasive constants: Faith, Learning, Community and Formation present as significant to mission in the conciliar and post-conciliar period. Faith provides the beliefs and values that shape and pervade all schooling experiences; Learning engages the liberating contributions of technology, pedagogy, content and knowledge informed by Christian anthropology; Community is founded upon relationships, stewardship, outreach, and inclusion; and, Formation nurtures identity through a focus on Christ and the integration of faith, life and culture as a continuing journey.

Purpose, goals and the 'elevator pitch'[81]

National goals for schooling in Australia focus on the development of successful learners, confident and creative individuals, and active and informed citizens. These goals are further developed by the National Catholic Education Commission (2017) in light of the 'far goal' of authentic human development centred in the model and message of Christ (Table 6).

Table 6. Purpose and goals of the Catholic school

PURPOSE
Holistic development centred in Christ
GOALS
❖ Challenging students to find, through God, meaning and value in their lives
❖ Forming an integral part of a church community in which all generations live, worship and grow together
❖ Critiquing our culture, and challenging community values, as an integral part of their Gospel mission
❖ Aiming to be welcoming and reflective communities whose most distinctive sign is the discernment of God's presence and their spiritual life
❖ Espousing values which unite Australia by promoting a citizenship infused by a commitment to social justice
❖ Encouraging students to develop an international perspective on their own country and how their country can identify and respond justly to its international obligations
❖ Developing a sense of historical perspective by reflecting on the development of societies and cultures over time, a story of human frailty but of continual efforts to live the Gospel message
❖ Giving priority to educating the spiritually and financially poor and being their advocates

[81] A term used to describe a verbal summary offered within a short space of time; akin to the experience of a conversation within an elevator.

Educational outcomes within the Catholic school while aligned with national goals reflect a particular philosophy of what it means to be human and to educate students towards being fully human within the social and cultural context of the nation. The three key core outcomes for students therefore are given additional meaning as a Christian anthropology provides the detail on the nature of being a successful learner, a confident and creative individual and an active and informed citizen (Table 7). These are the goals that reveal the development of the person, in relationship and advancing the community. They become the touchstones for curriculum development and interpretation and provide a basis for accountability to mission.

Table 7. A summary of student outcomes

National goals and student outcomes		
Successful Learners	Confident and Creative Individuals	Active and Informed Citizens
Appreciation of self and circumstances as the gracious gift of God	Understanding and application of the dynamics of interpersonal relationships	Recognition of one's place and responsibilities in an interdependent world
Self-worth as made in the image of God	Participation in multiple social environments (home, school, Church and community)	Service as a means of personal and communal development
Knowledge, skills, behaviours and dispositions across developmental areas	Development of quality relationships	Sacramental consciousness of God's presence within life

The 'elevator pitch' for the mission of the Catholic school is the executive summary that integrates the purpose, goals and relationships that define its life and culture. The substance of any 'pitch' might utilise the mission constants that arise from research and associated commentary, and conclude with an articulation of specific outcomes aligned with the national goals. One such example, (Sultmann, 2011), advanced the nature and purpose of the Catholic school, the elevator pitch, as "an ecclesial, life-giving, servant community with Christ as its cornerstone, the kingdom as its vision, evangelisation as its mission and education as its means for liberation."

INTEGRATION

Executive Summary

Telling his truth: the prophetic mission of the Catholic school in Australia has not changed since its humble beginnings in a colony of disadvantaged Catholics, to that of an established and respected educational service within an advanced social democracy. The philosophy of educating for personal and communal development, towards a civilisation of love, springs from the mission of the Church to live and spread the Gospel. It is a mission characterised by an anthropology of humankind made in the image of God and the call to give meaning and purpose to life through the revelation of Christ. The mission finds expression in constants of; its ecclesial nature, distinctive anthropology, community outreach, and its commitment to formation as integral to a new evangelisation within a changing community.

Reflection: "You are that tree"

The significance of Christ as cornerstone and the complementary engagement of the 'living stones' in support of Catholic school mission was highlighted by a newly appointed Bishop. Keen to reinforce the significance, privilege and responsibility of Catholic educators within the life of the Diocese, a Eucharist was arranged and celebrated with all Catholic school staff. The Gospel chosen was the story of Christ's encounter with Zacchaeus (Luke 19:1-10). It was Zacchaeus the 'small' tax collector who took the initiative of climbing a tree to satisfy an interest about Jesus. The strategy of Zacchaeus proved fruitful, for not only did he observe Jesus from the tree but became engaged in dialogue and was invited to host Jesus within his home. The Church leader, not wanting to miss the significance of the scene, reminded the gathering that they are encouraged to meet the Christ and support others in the process. In relation to the students, the Bishop expanded on the tree as a key metaphor and reminded teachers: "You are that tree, the means by which 'small' people may come to see, engage and nurture a relationship with the Lord."

Questions

1. **Head:** What inspires the development of your Catholic school?
2. **Heart:** What characteristics of the Catholic school most engages your heart?
3. **Hand:** How would you describe your school's mission within an elevator situation?

Activities

Theme: School culture

Goal: Articulating culture through images

Task: From the six images that follow, or others that you consider more appropriate, reflect upon and discuss the culture of your school.

- *School as machine:* an organisation made up of inter-locking parts, with each part playing a clearly defined role oriented to success and a mode of operation that is efficient.

- *School as political system:* an organisation similar to a system of government drawing on political principles to legitimate rules and factors that shape political life.

- *School as organism:* an organisation consisting of interrelated subsystems that will grow, develop, decline and eventually die in a natural environment.

- *School as culture:* an organisation based on shared meaning, sustained by values, beliefs, rituals and norms bound together by an authentic culture.

- *School as relationships:* an organisation dominated by relationships where individuals work collaboratively for communal and individual growth.

- *School as brain:* an organisation focused on intelligent strategies to define progress and overcome problems.

Activities

- **Theme:** Mapping culture
- **Goal:** Evaluating the pervasiveness of culture
- **Task:** Reflect upon and audit the nature of your school culture in terms of the following characteristics and then share with a colleague.

VERBAL CHARACTERISTICS	REFLECTIONS
Aims	
Goals	
Objectives	
Traditions	
Legends	
VISUAL CHARACTERISTICS	**REFLECTIONS**
Crests	
Mottos	
Uniforms	
Symbols	
Icons	
BEHAVIOURAL CHARACTERISTICS	**REFLECTIONS**
Ceremonies	
Language	
Structures	
Procedures	
Rituals	

Activities

 Theme: Mission integration

 Goal: Personal mission

 Task: Examine the school mission statement and develop your personal mission in relationship to that of the school. The following questions might assist your review.

- *What is the underlying meaning system* that shapes the statement?
- *What values* are nominated as significant to the school?
- *What aims* are offered as an expression of mission locally?
- *What meaning system*, *values* and *aims* can you emphasise within your role?

Theme: Mission counts

Goal: What is the nature of mission that lasts?

Task: The celebrated author John Steinbeck speaks of effective teachers being enthusiastic about their discipline and relational in their service. What are you most enthusiastic about in your role and how might your relationships be enhanced? The following questions might assist your review.

- *What* in your own educational history most impacted your learning?
- *What* are the most satisfying aspects in your current professional experiences?
- *What* relational characteristics offer most support to your students, colleagues, community?

CHAPTER FOUR
Living his life: Leadership as Christian praxis

Chapter Outline

CHAPTER FOUR	109
LIVING HIS LIFE: LEADERSHIP AS CHRISTIAN PRAXIS	109
INTRODUCTION	109
Reflection	109
At a glance	109
Focusing story: Pervasive Spirit	110
From your experience	110
THEMES AND MAIN IDEAS	110
An expansive and challenging canvas	110
Leadership: Images and paradigms	111
Myths and memes	114
Leadership movements	**116**
Leadership characteristics	116
Leadership behaviours	117
Leadership in context	117
Leadership forces	118
Leadership as co-responsibility	120
Leadership for learning	121
Leadership and ethics	123
Leadership and purpose	124
Leadership and Institute models	126
Leadership as Christian praxis	127
Church life as sacrament of Christ	127
Sign and instrument: summary characteristics	129
Touchstones of Christian leadership	130
Christian leadership practices	131
Leadership and transformation	**132**
Personal transformation	133
Relational transformation	135
Educational transformation	138
Organisational transformation	140
"What do we know for sure?"	**144**
INTEGRATION	146
Executive Summary	**146**
Reflection: Service and communion at the table	147
Questions	147
Activities	*147*

CHAPTER FOUR
Living his life: Leadership as Christian praxis

INTRODUCTION

Reflection

"When he had ceased speaking, he said to Simon, "Put out into deep water and let down your nets for a catch." And Simon answered, "Master, we toiled all night and took nothing! But at your word I will let down the nets." And when they had done this, they made a great catch of fish; and as their nets were breaking, they beckoned to their partners in the other boat to come and help them. And they came and filled both the boats, so they began to sink" (Luke 5:4-7).

At a glance

Living his life is the call to leadership as an expression of the Gospel. Sharing in the life of Christ is evidenced in a movement from singular to collaborative processes informed by his person and message and reflected in the schools' shared moral purpose.

The chapter introduces the theoretical platform for leadership through images that point to the subtlety and significance of leadership and the power of collaborative emphases. Limitations in leadership thinking are explored through myths and memes, and insights from progressive streams of leadership theory are outlined. The conclusion is drawn that the spirit of leadership in the Catholic school is sacramental in nature, applied in practices of service and communion and evidenced in transformation across personal, interpersonal, educational and organisational domains of school life. The significance of touch stones for leadership within a shared moral purpose are advanced and the essence of Christian leadership as Christian praxis is summarised.

Focusing story: Pervasive Spirit

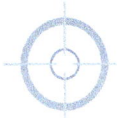

For more than four decades the late Reverend Bernard O'Shea held key leadership roles in Catholic Education within the state of Queensland and was a significant contributor to ideas and developments at a national level. On one occasion he was presented with the proposition that there could be a unique philosophy for Catholic school leadership, one developed to capture the particular tradition of the Church; a philosophy to distinguish it from other philosophies and herald something unique. His response to the proposition reflected his authentic faith, implied caution about triumphalism and drew from his extraordinary leadership experience. In due course the proposition drew the comment "While we live, discern, value and apply our tradition; the creative Spirit of God is present in all things, impacts all activities and is present across all time." In just a few words he gave expression to leadership in Catholic schools as being founded on something which is universal, present everywhere, but made distinctive in the Catholic school by foundations in faith and the invitation to enact mission through leadership.

From your experience

1. Do you consider your service in the Catholic school as an expression of leadership?
2. How might your leadership impact policy, organisational systems, processes and structures within your school community?
3. Are there examples of your leadership which manifest service and communion founded in a faith tradition?

THEMES AND MAIN IDEAS

An expansive and challenging canvas

The challenge to gather, analyse and synthesise leadership material is daunting as the diversity and development of thinking is already expansive and widening. A google search reveals 16.8 million 'hits' for the overall field of leadership; 223 thousand citations for educational leadership; and for leadership in Catholic schools, a staggering 29.3 million references. To say the least, the field is marked by extraordinary interest. Brian Caldwell in a thought provoking text,

Re-imagining Educational Leadership (2006), drew upon the image of the surfer in a 'barrel wave' to articulate the challenge. The scene conjures up simultaneously, the difficult, high risk and complicated nature of leadership in an environment that challenges. Caldwell concluded that the task of understanding and developing a practical and integrated perspective on leadership is akin to participating in an 'extreme sport.'

One of the most significant developments of the twentieth century was the emancipation of people within the new Republic of South Africa. The central figure in the process was the Republic's first President, Nelson Mandela. An anecdote about the President relates to a conversation he is believed to have had with a visiting colleague. The story speaks of the likely pride Mr Mandela would have possessed in achieving the Presidency and his sense of relief after so many years in apparent wilderness. The visitor is reported to have stated "Mr President, after almost three decades of imprisonment and frustration of immense proportions, you must be so excited and optimistic about the forthcoming changes predicted for the new South Africa." The response to the statement was simply "Ah yes; but imprisonment was the easy part, our greatest work lies ahead of us."

The full appreciation of the President's words may never be revealed, although it might be speculated he was implying that leadership should never be underestimated for it carries great challenge, privilege and responsibility. It is a significant and complex phenomenon which is seldom expressed in isolation and without some effect. It is something which is not necessarily fixed in time or location, nor does it hinge on the influence of a single individual. In a contemporary world it is expressed within a context of significant change and is often the subject of cynical commentary. Notwithstanding, it has the potential for enabling substantial vitality and growth and is a powerful influence on the personal, relational, professional and communal life within community.

Leadership: images and paradigms

Leadership is applied within a world of complexity, turbulence, high-velocity and continuous change and expectation. Within Australia, the Centre for Workplace Leadership revealed 75 per cent of employees sought better and more involved managers and leaders, with Gallup estimates indicating the resulting lack of engagement as costing $54.8 billion a year (Salicru, 2017, p.35). The conclusions of Salicru are that an appreciation of leadership in turbulent times carries the exhortation to 'keep it simple,' with story-telling and imagery being part of the process of understanding and action into which leaders are invited.

Imaging: the underground trains

An image of the complex and subtle nature of leadership can be observed in a phenomenon within the oldest and still functioning Catholic school within Queensland, Australia. The school is located in the central business district of the state's capital, Brisbane. It was begun by a layperson and for most of its history has been operated by the Irish Christian Brothers. It is recognised today for its longstanding tradition of service, outreach to a cross-section of students, innovative curriculum, commitment to renewal, and its historical 'train tunnel.'

Running deep below the school's recreational area is an old railway tunnel which links two major city locations. It is, even though of minimal length by world standards, Brisbane's equivalent of the underground. Constructed at a time when train travel had to support a fast growing and expanding city, the tunnel provides a critical role in the transport network which services the needs of commuters as they journey from one central point to another.

To the average observer it is now quite difficult to notice the tunnel and its passing trains. However, in the early years of the school's history, the era of the steam train, recognition was easy because of emissions, noise from rattling carriages and all manner of railway smells. With the onset of electrification, the tunnel and the trains became almost indistinguishable within the overall environment of the school. The only manifestation of the trains is a small central vent which provides some coverage to a large conduit to the tracks below.

The manifestation of the school's tunnel and its passing trains is symbolic of the expression of leadership within the life of the Catholic school. Similar to the evolving trains, the theory and practice of leadership have changed significantly. While leadership was once the domain of a particular individual with unique and noticeable characteristics, it is now more subtle and expressed more inclusively. It is, however, recognised as central to the life and culture of the organisation as it serves to build, bind and give authorisation to a host of directions, processes and determinations critical to mission.

Paradigms: Pre and post the iceberg

Paradigms are the means of conceptualising in new and radical ways ideas that provide foundational and substantive frameworks within which behaviour of a general form can be understood and shaped. Who can forget the paradigm shift advocated by President John F Kennedy in his often-quoted challenge "Ask not what your country can do for you, but what you can do for your country?"

A paradigm which characterises much of the initial thinking about leadership in contrast to more recent views is provided by Emeritus Professor Patrick Duignan, the inaugural head of the National School of Educational Leadership within the Australian Catholic University. The paradigm is illustrated in an image and story which offers insights into the myriad of complex encounters into which leadership extends and is expected to respond. In its telling, the image advances a level of clarity about leadership by contrasting 'old' approaches with 'new' perspectives.[82]

A story known to the majority of people living in the twentieth century is the one that tells of the fateful night in April 1912 when the ocean liner Titanic struck an iceberg and within two hours sank to the bottom of the ocean. The tale has been recounted in print and electronic media, literature and film, and to this day holds significance due to the enormity of the tragedy, its implications for ocean travel and the lessons in human nature that it reveals. One aspect of the disaster relevant to the current discussion is the nature of leadership exercised by its Captain, and others, pre and post the collision with the iceberg.

Duignan comments on the pre-iceberg paradigm (approach to leadership) by noting that there was some likelihood that the tragedy might have been circumvented in the first place. A litany of errors, within an illusory framework of certainty and over-confidence contributed greatly to the disaster. The captain was in control, 'at his table,' and the microcosm of the Titanic society was one where First, Second and Third class passengers were in their 'proper' places. It would have been unthinkable to challenge the beliefs and values that supported the actions, behaviours and relationships of the members of this mini society. Beliefs, values and commitments that contributed to a feeling of invincibility manifested in over-confidence, perhaps even arrogance.

The captain's leadership was based on authority and position. It was founded on hierarchy, patriarchy, control, and was ultimately, very lonely. Perhaps if the paradigm out of which the captain operated was different, there might have been a concentration of effort on 'other things' than on the need to create records and give scant attention to messages of warning and associated preparing and planning 'for the worst.' Clearly, the value of an alternative approach to leadership might have assisted the response to the tragedy, and, at best, even avoidance of it.

Duignan makes the point that leadership on the disastrous night in April emerged from unexpected quarters, especially from among the stewards. Some sacrificed themselves so that others might be saved while others simply kept to their posts while the evacuation occurred. The powerful scene recorded in the movie depicting the stoic and dependable role played by the musicians was testament to service in the greatest hour of distress. Given the pandemonium, it was amazing that some individual and collective harmony prevailed at all, and that so many people were saved.

---

82 Drawn from the keynote address by Professor Duignan, 2007.

Duignan further comments that the Captain of the Titanic responded in the only way he knew. His response mirrored what had worked for him as a highly respected captain of his era. Notwithstanding this reality, there were unfortunate leadership practices: lifeboats being inappropriately launched; third class passengers being kept behind locked gates; and disputes and arguments among officials that consumed valuable time. Conversely, there were also great acts of commitment and bravery which did much to support the unbelievable demands of an unworkable situation.

An analysis of a pre-iceberg leadership paradigm, in contrast to a contemporary approach, invites a number of potentially significant shifts that might have made a difference. However, outcomes from alternative approaches will never be known. What can be assured is that the pre-iceberg paradigm did not work effectively; particularly when alternatives within an extreme and problematic situation were required.

Within social events in the present age where discontinuity and rapidly changing conditions are the norm, the paradigm of leadership is called to be different. However, within environments that make demands of an increasing and diverse kind, there continues to exist the possibility that leadership may take the form of the lowest common denominator. That is, approaches based on misconceived or mistakenly gathered perspectives that present initially as appropriate and enticing, but can be destructive and unhelpful in the immediate and longer term. In this light an appreciation of the misconceptions about leadership act as a starting point for a deeper appreciation of quality leadership thinking and practice, aspects which might inform contemporary post iceberg responses.

Myths and memes

Paul Timm, Brent Peterson and Jackson Stephens suggest that the subject of leadership is permeated by myths to which they add "It would be useful to puncture" (1990, p. 134). In a similar vein, Wayne Dyer talks of the prevalence of "thoughts that were given to us by our families, our society, our culture" (Dyer, 2018) that can be so persuasive that they take over perceptions and direct behaviours in ways that are not necessarily advantageous or true. Dyer draws from the work of Richard Brodie who describes these inaccurate and given thoughts as memes, and argues their impact as being similar to a virus of the mind.

Memes are thoughts, beliefs, or attitudes in your mind that can be spread to and from other people's minds. Memes are ideas that are transmitted, like viruses, and take up residence in our heads. Their presence can influence our behaviour and limit us in ways

we don't even notice unless we make a real effort to examine what we think and why. Memes die hard because they've become who we think we are. They aren't necessarily good or bad; some may even serve our health and well-being (Wayne Dyer, 2018).

Silvia Pencak (2018) addresses the myths of leadership and contends that they need to be de-bunked in order to develop a mindset for leadership that reflects wisdom and truth.[83] While her identified set of myths include references to factors of age and attributes of attention seeking and affirmations, the myths articulated from Timm, Peterson and Stevens provide a broad illustration of how leadership can be mistakenly appreciated. Notwithstanding the accuracy, number and limitations of any set of myths and memes, the following examples begin to inform a leadership mindset seeking to be free from 'viral' leadership thinking.

Myth 1: "Leadership is a rare skill open only to a few."

The reality of organisational life is that everyone has leadership potential and that people may be leaders in one organisation and followers in another. Leadership opportunities are generally plentiful and within the reach of most people.

Myth 2: "Leaders are born, not made."

The reality of leadership is that it is not a gift of grace too abstract to be learned and practised. The title 'leader' is too often and too narrowly attributed to those whose actions take place in the most dramatic realms of human endeavour (e.g., Gandhi, Napoleon, and Churchill).

Myth 3: "Leaders are created by extraordinary circumstances."

The reality is that in most organisations leadership is needed on a daily basis and applied in all places, circumstances and interactions.

Myth 4: "Leadership exists only at the top of an organisation."

The reality is that without the leadership of many, so much of the organisation's enterprise and creativity would be diminished or lost.

Myth 5: "Leaders control, direct, prod, and manipulate."

The reality is that leadership is not so much the exercise of power itself, but rather the ability to empower others. Leaders align their energies with others, they pull rather than push, they inspire rather than command.

---

83 Silvia Pencak identifies seven myths about leadership: leaders being born not made; leadership comes with position; leadership comes with age; leaders don't make mistakes; leaders treat everyone the same; leaders want attention; leaders know everything.

Myth 6: "Leaders are charismatic."

The reality is that some are and others are not. Leaders can be fallible, flawed, and with no particular charm that separates them objectively from others. Charisma is the result of effective leadership not the other way around.

Myth 7: "Leaders seek and use power."

The reality of power is that it can be confused with subjugation and control. Power allows for the release of energy, and as with any form of energy, its value lies in how it is used.

Leadership movements

Leadership thinking can be observed in continuing and progressive movements each of which reveal particular variables of significance. What follows is a summary of the more dominant leadership movements that impact personal, relational, professional and communal life within the Catholic school. Within the discussion there is an attempt to develop more recent perspectives, particularly in view of their relevance to the mission of the Catholic school and their application to a wider group within its community.

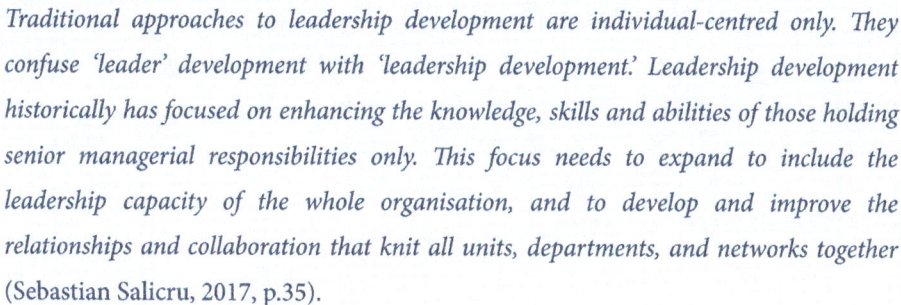

Traditional approaches to leadership development are individual-centred only. They confuse 'leader' development with 'leadership development.' Leadership development historically has focused on enhancing the knowledge, skills and abilities of those holding senior managerial responsibilities only. This focus needs to expand to include the leadership capacity of the whole organisation, and to develop and improve the relationships and collaboration that knit all units, departments, and networks together (Sebastian Salicru, 2017, p.35).

Leadership characteristics

Great man theories dominated early leadership thinking. They arose from the historian Thomas Carlyle during the nineteenth century when addressing the accomplishments of significant people of history. The theory was founded on the belief that leaders were great 'men,' born to rule, individuals who emerged at times when there existed gaps in the capacities of others.

Trait approaches sought to isolate those characteristics or traits which differentiated successful from unsuccessful leaders. Factors such as intelligence, personality, and attitudes were explored in an effort to explain and develop leader competencies.

Leadership behaviours

Behavioural theories acknowledge the limitations of leadership as solely reliant upon leader characteristics and turn to an examination of leader behaviours. The approach highlights two significant actions: the support offered by leaders to others; and meeting organisational goals through relationship and task management forces. Leader behaviours aiding relationship development include forging trust, friendship, support, respect and warmth. Behaviours which facilitate task completion incorporate defining goals, specifying roles and determining the necessary relationships and channels of communication.

Transformation and transactional models articulate the relationship between the person of the leader and the responses of those who follow. Leadership of a transformational form give importance to followers being educated in the nature of the task and the generation of motivation and inspiration for its successful carriage. Transactional theories centre on leaders identifying and addressing organisational attributes, particularly culture and mission, and pursuing the primary challenge of achieving outcomes through negotiation and agreement.

Servant leadership has its beginnings in the biblical tradition and is centred on religious values and processes. The model presents the leader as someone who is a servant first; listens before responding; fosters gifts of imagination and invitation; and is comfortable with non-verbal communication. Personal empathy and unqualified acceptance of others provides for sound leadership practice with personal responsibility and development being important to the overall leadership process.

Leadership in context

Situational leadership is a model of leading that is linked to the needs and conditions of time and place. That is, the behaviour of leaders reflects the contingencies of the situation and will vary in focus as circumstances change. In this view, there is no single mode of leadership that applies consistently as effectiveness is based on addressing the mix of contextual factors applicable to the situation.

Vision theories give priority to the vision of the organisation. This is an approach to leadership which is grounded in assumptions, beliefs, meanings and dreams about human nature, how people relate, society and its values (moral, political, religious). The model is conceptualised as the communal institutionalising of a vision and its primary protagonist is Professor Gerry Starratt.

The power of the leader is rooted in a vision from which followers can be energised.

It emerges from an ongoing dialogue among all members of the organisation and typically entails six facets, each of which interact dynamically:

i. the leader's power is rooted in a vision that is itself rooted in something basic to human life;
ii. that vision illuminates the ordinary with dramatic significance;
iii. the vision is articulated in such compelling ways that it becomes the shared vision of the leader's colleagues, illuminating their activities with dramatic significance;
iv. the leader implants the vision in the structures and processes of the organisation, so that people experience the vision in the various patterned activities of the organisation;
v. the leader and colleagues make day-to-day decisions in light of that vision, so that the vision becomes the heart of the culture of the organisation;
vi. the organisation celebrates the vision in ritual, ceremonies and art forms.

Starratt contends that there is no such thing as an ordinary day for the leader with a vision. Every day is full of new possibilities as each person is making decisions about themselves as persons, their self-worth, their abilities, their usefulness to society and their ultimate futures. "It is that sense of drama, flowing out of the leader's vision, which gives an electric quality to the words and actions of the leader and which drives the call to teachers (all) constantly to this same sense of drama in what they are doing" (Starratt, 1986, p. 6).

Leadership forces

Leadership forces (technical, human, educational, symbolic and cultural) are argued to provide for the direction and maintenance of organisational life (Sergiovanni, 1987, 1992). The technical force is the power of leadership through the execution of sound management techniques through planning, organising, scheduling, decision making, conflict resolution and team development. The human force encompasses the human resources aspect and requires interpersonal relationship competence. The educational force derives from expert knowledge in the areas of education and schooling. Expert knowledge is demonstrated in the promotion of teaching effectiveness, diagnosis of educational difficulties, curriculum, staff development and supervision. This force allows the principal, as leader, to be the 'expert practitioner' and provide for supervision and evaluation.

Important though the technical, human and educational forces are for promoting and maintaining quality schooling, two other leadership forces serve to promote authenticity. These leadership forces are symbolic and cultural in nature and draw attention to what is of value to the organisation.

The symbolic leadership force calls for modelling appropriate behaviour and actions, to give, as it were, explicit expression to the vision and goals of the organisation. The cultural leadership force is directed to establishing ways and means whereby that culture is transmitted to others.

Leadership through engagement addresses how leadership responds to a changing world. Amidst the rapidity and diversity of change, Drucker (1997, p. 16-17) speaks of two permanent tasks for the leader and poses four strategies. The leader's first permanent task is the assessment of organisational potential and possibility, and the directing of organisational resources accordingly. The second permanent task relates to the management of people so that strengths are enhanced and weaknesses minimised. This latter view establishes leadership as focused on the needs of others and less on the culture and dynamics of the service operation.

Drucker advocates four leadership strategies for organisations with an 'outside in' focus. The first is to examine and establish the nature of how 'business' is done. This is the need to recognise that organisations are not independent, but part of a larger whole. The implication is that partnerships, alliances and joint ventures will be necessary in order that goals can be achieved. The skills for the leader will therefore include negotiation and persuasion and, more significantly, an attitude of working cooperatively within and without the organisation's operation and sphere of influence.

A second strategy resides in the way work is organised and the nature of the workforce. Knowledge is becoming more important as is the move away from mass production. Organisations are becoming more knowledge based and the level of worker participation and responsibility continues to increase. Leadership in this context attends to how workers can be empowered to increase their management responsibilities. The implication is for an increasing emphasis on sharing responsibilities and identifying means for communication, co-operation and accountability among organisational personnel.

The third major strategy involves the need for organisations to become more self-regulatory. It will be necessary for organisations to integrate their business practices (e.g. appointments, promotions, placements, incentives) with the values of the organisation and thereby adopt more accountable and transparent values. The implication for leaders lies in personal witness and alignment with the culture of the organisation.

The fourth strategy for promoting an 'outside in' culture, relates to the use of information systems to understand what is necessary to pursue the organisation's mission. That is, leaders ask what information is necessary to assess strengths and weaknesses of themselves and their workforce to accommodate, generate and direct change. This implies a commitment to continuous learning and recognition of vulnerability in a climate of exploding knowledge and global interdependence.

Leadership as co-responsibility[84]

Parallel leadership entails processes which 'ordinary' people do extraordinarily well; this is leadership that allows for optional participation and observed in particular practices. That is, leadership of a parallel nature is not expressed uniquely as case studies reveal lasting change arises from a common set of leadership characteristics. Crowther (1999, 2001) provides an elaboration of these behaviours in a 'teachers as leader's framework' and identifies six core characteristics of a parallel leader (Table 8).

Table 8. Characteristics of a parallel leader

Articulates a clear view of the world	❖ Can articulate 'what ought to be' on important social issues ❖ Possesses personal views about social justice
Models trust and sincerity	❖ Has the respect of the community ❖ Demonstrates tolerance and understanding in difficult situations ❖ Regarded by peers as genuine
Confronts structural barriers	❖ Stands up for children, especially marginalised or powerless individuals or groups ❖ Influences the development and implementation of socially just policies ❖ Develops mutual relationships with authority figures
Builds networks of support	❖ Feels at ease with individuals and groups who assert cultural, ethnic and other differences ❖ Communicates with authority and is persuasive across diverse groups ❖ Organises tasks with relative ease ❖ Starts small and builds discipleship ❖ Nurtures a culture of success
Creates opportunities for individual success and recognition	❖ Adopts a 'no blame' attitude when things go wrong ❖ Searches continuously for new ideas ❖ Conveys a sense of optimism to others
Emphasises authenticity in pedagogy	❖ Aligns teaching to visionary ideals ❖ Values teaching as an important profession in shaping meaning systems ❖ Gets immersed willingly in the cultural context of students ❖ Builds problem solving skills

84 The ability or authority to act or decide on one's own, without supervision.

Distributive leadership is similar to parallel leadership but is more universally applicable. This view, also referred to as collective leadership (Salicru, 2017), is in keeping with the belief that all within the organisation can play an important role and that it is through teamwork and interdependence that goals are achieved. "Collective leadership involves all employees and means that everyone is responsible for the team or organisation's success and not just for their individual role. This means leadership is distributed, rather than being centred on a few individuals in formal positions of authority" (Salicru, 2017, p. 36).

Leadership for learning

Leadership for learning was given prominence in the address by Reeves (2008) in honour of William Walker, a legendary figure in Australian education. Drawing from a research base of 2000 school plans, Reeves identified a collective group of behaviours from principals and teachers as significant to enhancing outcomes for learning. These incorporated early, frequent and decisive intervention; personal connection with students; parent engagement; tutoring; managing student choice; in-school assistance; reformed grading systems; building a culture of commitment; strengthening people; a focus on student learning in professional development; and students concentrating substantial 'sacred time' to literacy (Reeves, 2008). Importantly, quality learning emerged from leadership from all members across the community engaging and co-operating in learning as a shared responsibility.

A synthesis of perspectives common to all leaders of learning was provided by Dempster (2009) in a landmark article geared to educators across the learning spectrum (pre-school to tertiary). Characteristic behaviours of significance included agreeing to and sharing a clear moral purpose for the school; engaging in disciplined dialogue; utilising evidence-based data in decision making; active professional learning; enhancing conditions for learning; monitoring curriculum and teaching; exercising distributive leadership; and connecting with parent and community support for learning. The conclusions of Dempster reinforced leadership for learning as a focused activity, intent on a particular goal with concentrated efforts directed towards the student as learner.

The learning organisation is characterised by the adoption and mastery of certain basic disciplines or 'component technologies.' The five disciplines that Peter Senge identifies are said to converge in ways that support innovation and builds long-standing change and transformation. The dimensions of systems thinking, personal mastery, mental models, building shared vision and team learning constitute the means for development which build a sense of the whole and advance people as active participants in shaping a preferred social reality.

> *Learning organisations are places where people continually expand their capacity to create the results they truly desire, where new and expansive patterns of thinking are nurtured, where collective aspiration is set free, and where people are continually learning to see the whole together. Moreover, the power of an approach to transformation that is centred in a unifying and integrating paradigm holds considerable advantages* (Peter Senge, 1990, p. 3).

Leadership within a learning organisation commits to processes that build organisational capacity as much as nurturing personal development. Systems thinking is the basis of this learning. It is the discipline that integrates the others, fusing them into a coherent body of theory and practice (Senge 1990, p. 12). It is the means for making sense of organisational questions and issues while offering a window into strategies that offer most leverage for effective change. Alongside systems thinking, there stand four other 'component technologies' or disciplines that can be mastered and integrated into everyday life (Senge 1990, p. 373).

Personal mastery is the discipline of continually clarifying and deepening personal vision through "focusing our energies, developing patience, and seeing reality objectively" (Senge 1990, p. 7). Mental models are the "deeply ingrained assumptions, generalisations, or even pictures and images that influence how we understand the world and how we take action" (Senge, 1990, p. 8). Shared vision incorporates "the capacity to hold and share a picture of the future we seek to create" (Senge, 1990, p. 9). Team learning is "the process of aligning and developing the capacities of a team to create the results its members truly desire" (Senge, 1990, p. 236).

Good to great organisations are characterised by Jim Collins (2001) as possessing outstanding leadership, somewhat unable to be named, but simply coded as Level Five. Level Five leaders possess qualities of Level 1, highly capable individual; Level 2, contributing team member; Level 3, competent manager; Level 4, effective community leader; as well as a set of attributes which set them apart. In summarising these special and additional qualities of a Level Five leader, Collins identified four persistent dualities: (i) a capacity to create results but with a compelling modesty; (ii) an ability to exercise unwavering resolve and yet possessive of a quiet and calm determination; (iii) an ability to meet standards but channel outcomes to the company and not to the self; (iv) an attitude of accepting responsibilities in times of challenge but in circumstances of prosperity to attribute credit to others and external factors.

Leadership and ethics

Leadership and ethics theories are intimately linked within decision making at all levels. Two models of significance are the *arenas of influence* on educational practice (Begley, 2011); and the *multiple ethical frameworks* (Shapiro, Stefkovich & Gutierrez, 2014). Both models permit decisions to be explored from alternative but complementary ethical perspectives.

Arenas of influence as significant in the determination of action. Acknowledging that the leader is at the centre of the decision-making process, Begley reveals the impact of the individual's immediate social situation, the group, profession, organisation, culture and transcendental as arenas of influence that impact determinations. Within the group setting, matters of interpersonal relationships apply; while within the professional and organisational arenas, elements of best practice and policy imperatives direct the leader's attention. At the same time, Begley encourages leaders to go beyond the school context and acknowledge the culture of the wider community as being important. As well, his inclusion of the transcendental arena permits the 'spiritual' to be an important influence. The framework allows for a deeper and wider understanding of potential action, with each arena offering particular insights while possessing a level of interdependence with all others.

The multiple ethical framework of Shapiro, Stefkovich and Gutierrez also provides lenses through which decisions might be critiqued by the leader. Ethics of justice, critique, care and profession applied individually and holistically allow for insights to be considered and serve as a basis for action. The ethic of justice is concerned with laws, rights and liberty; the ethic of critique with an examination of possibilities in terms of outcomes for students and others with concepts of oppression, power, privilege, authority, language, voice and empowerment, all being considerations. The ethic of care addresses relationships with issues of loyalty, trust and empowerment being emphasised. Finally, the ethic of profession speaks to ethical requirements of educational leaders in their carriage of responsibilities in terms of standards, quality service and authenticity.

The arenas of influence model and the lenses of multiple ethical practices provide a level of completeness to reflection and enable what Don Willower (1985) described as the ultimate goal of educational leadership as being 'at our best.' That is, decision making and strategic practice reflecting the complexity of organisational life and the diversity and importance of influences on individuals and groups. The resulting ethical practice is given deeper appreciation when it is tied to the organisation's purpose.

Leadership and purpose

Moral leadership entails influencing through a common and shared purpose, or morality. It reflects what each person, and the organisation as a whole might look like, 'at their best.' It involves coming to appreciate one's moral core as the basis of relating and working which leads to making right choices for authentic reasons. In this light, moral leadership, in the paraphrased words of Charles Burford, has much to do with character over characteristics, and developing and applying one's inner compass within the day-to-day life of the school.

> *The school leader's task is to deliver the promise made to an individual family when a child is enrolled and in so doing to serve the larger obligation to society and its future. This is no small task. It is complex. It is a noble service and it is entangled in the compromises and ambiguities of the human condition. Yet, in the midst of the mess and the complexity, the purpose is achieved and the promise can be honoured* (Anne Benjamin, 2002, p. 81).

The process of coupling is said to be integral to the development of a shared moral purpose (Burford, 2017). Coupling entails sharing, consensus building and engaging ownership of common values and ethics among staff.[85] It is the group's collective agreement on morals, ethics, and common values that underwrite all activity in the life of the school. It is where 'obedience to the unenforceable' arises because of an accepted covenantal commitment to a shared purpose. In this light, "leadership is the art of calling others to seek the truth; to explore the essence of one's being; to discover the spiritual chemistry of relationships; to make judgments about significance, rightness, wrongness" (Burford, 2017).

> *Carpenters become carpenters by building houses; pianists become pianists by playing the piano; managers become leaders by leading. The same is true of character: people become virtuous by practicing virtue and by living with moral mentors … Disciplined organisations reflect disciplined leaders whose honed abilities lead them to behave consistently, almost instinctively, in moral ways* (Thomas Sergiovanni, 2005, p. 112).

Authentic leadership seeks to align leader behaviours with the moral purpose of the organisation in which it is expressed. A comprehensive analysis of leadership research in Australia (Mulford, 2007) concluded that leadership no longer stands independent from the organisation and its core mission, nor is it independent of context. It entails the activation of complex and engaging processes, necessitates a commitment of the heart and is accountable.

---

[85] For detailed approaches to the identification of moral purpose as shaping professional practice see Begley (2006) and Branson and Gross (2014).

It possesses a 'how,' 'what,' and 'why' which reinforce its expansive nature, its level of potential and its challenge. In this context, Branson and Gross (2014) add that the starting point for leadership development begins with the formation of a capable leader in terms of the identification of their own values and convictions to make a difference in the mission of the school.

Leadership that addresses mission and engages moral purpose is characterised by Patrick Duignan (1987, 1998, 2002, & 2007) as being authentic in nature. Within a context where the culture of schools is complex, changing, elastic, uncertain, and at times unstable and usually value laden, Duignan advocates for leadership authenticity; leadership practices that direct and witness mission. With such a view, leadership takes on a personally symbolic frame of reference which focuses on the "Meaning of myths, the metaphors and rituals of collective life" (Duignan, 1998, p. 209). Authentic leadership is therefore a process of influence which is said to be professionally effective, ethically sound, and consciously reflective of purpose and practice being aligned with mission.

The practical implementation of authentic leadership is evidenced within literature which recognises processes of engagement with self and others within the moral purpose of the school. The five practices of exemplary leadership by James M Kouzes and Barry G Posner (2003), for example, set the pattern by confirming processes of modelling the way; inspiring a shared vision; challenging the process; enabling others; and, encouraging the heart. The emphasis is given to one's personal responsibility for engagement in what will be a multitude of situations and circumstances within the life of the school. Within faith-based schools the conclusions of Maddix and Estep (2017) draw upon similar leadership processes, specifically through the Spirit advanced by Christ. Again, five practical processes are identified: discovering self; serving a purpose; developing shared vision; creating change; and, empowering others. These are the processes that evolve from an attitude of servant and collaborative leadership and provide the challenge to nurture personal transformation as a basis for effective leadership.

A further and critical analysis of leadership within culture, specifically the culture of the Catholic school, is offered by Branson, Marra and Buchanan (2019). Their comprehensive overview of leadership theory generates a hypothesis for authentic leadership being supported by transpersonal relationships. The research provides a platform for understanding and applying multiple leadership expectations and practices on the basis of quality relationships. The essence of transpersonal leadership is said to engage people through relationship "that seeks to create a culture based upon the shared values of trust, openness, transparency, honesty, integrity, collegiality and ethical practice" (p. 4). This research, when integrated with principles of Neuroscience (Braden, 2017,

Chopra, 2017, Dispenza, 2007 & 2012), supports the process of understanding why some leaders are more successful than others and how and where behaviours are stored in the brain and applied automatically.

When high quality leadership is understood as essentially a transrelational phenomenon, the educational leadership practice of the Catholic school principal will simultaneously fulfill their Catholic and educational leadership responsibilities. (Chris Branson, Maureen Marra & Michael Buchanan, 2019, p. 1).

Leadership and Institute models

Models and exemplars of leadership activity for principals and teachers are proposed by the Australian Institute for Teaching and School Leadership (AITSL). The resources of AITSL constitute an extraordinary wealth of material for reflection and action, particularly in terms of where and how the moral purpose of the school can be enacted with purpose and authenticity. While reflecting only a fraction of the detail within AITSL documentation, Table 9 highlights the areas of leadership focus which have gained national ascendancy.

Table 9. A summary of leadership responsibilities

TEACHERS	PRINCIPALS
❖ Know students and how they learn	❖ Leading teaching and learning
❖ Know the content and how to teach it	❖ Developing self and others
❖ Plan for and implement effective teaching and learning	❖ Leading improvement, innovation and change
❖ Create and maintain supportive and safe learning environments	❖ Leading the management of the school
❖ Assess, provide feedback and report on student learning	❖ Engaging and working with the community
❖ Engage in professional learning	
❖ Engage professionally with colleagues, parents/carers and the community	

Within the wider arena of leadership, the Institute of Managers and Leaders (IML) also provide substantial commentary and resources on the practice of leadership. The current position of this professional body is that it is "timely to move leadership and management from relatively loose and informal constructs to having professional standards and a mature base of knowledge" (Tarrant, 2017).

This goal is argued as 'a road less travelled.' It is however, one that begins with a conceptualisation of leadership as primarily centred on vision and thereafter entailing skills of setting strategy; defining culture; leading people; making decisions; applying ethics; being inclusive; and networking. The conclusion of Deborah Tarrant, 2017 is that this leadership puzzle requires proactivity through mentoring and networking, planning, personal development, time management, building relationships, and balancing the macro with the micro in a context of the organisation's primary vision expressed through mission.

Leadership as Christian praxis

An assessment of leadership directions within an evolving and compelling body of research and practice points to a focus on mission which is advanced though personal and communal engagement, authentic witness and capabilities exercised within a shared and ethically founded vision. In this light, leadership within the Catholic school is challenged to further the role of Church in advancing God's mission through the agency of all in personal, relational, professional and communal ways. This is the paradigm that offers meaning, sustains service and nurtures communion through the action of the Spirit. It is a paradigm that is centred in the Gospel, expressed within Church and is professional in character. It is leadership in the Catholic school that is praxis based, open and life-giving to its community.

> *If you want to make minor improvements in your behaviours, relationships and organisations, work on attitudes and behaviours; but, if you want to make major improvements, quantum leaps, work on paradigms, and behaviours and attitudes will follow* (Stephen Covey, 1992, CD).

Church as sacrament of Christ ———

The Second Vatican Council provided a clear and emphatic focus on Christ as central to the life of the Church and reinforced this relationship when it argued "By her relationship with Christ, the Church is a kind of Sacrament, or sign and instrument of intimate union with God and of the unity of the whole human race" (LG, para. 1).

The consideration of the Church as Sacrament[86] signals the activity of God in the world and confirms the Church as the basic Sacrament from which the formal Sacraments flow. This position has also been advanced to include "The activity of Christian communities is also sacramental, even though certain actions,

---

86 A definitive work on the Church as Sacrament is offered by the Belgium Theologian, Edward Schillebeeckx.

the sacramental liturgies, may be more formally and explicitly singled out as Sacraments" (Cooke, 1983, p. 235). In a similar vein, the Catholic school as proceeding from the heart of Church is sacramental in nature. This concept of the universal Church and its particular communities as being imaged as a Sacrament offers a 'root metaphor,' a foundation upon which the school's mission and leadership practice might be articulated (McBrien, 1988).

> *In history, the Church is the universal sacrament of the salvation and life that comes from God. Revealing the mystery of God's will, God gathers Church together from amongst all peoples, in order to admit all 'people' to communion with God in the Holy Spirit and through God's Son* (Australian Episcopal Conference, 1970, para. 4).

The connection between the nature of Sacrament and the daily life of Christ's followers within communities is developed by Martos (2009) in a discussion of the Paschal Mystery and the Kingdom of God. The Paschal Mystery is elaborated as "Something that Jesus did a long time ago but that has had an effect on humanity ever since, especially on Christians" (Martos, 2009, p. 185). It entails the life, death and resurrection of the Lord which is argued to have relevance for the community and how it celebrates the remembrance of Christ through the action of the Spirit. It is the story that offers to all who serve and relate within the environment of the Catholic school, a window into a leadership imagination shaped by the Spirit.

The further link between the Sacraments and everyday leadership practice is through the paradigm of the Kingdom of God whereby "The Church has but one sole purpose that the Kingdom of God may come" (GS, para. 45). Like the Paschal Mystery "The Kingdom of God is not food and drink but righteousness and peace and joy in the Holy Spirit" (Romans 14:17). Given repeated attention in the documents of Vatican II and the Christian Scriptures, the Kingdom of God preached and witnessed by Christ is not limited to the ministry of the ordained; but is also "The special vocation of the laity within the 'temporal affairs' that constitute their life" (LG, paras. 31 & 36). The Kingdom vision is therefore intimately linked to the Paschal Mystery for it makes explicit the mind and action of Christ as life is encountered in community.

> *Whoever came in contact with one of these believing communities was truly in contact with the presence of the risen Lord ... The community was effectively acting as a Sacrament of the risen Christ ... It was the entire existence and activity of the community that was sacramental* (Bernard Cooke, 1983, p. 72).

Sign and instrument: summary characteristics

Christian leadership involves a balanced integration of the intellectual, moral, spiritual and seeks to awaken 'capacity for self-transcendence.'[87] It is a conceptualisation that Maher (2017b) advances is integral to the ecclesiology of Pope Francis; an ecclesiology that is based on the spiritual exercises of St Ignatius and evocative of three questions "What have I done for Christ?" "What am I doing for Christ?" "What should I do for Christ?" It is leadership that recognises the Spirit of Christ as incarnational and the desire to be contemplative in one's actions. In the summary of Maher (2017b), it is, 'making Christ present in our actions, our leadership.' Its' essence is sacramental in nature in that mission is the intention (being instrument) and shared mission (being in communion) its' sign.

The practice of leadership has as its focus two interdependent themes: the 'why' and the 'how' of leadership. As Charles Burford argues, the essential and only leadership questions are "Why are we doing this; and, how might we do this in ways that reflect this purpose?" These are the questions of leading for mission and leading in ways that witness mission. It is leadership which is an instrument and sign of the moral purpose of the Catholic school. It is leadership that is open to all and situates the leader in an encounter with self and others. It is leadership which reflects the Spirit of God and the model and message of Jesus. It is leadership that simply asks what Christ might think, feel and act in this situation. It is leadership that allows us to "Think of ourselves as representatives of God bringing his power, his wisdom, his heart, his mind to the world" (Barron, 2016, p. 32).

Mission as instrument

Drawing on the Christian scriptures "Just as the Son of Man came not to be served but to serve, and to give his life a ransom for many" (Matthew 20:28), the late Pope John Paul II (1979) argued that service is not merely an obligation as some form of social membership but a call to vocation. It is a response to Christ's personal invitation to 'follow me' (John 1:43). This 'following' occurs within a community who build up the Body of Christ and remain in unity, in communion with the whole.

The call to service in Oceania by Pope John Paul II is one that harbours 'no time for complacency' (EO, para. 39). The challenge lies in presenting the Good News in a way that brings "hope to the many who suffer misery, injustice or poverty. The mystery of Christ is a mystery of new life for all who are in need or in pain" (EO, para. 41). The task is to present Christ in new ways, so that the

---

[87] A concept drawn from the writing of Fr Bernard Lonergan SJ as discussed by Professor Anthony Maher (2017b).

power of his Spirit can be realised. "This call to mission poses great challenges, but it also opens new horizons, full of hope and even a sense of adventure" (EO, para. 39).

Communion as sign

Communion is essentially about relationship, membership, participation and shared beliefs and values. The Second Vatican Council (LG, para. 6) spoke of the Church as a communion,[88] one based on all its members being united to Christ, and the communion of members as the one Body of Christ. The concept of communion is not a sociological concept but a theological understanding of what it is to belong to the Church.[89]

> *The Church as communion is the new people, the messianic people, the people that has for its head Christ ... as its heritage, the dignity and freedom of God's children ... for its law, the new commandment to love as Christ loved us ... for its goal, the Kingdom of God ... established by Christ as a communion of life, love and truth* (CL, para. 19).

Communion implies that the wisdom of the Holy Spirit be sought and the 'body' to be informed. This is at the core of leadership where consultation and collaboration advance mission. It is more than searching for the right answers and building ownership of what otherwise might not be acceptable. It is about commitment and faith in the movement of the Holy Spirit within the body of the Church generally, and within the community of the Catholic school in particular.

Touchstones of Christian leadership

The concept of a touchstone draws from the tradition of assessing rocks that appear to be gold at first glance, 'fool's gold,' because of their outward appearance particularly in terms of colour. The rubbing of the sample against a touchstone and examining its impressions allows for an assessment of its true value. In a similar way, leadership as Christian praxis can be assessed for its authenticity by touchstones that reveal its true essence.

The touchstones for leadership in the Catholic school are argued by Burford (2017) to entail three principles: Incarnational, seeing the Spirit of Christ in people, relationships and creation; Contemplative, encountering the Spirit through information gathering, reflection and informed decision making; and Ecclesial, living and applying the history, traditions and religious nature of the faith from which the moral purpose of the school arises.

---

[88] Walter Kasper in Theology and Church (1989, p. 149) argues that of all the ideas that emerged from the Second Vatican Council, perhaps the guiding one was that of communio – communion.

[89] The Extraordinary Synod of the Council in 1985 and the Synod of Oceania in 2001 declared the Church to be essentially a mystery of communion. The Oceania Synod Fathers emphasised that 'communio would be the theme and aim of all evangelisation in Oceania and the basis for all pastoral planning' (EO: 52).

These principles (incarnational, contemplative and ecclesial) provide the evaluative check, the touchstones for examining the authenticity of leadership practices that unfold in a myriad of activities and engagements in the daily life of the school (Figure 11).

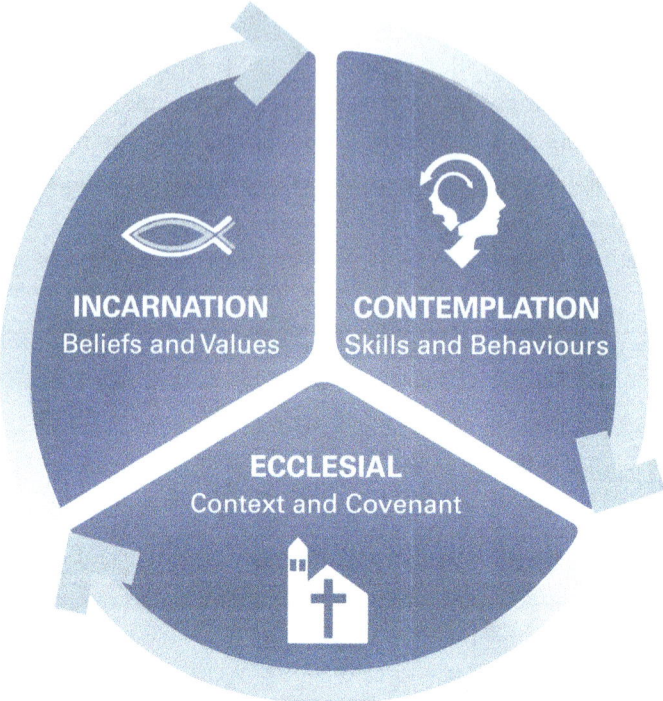

Figure 11. Christian praxis leadership principles

Christian leadership practices

The practice of leadership as instrument and sign of Christ conjure up all manner of tangible and intangible activities and processes. These practical, observable and at times 'hidden' manifestations reflect the integration of faith and life and become part and parcel of everyday culture within the Catholic school.

Table 10 summarises the potential impact of leadership on four mission constants (faith, learning, community and formation) developed in Chapter Three. This is leadership which is both instrumental in pursuing mission and being sign through behaviours that accord with the mission and goals of the school. While not exhaustive in its presentation, nor independent in their relationship, the table reveals how leadership nurtures elements of mission and in the process gives witness to these same characteristics.

Table 10. Leadership for mission in the Catholic school

MISSION	LEADERSHIP
INSTRUMENT	SIGN
FAITH	
❖ Founded on person and message of Christ ❖ Personal and communal in nature ❖ Attentive to Church tradition ❖ Inclusive and outreaching	❖ Commitment to a shared mission; ❖ Supported by an ecclesial community ❖ Expressed through spirituality ❖ Values of joy and hope
LEARNING	
❖ Prophetic and liberating ❖ Alignment of purpose, goals, programs, processes, systems and structures ❖ Relevant and responsive pedagogy ❖ Responsive to needs	❖ Catholic anthropology of the person ❖ Quality practice and relationships ❖ Religious climate ❖ Authentic culture
COMMUNITY	
❖ Servant community ❖ United in Spirit ❖ A home and school of communion ❖ Renewing for service within the world	❖ Shared beliefs and values ❖ Connected to Church ❖ Learning community ❖ Dialogue with context and culture
FORMATION	
❖ Integration of faith, life and culture ❖ Formation for mission ❖ Systematic planning ❖ Progressive and developmental in nature	❖ In dialogue and connection with 'story' ❖ Continuing transformation of the 'head, heart and hand' ❖ Witness, religious literacy and faith practice ❖ Personal readiness and commitment

Leadership for transformation

The expression of leadership as Christian praxis impacts an array of personal, relational, professional and organisational understandings, intentions, structures, processes and behaviours. Central to these manifestations is the pervasive force of leadership as a dynamic and creative Spirit, possessing an influence on all life and culture and providing opportunity and possibility for transformation.

Personal transformation

The vocational call of the teacher is a spiritual response for "as teachers, we are called to be more than mere dispensers of information with the associated challenge of "Who among us has not been concerned with covering the material?" (Durka, 2002, p. 39). The challenge is to think of ourselves as moral beings who are concerned with defining our life's purposes in a way that models for students a quest for doing the same. "Young people are more likely to be affected by teachers who themselves are questioning, pondering and learning" (Durka, 2002, p.52).

The Teacher's Calling (Durka, 2002) invites the challenge of understanding, feeling and living an imagination of how an authentic mission can be engaged at a personal level. Similar to the shift, *metanoia*, expressed by Christ as a prerequisite for the Kingdom, a Gospel imagination for the Catholic school involves a personal way of thinking, feeling and acting in light of the model and message of Christ. It is the invitation to know, integrate and act in ways that advance mission through personal encounter and engagement. To paraphrase David Hunt, it is to "Begin with yourself, do not begin out there. To begin with ourselves is to stop and reflect, to enter into our inner life, to connect with what we feel and believe, and so set an inner foundation for continuing our life's journey" (Hunt, 1991).

> *Your responsibilities make demands on you that go far beyond the need for professional skills and competence ... Through you, as through a clear window on a sunny day, students must come to see and know the richness and the joy of a life lived in accordance with Christ's teaching, in response to his challenging demands. To teach means not only to impart what we know, but also to reveal who we are by living what we believe* (Pope John Paul II, 1984).

Figure 12 is indicative of the movement in head, heart and hand as a Gospel imagination is engaged at a personal level. It depicts a shift from the centrality of the ego to a spirituality which is centred in God and a Gospel imagination integrated by principles of alignment, empowerment and engagement. Outcomes become evident in ways that illustrate a movement from doing to observing, increasing awareness, and becoming more responsibly active in pursuing a movement from partial to full life in the Spirit. The indicators of transformation are seen in respect, graciousness, trust and forgiveness (Rolheiser, 2011) and captured in the primary movement from paranoia to metanoia, or, the movement from trust in self to trust in God (Figure 12).

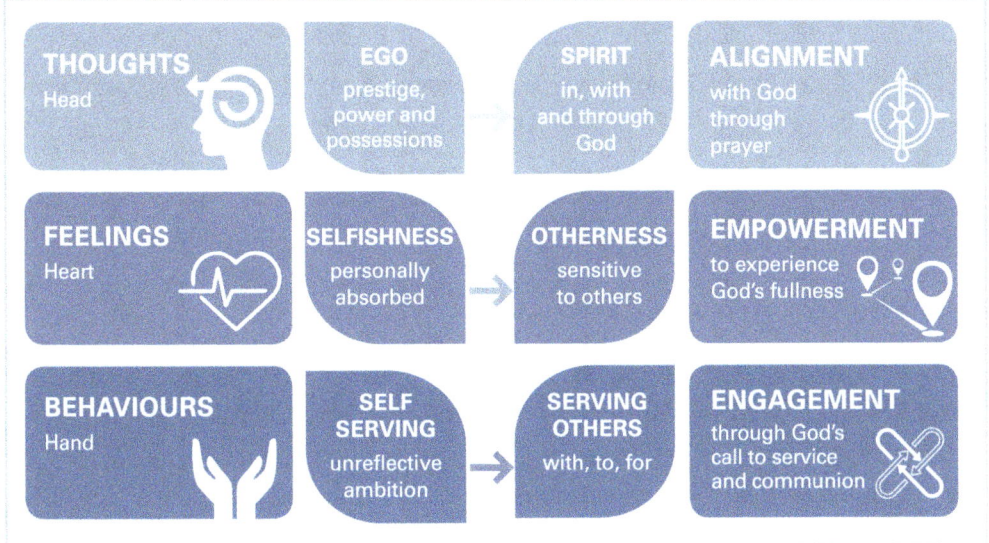

Figure 12. Shifts for personal transformation

The nature of 'shift,' the Gospel invitation to *metanoia*, is discussed by Dyer (2007) in terms of a movement from the morning to the afternoon of life; a transition from ambition to meaning; and a journey towards a renewed sense of trust in the source of all life. Characteristic outcomes of this movement include finding one's passion, dissolving superficial needs, being guided by something bigger, and exercising independence from the affirmation of others and the expectations of self. In essence, it entails a movement from the false self to the sacred self, or, a spirituality of descent (Rohr, 2003). It is a focus on the sacred in life, a God realisation that finds expression in a Kingdom view, or for Dyer 'being in the moment and not being attached,' 'living the virtue,' 'dissolving worldly ambitions,' 'entering a dark room with light,' and 'surrendering to experience abundance.'

In an information age where knowledge is the new currency, teachers are said to constitute the new social class that not only broker this 'gold' but also give principal witness to how it might be used. In this light, the content of the curriculum becomes as important as the means by which it is shared relationally. The words of Pope Paul VI are prophetic "people listen more willingly to witnesses than to teachers, and if people do listen to teachers, it is because they are witnesses" (EN, para. 41). Stated in practical terms, and with a view to integrating notions of content and process, Miller (2007, CD) advances "It is in the witness of caring, building relationships, demonstrating justice and modelling a search for the truth that teachers display their worth."

> *As from the first moment that a student sets foot in a Catholic school, he or she ought to have the impression of entering a new environment, one illumined by the light of faith ... in a Catholic school, everyone should be aware of the living presence of Jesus ... the Gospel spirit should be evident in the Christian way of thought and life which permeates all facets of the educational climate* (RDECS, para. 32).

Relational transformation

Missiologist Stephen Bevans SVD (2013) proposes that mission is ultimately God's mission with the task of the leader being to point out and contribute to God's work. As God's nature is to relationship, so too humanity joins in God's work by striving to operate relationally. In this light, relational transformation invites a view of social reality, skills of interpersonal effectiveness and functionality in groups that are intent on serving mission and demonstrating communion in commitment and action.

Social reality

The German philosopher Jürgen Habermas uses the terms 'system' and 'lifeworld' to describe two aspects of social reality. Everything that exists in the social world, the world of people, may be classified as belonging to the lifeworld or system. The lifeworld is a subjective world of visions, values, beliefs, principles, dreams, intuitions, needs and desires. While there are aspects of the lifeworld that are quite individual and unique, there are aspects of this world that are shared in common and are identified as culture. One's lifeworld is a powerful force, a source of energy which drives individuals and groups in a particular direction. The energy is seen in personal actions as well as normative action which emerges when members of the community act in accordance with a shared vision of reality.

The world of the 'system' enables societies to engage in production through schemes, plans, processes, strategies or procedures which people invent to produce goods and services. Systems are concerned with the regulation of the various parts of the production process into an efficient whole for the purpose of control, efficiency and productivity. As with the lifeworld, systems may be either positive or negative. Positive systems achieve outcomes that minimise costs in human and material kinds whereas negative systems are ineffective in terms of satisfying lifeworld visions and values and efficient production. Where the lifeworld is the setting for expressive and normative action, the system is the context for both teleological and strategic action. Teleological action involves the actor using logical and scientific methods to achieve a desired outcome.

The acknowledgement of the positive and negative elements of the lifeworld and the system leads Habermas to conclude that human development requires the integration and balance of the lifeworld with the system. The ideal is that each should provide a mutual service and so compensate for any negative forces associated with the other. The process for achieving this balance is one of 'communicative action.' This is action that is grounded in awareness, facilitates good choices, engages all relevant people and leads to authentic action. It is a process that balances and holds in a creative tension the movement from leader centred to group centred behaviours. It is a process that engages relationship in ways that respect, empower and advance shared mission. (Table 11).

Table 11. A continuum of leader behaviours

Leader-Centred ⟶ Group-Centred						
Leader decides announces decision	Leader decides sells decision	Leader presents ideas invites questions	Leader presents tentative ideas subject to review	Leader presents alternatives group decides	Leader defines boundaries group decides	Group defines boundaries and decides
Leader behaviours						

We each have a separate, unique and individual identity but at the same time are members of a community ... the construction of patterns that exist in the psyche of the person, our individual identity, is a form of psychological DNA ... immersion within groups helps to provide shape and direction to our lives; the groups that surround us impact our sense of identity (Norman Amundson, 2003, p. 41).

Skills and relationships

Integral to balancing lifeworld and system factors in the social reality of the Catholic school is the application of interpersonal skills. These skills are operative in relationships of varying intensity: awareness, surface relationships and mutuality. At the level of awareness there may only be a recognition of another's presence while at the surface level there may exist some shared knowledge. However, at the mutual level there is an openness and sharing of one's personal self and being open to growth induced by others. Interpersonal development involves not only the movement from awareness, to surface relationships, to mutuality but the assessment of relationship development in light of lifeworld and system expectations. Lifeworld and system influences not only impact on the one-to-one relationship level but are also experienced within group environments. Groups, like individuals and organisations, possess their own life and possess characteristics all of their own. Hence, an important consideration within the field of relationships is an understanding of how relationships are experienced within groups.

Group development is an accepted phenomenon within organisational and interpersonal literature. While different names are attached to varying stages of group development, agreement exists that there are at least five discernible stages (forming, storming, norming, performing and mourning) with each stage characterised by group actions. Each group stage is associated with particular group tasks and within each stage there are interpersonal challenges requiring different structured experiences. At the same time, group participation can vary with members demonstrating a range of behaviours that attract specific attention. Characteristics of blocking, competing, seeking sympathy, desiring attention, focusing on pet concerns and withdrawing, all being possible within the range of personal and interpersonal dynamics that constitute group performance. In such circumstances, the skills of group members in communication, problem solving and conflict resolution become significant.

Having Spirit means focusing on the good within and the positive aspects of what happens around you and using the energy that flows from that to create the environment for your staff to produce, learn and expand their horizons. In purely economic terms, this will improve the performance/output of your staff because just as a home is a comfortable place, so too can a workplace be. My particular hobby horse is that leaders often neglect all but the mental conditioning of their bodies and wonder why nothing works well. It is important to feed and encourage our mind, emotions, physical body, as well as our Spirit, and for all of these to work in harmony. When they are not in harmony, it is important to take the time to listen, and to act to restore the balance (Paul Parfenow, cited in Bennett & Mathieson, 2002, p. 39).

An approach to interpersonal relationships in support of mission; one based on participation, collaboration, shared decision making, recognition of difference and gifts, is summarised in the goal of sharing wisdom. Mary Benet McKinney OSB (1987) advances that the approach has three core components: implications in the way interpersonal relationships are understood; process imperatives that signal what is valued; and stances that need to be taken in terms of the actions that arise. The summary in Table 12 outlines these characteristics which reflect aspects of the head, heart and hand in promoting quality and authentic interpersonal relationships in support of the moral purpose of the school. It is a movement from the 'I' to the 'We' in thinking, feeling and acting interpersonally (Table 12).

Table 12. A shared wisdom model for inter-personal engagement

DOMAINS	Continuum of Expression — The 'I' to the 'We'
IMPLICATIONS - Beliefs about sharing wisdom	
❖ We must share our wisdom to secure meaning ❖ We must hear, respect, and treasure one another's wisdom ❖ We must work for a climate that is open and respectful	
PROCESS - Engaging others in shared wisdom	
❖ We must understand the differences in personality types ❖ We must learn to use process skills – communication, conflict resolution, problem solving ❖ We must take time for reflective prayer ❖ We must take time to gather the wisdom ❖ We must learn to accept the discerned wisdom as the will of the Spirit	
STANCES - Action in advancing shared wisdom	
❖ We must be open to new ways of thinking and feeling ❖ We must be open to information and data collected by others ❖ We must be willing to let go of the need to control ❖ We must be willing to let go of the need to win ❖ We must let go of the need to be always right ❖ We must be willing to leave the familiar and risk the unfamiliar	

Educational transformation

The challenge to educate authentically is to engage the complexity and holistic integrity of the person, community and creation. At the core of this growth is the recognition of an evolution from the created order, reclaiming the sacred sense of life as gift, rediscovering interdependence with people and nature, and engaging in a world where all is interconnected.

The human story does not exist in isolation from the story of life, the earth, and the cosmos. Physicists, palaeontologists, archaeologists and sociologists offer fascinating perspectives on human evolution and humankind's planetary presence as a very recent phenomenon. Scientific evidence reveals human footprints on the earth made by 'homo ambulans' 3.6 million years ago, the creative use of hands by 'homo erectus' two million years back, the growth in self-reflection by 'homo spiritus' 70,000 years past, and the consciousness evidenced in Paleolithic art created by humans in the comparatively more recent time span of 30,000 years. This very ancient history is testimony to an evolving ancestry of almost unbelievable proportions and indicative of the need for education to respond in ways that connect, inform, empower and give flexibility and continuity to learning.

The provision of education within Australia is shaped by the reform agenda of the Australian government which promotes national goals for schooling and service delivery principles of excellence and equity. For Catholic schools these goals and principles are interpreted from a particular view of the human person and pursued through practices of personal liberation and community contribution. Such emphases have characterised Catholic schools from the beginning of British settlement and are evident in a multiplicity of educational transformations, most noticeably in relation to perspectives about students, learning, curriculum and pedagogy (Table 13). Integral to these educational perspectives is leadership which shapes and guides educational thinking and practice through the lenses of the vision and mission of the school.

Table 13. Traditional to contemporary educational perspectives

TRADITIONAL	TO	CONTEMPORARY
STUDENTS ... HUMAN BEINGS CREATED IN THE IMAGE OF GOD		
Education as a basic right	→	Education as a right, incorporating empowerment for personal and communal life
All learners are similar	→	All learners possess inter and intra individual differences
Student development as predictable	→	Student development as sensitive to quality intervention
LEARNING ... INTEGRATION OF KNOWLEDGE AND EXPERIENCE		
Learning as a cognitive and largely passive receptive process	→	Learning as a cognitive, multi-sensory, dynamic and interactive process
Learning as a 'lock step' graded process	→	Learning as a continuous process
Learning occurring at fixed stages in life	→	Learning as a life-long experience
Learning as a set of independent and isolated experiences	→	Learning as an interdependent and integrated experience

TRADITIONAL	TO	CONTEMPORARY
CURRICULUM ... MEANS FOR EXPRESSING VISION AND MISSION		
Religious education as the centre of faith development	→	Religious education as a key learning area, complemented by faith expression within the relational and religious dimension of the school which is sensitive to the needs of students from multiple faith traditions
Curriculum as the formal instructional experience	→	Curriculum as the totality of school experience
Independence of formal subject areas	→	Interdependence of key learning areas
Curriculum of the 'basics' (literacy and numeracy)	→	Curriculum of the 'new basics' inclusive of 'old basics' and key competencies for on-going learning
A curriculum of confined knowledge and skills	→	A curriculum of expanding knowledge and skills
PEDAGOGY ... THE FACILITATION OF HOLISTIC DEVELOPMENT		
Classroom as the sole learning environment	→	Classroom as a base learning centre networking with other learning environments
Teacher as information provider	→	Teacher as facilitator, co-learner and model
Utilisation of specific teaching resources	→	Creative use of multiple teaching resources
Teaching focused on 'inputs'	→	Teaching focused on process, essential learning and outcomes
Teacher as the centre of the classroom	→	Student and teacher as integral to the learning process in an inter-connected age of information
Technology as a relatively distant support to learning	→	Technology providing a gateway to accession of changing knowledge, pedagogy and assessment

Organisational transformation

Organisational transformation is focused on upgrading services to address needs, capitalising on the existing diversity of personnel talent, achieving best practice and reforming management to meet new and emerging implementation requirements. For organisations providing a service within a philosophy based on the person and message of Christ, this culture can be described as mission-centred both within and without.

> *Even if people are not consciously aware of it, there is a sense of spirit in every organisation. It can be referred to as 'collective vision,' 'morale,' 'life force,' 'teamwork,' 'energy,' or 'corporate culture.' None of these terms is an adequate description of organisational spirit but each is often used as a substitute for 'spirit' in situations where the speaker wishes to avoid the potential embarrassment of using a word that seems 'touchy-feely'* (Vicki Bennett & Ian Mathieson, 2002, p. 38).

Transformation within a Catholic Christian community has the distinctive goal of living in accord with the Gospel. Renewal involves an appreciation of Church mission as responsive to contemporary needs and presumes and promotes a connection with the Divine through contemplative dialogue.

> *The path of contemplative dialogue, the practice of engaging collective awareness in organisations is said to be a synthesis of the work of many people from many fields. Taken together, this mix of theory, skills and values produces new possibilities for understanding and engaging relationships, communities and organisations with depth, compassion, and effectiveness* (Steven Wirth, 2012, p. 2).

The movement from 'darkness' to 'light,' 'being people of life and for life' (EV, para. 78) within managerial practices is the challenge to be authentic to the Gospel in processes, systems and structures. It involves practices that are open to all, the outcomes of which contribute to the growth of the community and the renewal of society overall (EV, para. 101). The journey is said to be rooted in building up the Christian community (EV, para. 95) through being open to the truth through the action of the Spirit. This is the essence of organisational transformation in light of the Gospel.

> *Insofar as the process of contemplative dialogue works with what is most essential about the human persons, it requires no explicit language or particular belief system to be effective. It makes no effort to 'change' or 'fix' participants. Rather it assists them in touching what is most central and trustworthy in their human experience, and speaking of it with deep integrity* (Steven Wirth, 2012, p. 3).

The essence of contemplative dialogue is becoming awake within organisational life. It is being attentive to what is going on and looking to engage this mystery "in ways that allow us to know it more intimately, more productively, and with far richer understanding. It is a way of being in relationship to the ordinary reality about us that makes available not just the visible and material qualities, but also the less tangible depths that lie hidden beneath mundane circumstances" (Wirth, 2012, p. 6). It is argued to involve three inter-related practices: contemplative noticing or mindfulness (to take a long compassionate look at the real); adoption of a non-defended learning stance (a commitment to the truth and developing collective commitment to the common good); and, non-violence (adoption of group safety and people engagement that allows fundamental problems to be solved).

Values and strategies of contemplative dialogue in organisations provide a framework for intentional action. Guiding values of sharing information, supporting free and informed choice, and sharing responsibilities for implementation and monitoring of actions provide the foundations for strategies identified by Wirth (2012, p. 23) as including:

- Creation of environments in which members are supported in authentically engaging the issues before them;
- Sharing control with those who have competence and who are involved with the issue;
- Combining advocacy with inquiry rather than one-sided advocacy; and
- Working together to reduce personal blind spots and inconsistencies.

Practices of contemplative dialogue reflect Gospel values. The value of justice is evident through inclusiveness and openness to the Spirit; common good is realised in the building of awareness and interdependencies among people; truth and peace are reflected in the non-violent and open dynamics of the process; and freedom and liberation flow out of processes of co-creation. Consequences from the process are argued to include personal growth for the individual; organisational capacity building for addressing threatening or embarrassing situations; identification and dealing with 'the undiscussable' which can be destructive to personal and organisational service and development; nurturing deep learning which combines the solving of simple problems in processes that incorporate the revealing of assumptions and beliefs as to action; and, the development of constructive group behaviours.

> *The way to engender a sense of spirit in an organisation is to create an environment which encourages it, to nurture it, to select people who will be responsive to it and to behave in ways that encourage others to live it* (Vicki Bennett & Ian Mathieson, 2002, p. 39).

Table 14 summarises the changes in behaviours when the Spirit of the Gospel informs perspectives within a cluster of organisational domains. In the examples offered, traditional organisational behaviours are contrasted with perspectives that reflect a Spirit based contemplative culture centred on a Kingdom vision. The continuum of expression identifies the impact of this shift. The culture which is encouraged is one where the Spirit of God directs action, with values of truth, love, inclusion, trust and freedom providing the foundations for organisational life (Table 14).

> *Has not all our discussion of our structures and their mutual relationships not put the sociological and institutional dimension too much in the foreground? Haven't we talked too much about the Church and too little about Christ? ... Our view of Church must be not only sociological but also supernatural ... What we can do is infinitely inferior to the one who does real reform* (Joseph Komonchak, 1987, p. 736).

Table 14. Shifts in organisational transformation

ORGANISATIONAL DOMAINS	Continuum of Expression	
	Traditional →	Spirit Centred
Purpose		
Vision	Decreed from	Shared with
Mission	Working for	Identifying with
Ministry	To others	With, to and for others
Identity	Within group	Within and beyond group
Governance		
Authority	Centralised/singular	Devolved/collegial
Accountability	Private	Transparent
Purpose	Regulatory	Empowering
Management	Independent	Interdependent

ORGANISATIONAL DOMAINS	Continuum of Expression Traditional → Spirit Centred	
Human Resources		
Leadership	Leader and followers	Leadership by all
Communication	One way	Mutual sharing
Improvement	Service focused	Needs based
Performance	Inspectorial	Shared discernment
Culture		
Personnel	Instrument for purpose	Dignity and worth
Relationships	Self-serving	Team centred
Community	Belonging	Shared beliefs and values
Success	Normative	Developmental
Organisation		
Data	Presumed	Evidence based
Design	Incremental growth	Focus on purpose
Partnerships	Few and simple	Many and complex
Strategy	Self-focused	Open to clients and context

"What do we know for sure?"

Chapter Four has focused on leadership and drawn the conclusion that within the Catholic school, leadership is an expression of Christian living, shared Christian praxis, the process which brings faith to life and life to faith. It is leadership that invites courage and trust, themes central to the Kingdom of Christ and the context of leadership in the early Church. Described by Miller (2007, video) as 'the great educational emergency,' it is a challenge that holds no limits and is offered to all within the community of the Catholic school.

Leadership as Christian praxis is that 'special something,' the 'deep vocational commitment' described as 'spiritual capital' (Grace, 2010, p. 117) and characterised by a spirituality which animates, inspires and operates dynamically. It is a form of leadership which arises from Christian discipleship and shapes meaning and action within Catholic school settings.

In its essence, spiritual capital incorporates personal witness to faith practice, action and relationship evidenced in personal and professional endeavour. Characteristics of spiritual capital reveal a personal relationship with God, in Jesus and the Saints through the indwelling of the Spirit (Gerald Grace, 2010, p. 125).

The call to leadership as Christian praxis in a post-modern society is similar to the invitation to those within the infant Church (Morwood, 1997; O'Loughlin, 2007). Moreover, Morwood adds that if 'tomorrow's Catholics' are to give expression to their faith, then their leadership will need to draw from a spirituality based on "the foundational" (1997, p. 136). The fruits of the task are significant as they allow for "participation in decision making, being heard on important issues, allowing God's Spirit to be creative among us, and taking seriously that God's Spirit is active in the body of the Church" (Morwood, 1997, p. 127).

The legendary broadcaster Oprah Winfrey is known to have asked "What do you know for sure?" Notwithstanding the challenge, the value of the question encourages a response that 'gets to the chase' as experience and reflection are interrogated and a summary is ideally forthcoming and hopefully of some use. The response to the question in relation to leadership, specifically conceptualised as Christian praxis, is that what is known for sure, can be seen in at least the following conclusions:

- Leadership is founded on the vision and mission of Christ;
- Leadership is centred in the Spirit;
- Leadership is manifested in a learning community;
- Leadership is open to all;
- Leadership engages the agenda of the world;
- Leadership heralds blessing of known and unknown forms; and,
- Leadership is supported through continuous reflection and formation.

Leadership as Christian praxis involves a "call to growth and a continual process of maturation" (CL, para. 155). The concept is reinforced by the theme of the diligent vinedresser "I am the true vine, and my Father is the vinegrower. He removes every branch in me that bears no fruit. Every branch that bears fruit he prunes to make it bear more fruit" (John 15:1-2). The implication is that it is the Spirit of Christ that provides for transformation according to the will of the Father, under the guidance of the Holy Spirit (see CL, para. 156). Within the mission of the Catholic school this formation in leadership becomes "an ever clearer discovery of one's vocation and the ever-greater willingness to live it so as to fulfil one's mission" (CL, para. 156).

INTEGRATION

Executive Summary

Leadership is one of the most talked about, researched and theorised activities within community and organisational life. While daunting in its conceptualisation and comprehensive in its application, it is accessible to all and central to life within the Catholic school. Foundations lie in enacting the Spirit of Christ, processes reach into personal, relational, professional and communal domains and outcomes are evidenced in transformations of known and unknown forms. What can be said for sure is that within the Catholic school it is Spirit centred, experienced as Christian praxis and provides a significant expression for alignment by the living stones with the cornerstone of Christ.

Reflection: Service and communion at the table

My wife and I shared an experience of table service in a small but memorable way during an extended time in Sydney. For months, literally, we had been advised that there was a 'little coffee shop' on Victoria Street that should not be missed. We would pass by it daily, and, because of the overflow from its narrow confines onto an already busy footpath, we would tend to 'write it off.' We were, however, always intrigued by the crowd and the acceptance by clientele of less than ideal physical circumstances. It took a while before our curiosity gave way to having a 'coffee at Bar Coluzzi,' the trading name brandished on an old sign outside, which also contained the words, 'serving people for over 40 years.' It was not long after that first cappuccino that we began to understand its attraction. It was a place where table service was excellent, and, more significantly, where communion was fostered intensely. Community knowledge, acceptance and relationship existed not only between the owners and patrons, but also were encouraged among the patrons. People knew people and were encouraged to connect without pressure. Experiencing Bar Coluzzi once, then going back repeatedly, confirmed it as a place to gather and share life, a place of quality service and communion at the table.

Questions

1. **Head:** How can leadership be articulated as 'kingly' in nature?
2. **Heart:** Do you 'feel' a commitment to leadership as Christian praxis?
3. **Hand:** What behaviours would characterise your leadership style?

Activities

- **Theme:** Self-awareness
- **Goal:** Profiling capabilities
- **Task:** Personal reflection and perceptions of a trusted colleague provide a contribution to leadership self awareness

STRENGTH AREAS Perception	GROWTH AREAS Perception
Self	*Others*
Self	*Others*

- **Theme:** Imaging leadership
- **Goal:** To develop an image/s of leadership
- **Task:** Consider the leadership image from *The Renewal of Personal Energy* (Hunt, 1992, p. 56) and identify an image that reinforces your leadership approach?

> *My image is of myself holding a bouquet of multi-coloured balloons. These balloons are unlike other balloons. They are not filled with air but rather with my developed and underdeveloped qualities. Some of the balloons are large (my developed qualities)*

Activities

and have long strings so they soar above the others. Other balloons are small (my underdeveloped qualities) with shorter strings so they tend to bob below the larger ones. Other people around me are also holding balloons of various sizes on varying lengths of string. The fun part comes in sharing balloons because it gives my smaller balloons a boost and helps them soar a little higher.

 Theme: *Dadirri*

 Goal: Listening deeply

 Task: Deep listening, *dadirri*, is a natural and contemplative process that occurs in practices of sustained silent listening. Consider occasions when *dadirri* was invoked and note your reactions about such.

....
....
....
....

 Theme: Becoming the change

 Goal: Leadership action

 Task: Mahatma Ghandi provides the challenge: "become the change you want to see in the world." What single strategies for change exist in the following?

- ❖ *Personal:* my relationship with my inner-self will be enhanced by…
- ❖ *Relational:* My relationship with my colleagues will be enhanced by…
- ❖ *Professional:* My relationship with my professional duties will be enhanced by…
- ❖ *Communal:* My relationship with my community will be enhanced by…

CHAPTER FIVE
One garment: Ministry as integration

Chapter Outline

CHAPTER FIVE	150
ONE GARMENT: MINISTRY AS INTEGRATION	150
INTRODUCTION	150
Reflection	150
At a glance	150
Focusing story: Jigsaw	151
From your experience	151
THEMES AND MAIN IDEAS	151
Oneness of mind and Spirit	152
Thriving in the new normal	152
Mind: the brain and body relationship	154
Mind and spirit relationship	156
Ministry	165
Professional vocation	166
Five-star aspirations	167
Spirit encounters	169
Legends in the Spirit	171
Fruits of the Spirit	174
Prayer and meditation	176
Living consciously	179
"Why was it so?"	181
Ministry: Perspective and capabilities	181
Researching capabilities	184
A metaphor for capabilities	191
Gauging priorities	193
INTEGRATION	194
Executive Summary	194
Reflection: The essence of ministry	194
Questions	194
Activities	195

CHAPTER FIVE
One garment: Ministry as integration[90]

INTRODUCTION

Reflection

"Fundamental to Christian discipleship is the experience of being called like Matthew. "As Jesus was walking on from there he saw a man named Matthew sitting by the customs house, and he said to him, 'Follow me.' And he got up and followed him" (Matthew 9:9). In Baptism, all Christians have received the call to holiness. Each personal vocation is a call to share in the Church's mission; and, given the needs of the new evangelisation, it is especially important now to remind lay people in the Church of their particular call. The Synod Fathers "rejoiced in the work and witness of so many of the lay faithful who have been an integral part of the growth of the Church in Oceania"" (EO, para. 43).

At a glance

The vocation of the educator in the Catholic school is ministerial in that it reflects foundations in faith through the expression of spirituality, mission and leadership. The concept of one garment images the integrative nature of this ministry expressed within and beyond the school community.

The chapter develops the concept of ministry through four related themes: oneness of mind and Spirit; ministry as vocation; Spirit engagement; and capabilities. The theme of oneness in Spirit explores the relationship of ministry and neuroscience while the discussion of ministry gives a focus to the ideal within the life of the school. Spirit engagement elaborates on ministry witness, and, ministry capabilities are identified as generic to ministry practice and formation.

---

90 The image of garment is drawn from two sources: Saint Paul who encourages followers to be clothed in Christ; and Ronald Rolheiser who speaks of one's internal and external garment in *Sacred Fire*.

Focusing story: Jigsaw

Holidays can be periods of renewal when the stresses and tensions of work give way to a variety of alternative experiences. As part of the usual 'trip away,' how often have we taken a jigsaw puzzle and left it on the dining table for completion as inclination allows? Interestingly, over the course of time, the 'puzzle of a thousand pieces' gradually is completed as the 'picture on the box' comes to life. The picture is always in a process of completion, never fully whole until the last piece is in place. Even when the scene is finished, one has the impression that it too is part of something much bigger, something beyond the limited square that is now whole.

From your experience

1. How important is the alignment of personal beliefs and values with the processes, structures and relationships within the school community?
2. In what ways have you experienced this alignment?
3. What are some practical priorities in ministry formation?

THEMES AND MAIN IDEAS
Oneness of mind and spirit

Chapter five integrates the discussion of foundations in faith, spirituality, mission and leadership through the practice of ministry within the mission, life and culture of the Catholic school. At the heart of this process is understanding, experiencing emotion, and engaging behaviours that reflect connection and support betterment.

Not long after taking on a leadership role in a professional association the opportunity to share one's vision arose. The invitation was a privileged experience to research and reflect on the importance of values, the mission of the organisation and the leadership that was required within changing and challenging times. The response entailed a reflection on 'looking inwards and outwards' in personal, relational, professional, and organisational terms. While the presentation appeared to possess some value, it was only at the reception afterwards that I appreciated the significance of 'going deeper,' specifically at a personal level. The comment from a colleague reinforced the point. "I really enjoyed that 'inner' perspective, where might I find out more?" The exchange was such that the notion of 'going within,' while a good one, is just a concept that presumes an appreciation of 'what is it that lies within, where can it be found, how might it work, how can it be developed, and what means exist for sustaining it?" In its simplest form it is the conversation about what constitutes the whole of self and how the self might be understood, developed and integrated within life as a whole.

> *To understand the whole, it is necessary to understand the parts. To understand the parts, it is necessary to understand the whole. Such is the circle of understanding. We move from part to whole and back again, and in the dance of comprehension, in that amazing circle of understanding, we come alive to meaning, to value, and to vision. The very circle of understanding guides our way, weaving together the pieces, healing the fractures, mending the torn and tortured fragments, lighting the way ahead - this extraordinary movement from part to whole and back again, with healing the hallmark of each and every step, and grace the tender reward* (Ken Wilber, 1997, p. 1).

The discussion of mind and spirit is undertaken with substantial reservation but equally with significant interest. The reservation is on the grounds of the complexity of the science in language and concept, the recency of this knowledge, and the expansive and connected forms in which the understandings are presented. Notwithstanding the challenge, the relevance for ministry as an integrative expression of spirituality, mission and leadership holds much anticipation.

Principles and practices from mind and spirit research are relatively recent in their identification, particularly in western science although their identification and significance are not new for some cultures. However, what is commonly accepted is that once held intuitive beliefs about their nature and relationship are now being explored scientifically and contributing to applications in multiple arenas of human endeavour.

Thriving in the new normal[91]

Personal and social experiences in the everyday reveal a 'new normal.' Climate is changing, debt is increasing, esteemed institutions are less trustworthy, populations are exploding, energy needs are expanding, gaps between rich and poor are increasing, and the effects on individuals, groups and institutions are felt comprehensively. The world of the past, the one that offered security,

---
91 A term used by Gregg Braden, 2013, to describe contemporary social reality.

predictability and stability is now changed and there is 'no going back' (Coleridge, 2017). Rather, the challenge and invitation are to go forward. "It is a time of "graceful urgency to do what we need to do to respond to the crises of our time" (Braden, 2013, DVD)[92].

Meaningful engagement with the present can be bewildering, if not daunting and potentially frightening. There is no avoiding what sociologists and technology 'wizards' are saying and demonstrating already exists and what might be 'around the corner.' The world already has self-driving electric vehicles, 3D printing, computerised watches, energy producing households, artificial intelligences replacing professional services, and creative companies establishing new processes and relationships not seen before. It is the dawning of a new revolution, an exponential age, a time when predictability is not possible and yet responses beyond survival are needed to address the avalanche of the new and the opportunities within the new.

A central aspect of the discussion about mind and spirit is the nature of their relationship. This understanding while possessive of an expansive history across time and cultures is relatively new. Within this more recent period, the last 300 years, reference to the French philosopher René Descartes (1596 - 1650), the mathematician Isaac Newton (1643 - 1727), and theoretical physicist Albert Einstein (1879 - 1955), often figure in the conversation. It was Descartes who proposed that matter and spirit are separate; Newton who introduced scientific method to measure and predict material phenomena; and Einstein who revealed the nature of energy as incorporating elements of matter and speed. Each scientist, while contributing to understandings within their unique time and available resources, provided perspectives which today continue to be explored, debated and enhanced.

The question of "Where to from here?" provokes immediate disclaimers of knowledge inadequacy, limited experience, and the arrogance of predictions in a reality that is so changeable. However, within a Christian meaning system, the cardinal virtues of faith, hope and charity spring to mind as first, traditional and honoured responses within a 'new normal.' These virtues have held steadfast despite the prevailing zeitgeist[93] across millennia. Faith provides a sense of trust in 'something' within and yet beyond the self and community; hope sustains the disposition of perseverance and anticipation of betterment; and love is the connection that nurtures oneness and relationship in the search that is experienced within self, others, institutions and creation. Significantly, faith is the time-honoured tradition, 'a belief,' 'a hunch' that there is a 'life force' that holds everything together, gives meaning and purpose to existence, and provides for relationship in an environment that is connected.

92 Gregg Braden is internationally renowned as a pioneer in bridging science and spirituality.
93 Zeitgeist is the defining spirit or mood of a period of history as shown by the ideas and beliefs of the time.

Mind: the brain and body relationship

The mind of a person is the capacity to think and to feel together (Dispenza, 2012, 2014, 2017). It is to act in harmony in ways that enhance the function of the whole and so "create coherence between our beliefs and the reality we experience" (Lipton, 2016, p. 139). It is the expression of the human as a single integrated and aware organism in relationship to its own uniqueness and in relationship to others and the environment. This life situation, however, is not the full expression of our life (Tolle, 2004, 2005). That is, the wholistic nature of our being is constituted by the integration of the mind and Spirit in ways that are individualistic and unique; the expression of which is described as the 'soul' of the person.'

An understanding of the mind, the brain and body relationship, is founded on terminology and understandings commonly used by professionals but not always appreciated by newcomers to the science. Without being expansive, and acknowledging one's disciplinary limitations, the basic foundations underpinning brain and body relationships include, but not limited to: the nature of cells, brain structure, plasticity, brain and body communications, and, quantum field theory.

Cells

Cells are the smallest structural and functional unit of every living organism and possess the unique ability to store and communicate information between each other (Dispenza, 2014, p.15). Cells group together as tissues with a similar structure and work together for a specific function as organs. Within cells there are proteins; large, complex molecules that are required for the structure, function, and regulation and reproduction of the body's cells, tissues and organs.[94] Also within each cell, there are genes that constitute the fundamental physical and functional unit of heredity and reflect adaptation to the environment.

Brain structure

The brain comprises three significant anatomical units.[95] The first, Hindbrain (the behaving brain), manages the autonomic nervous system that acts largely unconsciously and regulates bodily functions such as heart rate, digestion, respiratory system, pupillary responses, urination, and sexual arousal. The second, Midbrain (the feeling brain), takes in sensory information (sight, hearing, smell, taste and touch) and incorporates this within the limbic system which regulates, and controls drives, as well as emotional responses and memory.

---

[94] Deepak Chopra is a respected endocrinologist who discusses the nature of proteins in cell reproduction by asserting ninety eight percent of the atoms of the body were not there a year ago. It is as if you lived in a building whose bricks were systematically taken out and replaced every year... "what I am calling intelligence takes on the role of guiding this change so that we do not collapse into a heap of bricks" (Chopra, 1990, p. 48-49).

[95] In the 1950's and the 1960's, the US psychologist, Paul MacLean, developed a theory of the triune brain.

The third, Forebrain (the knowledge brain), is the cerebral cortex made up of two hemispheres which store knowledge and enable thought. While the brain might be viewed anatomically as comprising separate functions, the root of all thoughts, emotions and behaviours is the communication between neurons. These are manifested in the synchronised electrical pulses from neurons communicating with each other via neuro-transmitters. These are "the runners that race to and from the brain telling every organ inside of us of our emotions, desires, memories, intuitions and dreams" (Chopra, 1990, p. 58).

Brain plasticity

The once held belief that the brain was hard wired is now replaced with the concept of neural plasticity. Plasticity is the flexibility of the brain to change in accord with what is thought, chemically transmitted, and behaviourally experienced (Doidge, 2008; Dispenza, 2015). The process entails the "brain's ability to change its synaptic wiring by learning information and recording experiences and to maintain a modified state of being" (Dispenza, 2014, p. 11). Described as Hebbian Learning,[96] this is the process of neurons 'firing and wiring together' in new and different forms to impact gene modification and enhance new behavioural practice and wellbeing (Braden, 2017; Doidge, 2007; Greenfield, 2000; Winston, 2003). Moreover, the recognition and activation of neurons in the heart and the 'gut' reinforce the nature of the whole body being in relationship, and the capacity for plasticity of the brain to be impacted by thinking, feeling, behaving, and intuiting as the brain sends and receives signals all over the body (Benson, 2014).

Brain and body communications

The exploration of the dynamic relationships within the body (Braden, 2017, Chopra & Tanzi, 2018, Dispenza, 2017, Lipton, 2016, 2017) are forging a new frontier of inquiry and application according to Caroline Myss (2017). It is an arena of theory and research which draws together and explains relationships in ways not understood previously nor necessarily applied in a range of settings.[97] The nature of these relationships is summarised by Bruce Lipton; "If I change my beliefs about life I change the signals that are going through my body and adjust the function of cells" (Lipton, 2017). In other words, rather than being passive recipients of environmental signals (the survival response),

---

[96] Hebbian learning is when a synapse between two neurons is strengthened when the neurons on either side of the synapse (input and output) have highly correlated outputs.

[97] One example offered by Maureen Marra is on the work of David Rock under the banner of Neuroleadership which combines neuroscience and leadership. It works on the basic principle that the human brain has ancient responses in that it moves towards rewards and away from threats.

human beings can reverse the pattern and learn to manage these experiences in ways that induce learning and development (the creative response).[98]

Quantum field theory

The definition of 'quantum' in Physics is the smallest amount of an entity involved in an interaction. In terms of human relationships, a quantum way of considering reality is to view these relationships as offering endless possibilities through proactive and life directing engagements between the world of the mind and the environment (Dispenza, 2014, p. 32-33). Supporting this understanding is the concept of wave energy which refers to an oscillation accompanied by a transfer of energy that travels through a medium (space or mass). Wave energy is imperceptible to human sensations, is unpredictable in direction but is scientifically demonstrated in the relationships between matter which is more energy than particle. Braden (2013), for example, points to the composition of the atom as predominantly empty space with 99.9 per cent of it comprised of energy. Moreover, the universe is argued to be 96 per cent empty space which comprises waves of energy that connect and extend it via electromagnetic fields.[99]

Mind and spirit relationship

The relationship between Science, in exploring aspects of the mind, and Religion, in nurturing the life of the spirit, is significant for it holds together minds and hearts to make sense of the world. In this regard, Science and Religion offer differing perspectives of a single reality. The role of Science is to unravel functionality, and the role of Religion is to provide meaning. "Science takes things apart and Religion puts things together. This is the biggest picture, and the biggest picture is always the best picture" (McGrath, 2018).[100]

Science is concerned with theories and explanations about the mysteries of the universe. Religion is concerned with the quest for ultimate (telos) meaning of these mysteries. The breakdown of relations between science and religion after the 18th century left both science and religion impoverished. Science without religion ignores the enduring power of the numinous[101] in humanity and mystical ways of knowing. Religion which ignores science becomes less credible in a scientifically conditioned world (Kevin Treston, 2018, p. 66).

---

98 Every thought, feeling, and emotion creates a molecule known as a neuropeptide. Neuropeptides travel throughout your body and hook onto receptor sites of cells and neurons. Your brain takes in the information, converts it into chemicals, and lets your whole body know if there's trouble in the world or cause for celebration. Your body is directly influenced as these molecules course through the bloodstream, delivering the energetic effect of whatever your brain is thinking and feeling (Deepak Chopra, 2018, AZ Quotes. 1508011).
99 The theory of morphogenetic fields offers insights into the relationship of matter and energy and argues that fields of energy extend beyond matter and members of social groups.
100 Compounding and balancing these positions is the work of Professor Jordan Petersen, the renowned clinical psychologist who seeks meaning and learning through the application of Scripture.
101 Numinous refers to mystical, spiritual, magic, supernatural, magical.

A common reference to the 'body' within Christian religious traditions was to use the phrase 'temple of the spirit.' These words signify the presence of the Holy Spirit as pervasive and sacred. The presence of the Holy Spirit is seen in the attitudes of mystics and saints who refer to the reality and operations of the body in relationship to the spirit. The statement on the memorial grave of Australia's first saint Mother Mary MacKillop RSJ, for instance, signifies the presence of something beyond the 'material;' "We are but travellers here." The words are a reminder of the integrated nature of the spirit that possesses an existence beyond the material nature of human life but significantly guides the actions of the person during life. In presenting the essence of this Spirit, Marianne Williamson (2004) draws from an early nineteenth century reflection.

No longer seek God in the heavens above or the earth beneath, or in the things under the earth, but recognise God as the great fact of the universe, separate from no place or part, but revealed in all places and in all things and events, moment by moment. And as eternity alone will exhaust this momentary revelation, which has sometimes been called the ETERNAL NOW, thou shalt thus find God ever present and ever new; and thy soul shall adore God and feed upon God in the things and events which each new moment brings; and thou shalt never be absent from God, and God shall never be absent from thee (Thomas Upham).[102]

Within the Christian tradition the Holy Spirit is a life force that is named, prayed to, gathered in, and experienced individually and communally. Notwithstanding this enthusiasm, Bruce Lipton (2016, p. 203) indicates that within some scientific circles the word 'spirit' is as warmly embraced as the word 'evolution' is in fundamentalist circles. In addition, probing questions on the presence and nature of spirit illustrate that it is not easily understood and recognised. Mindful of the questions posed earlier in this chapter, Wayne Dyer asks, "Where are you looking?" Brandon Bays inquires "If you do 'look inside' what do you see?" and Stephen Covey adds "If you do observe something special what keeps you facing this true north?" These are the challenges of becoming attentive to the life of the spirit, which from a Christian perspective possesses a unique interpretation.[103]

---

102 Thomas Upham (1799 - 1872) was an American philosopher, psychologist, pacifist, poet, author, and educator. He was an important figure in the holiness movement. He became influential within psychology literature and served as the Bowdoin College Professor of Mental and Moral Philosophy from 1825-1868.

103 Holy Spirit: "The relationship of love between Christ and the Father, revealed in the life of Christ and evidenced in the love of people for one another." Spirit: "God given and integral to human nature, it shapes and guides behaviours but is not centred in religious beliefs and practices."

Multiple commentators on the nature of spirit (Eckhart Tolle, Wayne Dyer, Louise Hay, Ronald Rolheiser, Richard Rohr, Deepak Chopra, Esther Hicks, Caroline Myss, Marianne Williamson, Thomas Merton, Henri Nouwen) point to the role of spirit in monitoring and controlling thoughts, feelings and actions. This is the spiritual self that is not centred in thought but uses thought; applies wisdom that is not dependent on the neurological system but is argued to be found in every cell; is not physical in nature but has a profound influence on all behaviour. It is a presence that embraces and shapes every action and is variably described as 'Spirit,' 'Holy Spirit,' 'True Self,' 'Sacred Self,' 'Source,' 'Stillness,' 'Silent Witness,' 'Internal Navigator,' 'Voice Within,' 'Higher Consciousness,' 'Universal Intelligence,' 'Inner Being,' 'Mystery,' 'God.' It is the means for managing the mind (body and brain relationship) which is found in the integration of cognition (thinking), affect (feeling), and behaviour (experience), see Figure 13.

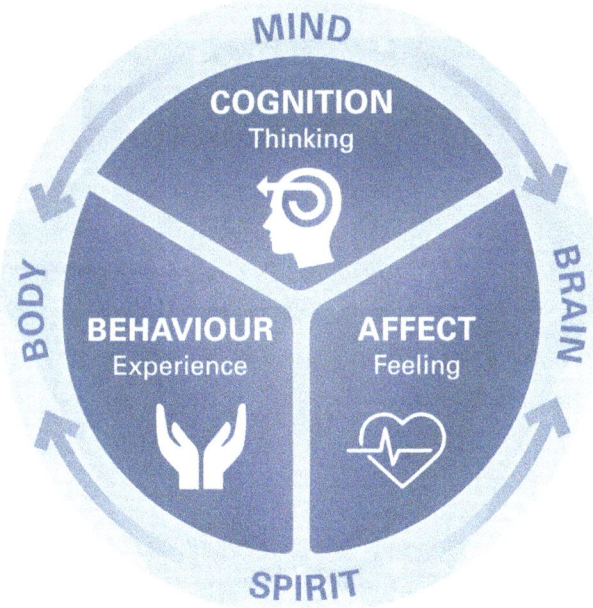

Figure 13. Personal integration through life in the Spirit

While the action of the spirit is observed in relation to the individual, this action of the spirit creates patterns of energy that go out from the self and influence the group (Braden & Dispenza, 2013). This energy, wave energy, is shown to connect with and impact patterns of behaviour that are not necessarily measurable but are able to be experienced. For instance, within the community of a Catholic school how often is the comment made "The staff here are simply wonderful," or, "I love working in this space, there is something special here," and, "This is a great place to be, people are so good." Our intuitive self identifies these experiences, connects with them and in turn, adds to or subtracts to that which already exists. The Second Vatican Council referred to the relational nature of this experience in the word '*communio*' an experience of shared values and beliefs found in relationships informed by the Spirit of Christ.

An example of the movement of the universal Spirit beyond the school environment is offered by Maureen Marra when commenting on the recent cave rescue in Thailand.[104] In this illustration, people gathered around a common purpose with a clear goal that they all believed in. Many risked their lives in the effort to save the stranded 'Wild Boars' soccer group for no personal fame. One of the rescuers is quoted as saying "The teamwork that they went through to get them out was quite phenomenal. It showed what people can do when they all collectively come up with a way to do something that has never been done before, and work together. Everybody played a part, and everybody volunteered to go there and help out. It was nice to be a part of that and I would do it again given the option." This is the way humans can behave. From an evolutionary perspective, rescuing others presents as not only part of the human condition for survival of the group but also manifests the level of care and outreach through the activation and guidance of the Spirit.

Thinking about these well-known facts has led me to three conclusions. First, that intelligence is present everywhere in our bodies. Second, that our own inner intelligence is far superior to any we can try to substitute from the outside. Third, that intelligence is more important than the actual matter of the body, since without it, that matter would be undirected, formless and chaotic (Deepak Chopra, 1990, p. 45).

The expression of the Spirit of Christ is evident in a multitude of personal and organisational forms within the Catholic school. In short, the life and impact of the Spirit can be evidenced in people, relationships, professional practices, communal living and organisational culture. Research on the culture of Catholic schooling in Australia was pioneered by Brother Marcellin Flynn FMS. Defined as "The way we do things around here" (Flynn, 1989, p. 22), Flynn argued that culture was significant to student outcomes, expressed uniquely, evident in component elements, centred on relationships, shaped by the curriculum, and impacted mission. Notwithstanding the significance of culture within these respective arenas, Flynn offered a deeper appreciation of culture by arguing that

---

104 The 'cave experience' records the 18-day entrapment of a group of 12 soccer players and their coach in a cave in Chiang Rai, Thailand. A global community of specialist rescue teams came together to relieve a traumatic and exceptionally dangerous situation that was associated with prolonged media and social interest in July 2018.

it encompassed "the Christian message as it is experienced by the school community" (Flynn, 1989, p. 23). That is, Catholic school culture at its foundational level was shaped by the Spirit of Christ and seen within the total fabric of the school (Figure 14).

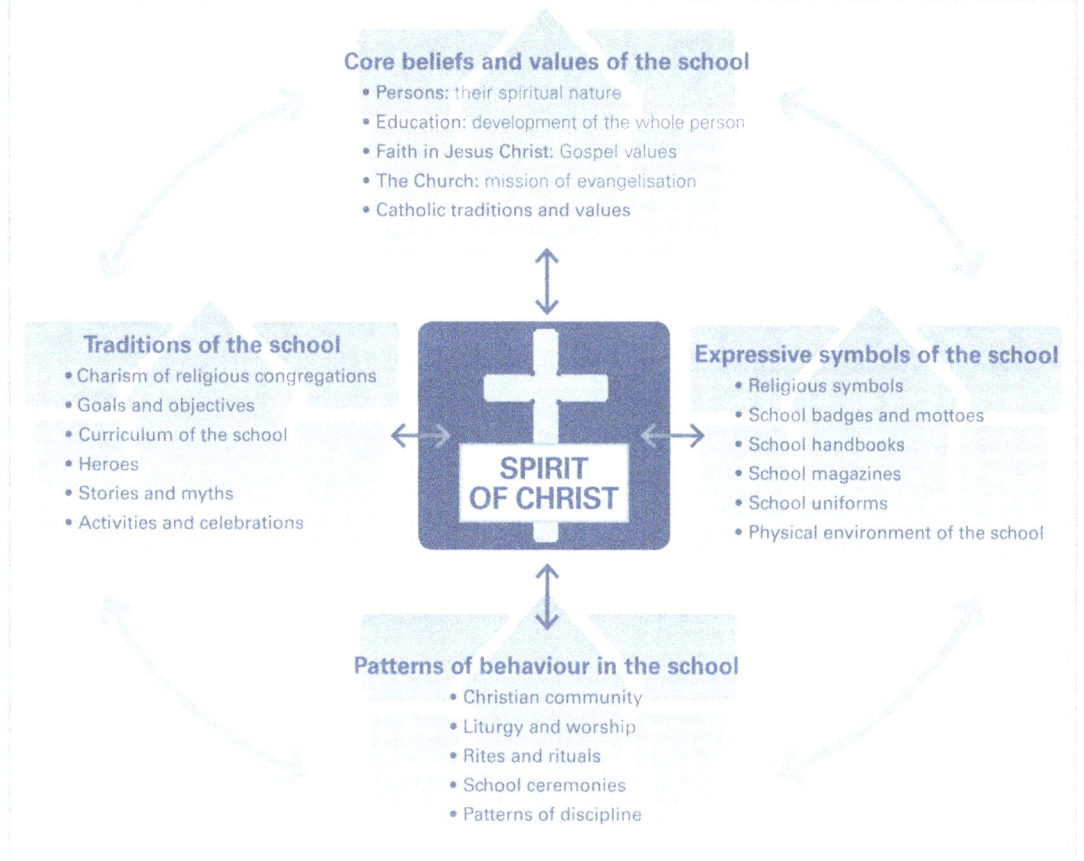

Figure 14. Expressions of the Spirit in the culture of the Catholic School[105]

Applications

Linkages between the worlds of Science and Spirit invite consideration as to their application more broadly. Lipton argues that "These realms (science and spirit) were split apart in the days of Descartes centuries ago. However, I truly believe that only when Spirit and Science are reunited, will we be afforded the means to create a better world ... This is the world of quantum physics, in which matter and energy are completely entangled" (Lipton, 2016, p. 203).

---

105 Figure is drawn from the work of Marcellin Flynn FMS, 1985.

The relevance of mind (brain and body), and spirit research is evident in new and complementary treatments that address 'disease' through increased awareness and self-initiated personal processes (Thompson, 2017). The emerging sciences of Psychoneurology and Psychoneuroimmunology (PNI),[106] for example, together with validated interventions in mindfulness; exercise; music; yoga; sound frequency; social attachment; memory releasing; meditation; and expressions of gratitude point to an expanding and enriching body of practices in support of human flourishing at personal and relational levels. At the same time, the relevance of mind and spirit connections is argued to offer "each person the ability to shift their energetic field towards more care, appreciation, gratitude, and compassion with deep connection to your heart." It is the process that science and technology can now monitor (Braden, 2018, p. 21). Evidence in support of the proposition is offered from health research on radical remissions (Turner, 2017); the success of medical mediums (William, 2017); unexpected outcomes from control and placebo studies (Hamilton, 2017); the impact of healing based on prognosis conversations (Beckwirth, 2017); bio-chemical changes to the body from meditation (Lipton, 2017); and, holistic therapy techniques (Brogan, 2017).

The study of Turner holds interest as it examines multiple interventions and synthesizes findings from a significant sample size. The research engaged 1500 people and incorporated 250 interviews. Across the full subject group, seventy-five practices were identified as significant. However, a common set of nine factors were found to be consistent with all recorded health transformations. Notably, of these nine factors, there were only two that were of a physical nature: a radically changed diet; and use of herbs and supplements. The seven other non-physical interventions included, taking interest and care of health; following intuitions; releasing suppressed emotions; increasing positive emotions; embracing social support; deepening spiritual connection; and, possessing a strong reason for living. In short, what counted in cases of all radical remissions were mental, emotional and spiritual factors.[107]

---

[106] Psychoneurology is a drug-free alternative to traditional psychiatric and psychological approaches. The principle of Psychoneurology is that each individual human being is already perfect and complete and thereby can achieve health and success by integrating new resources or learnings. Psychoneuroimmunology (PNI), also referred to as Psychoendoneuroimmunology (PENI), is the study of the interaction between psychological processes and the nervous and immune systems of the human body.

[107] Commentary by Joe Dispenza (2013) also reinforces a small number of influences that characterise spontaneous remissions. These include: belief in a higher intelligence; commitment to recovery and new management based on understanding of negative processes; changes in thinking about stressors and the creation of a new self; and linking intentional thinking with elevated emotion.

Dispositions

The implications of mind and spirit relationships encourage ministry to be pursued with elevated enthusiasm and understanding. Again, without being exhaustive, ministry within the Catholic school can draw from mind and spirit understanding and be appreciated in its holistic and dynamic nature, shaped by Spirit, and, practiced in the quantum field. Perspectives include:[108]

- ❖ The world is a graced place of energy and matter held together by an infinite intelligence;
- ❖ The Christian tradition names this intelligence as the life-giving energy of God, self-giving love which is dynamic and efficacious;[109]
- ❖ There is intelligence, a Spirit, within every person that directs the processing of information, registers feeling and influences behaviours;
- ❖ The perfect integration of the human and the Divine Spirit is found in the person of Jesus, the Christ;
- ❖ Christ is the ultimate model for ministry seen in his relationship with the 'Father,' and his vision and action in the world;
- ❖ The Catholic Christian Church celebrates, witnesses, teaches, serves and builds community in the Spirit of Christ; and,
- ❖ Ministry within the Catholic school manifests the Spirit in multiple and dynamic ways.

Living in ways that empower an awareness and a creative response by the Spirit entail the examination of old patterns; confirming those that 'work,' and the creation of new approaches that align with the reality of the new normal. In summary terms, new approaches integrate dispositions that recognise the infinite nature of the quantum field and the interactive capabilities of the person in engaging thought, emotion and behaviour. This cycle of thinking and feeling is compounded by revelations such as 95 per cent of memories are subconscious and the norm for thinking entailing 60,000 thoughts a day with 90 per cent repetition (Dyer, 2007; Tolle, 2005).

Dispositions which align with a creative response within the 'new normal;' an increasing emphasis of being over doing; engaging wave energy over a focus on 'particle;' and viewing life as a connected whole are offered for consideration. The propositions possess implications for behaviour and wellbeing in ministry and serve as a background to its practical application.

---

[108] The words of Richard Rohr when commenting on the Trinity, "it is the ultimate presumption" are similarly applicable in offering conclusions of this form.

[109] Efficacious in this context is having the power to produce a desired or intended result.

Being more connected to Spirit

Sustained creative development arises from coherence within the mind and connection with the Source. In the challenge of Norman Amundson (2003), it involves finding ways to 'still our minds' during chaos and to find new ways of staying in the 'flow and of continuing to make sense of our lives' (p. 97). It is to "create a coherent signature every day ... Create your new life and give thanks for it" (Dispenza, 2013, DVD). It is first engaging the Spirit of Christ prior to witnessing this Spirit in going out from Christ.

Being less constrained by time

Giving less attention to time is the disposition of not 'pushing' for outcomes and therefore 'letting things come.' The strategy entails minimising one's personal need for success and so becoming less fearful, frustrated, anxious and disappointed as outcomes may not accord with expectation. It is the commitment of 'letting go and letting God' in ways that are fashioned from belief, trust and experiential learning. It is allowing time and the Spirit to work in the quantum field in ways that are trusted and potentially contrary to expectation.

Being appreciative through language

This is the disposition of 'feeling compassion.' Thanks, Appreciation and Gratitude (TAG) are argued to precipitate patterns of wave energy emanating from the heart that are said to be 100 times stronger than any other organ in creating a magnetic field (Braden, 2013). This is the process of engaging, blessing and sharing Spirit that is confirmatory and life-giving. It is recognising the presence of the Spirit in the myriad of actions and happenings in the 'world around us' and commenting affirmingly about such.

Being less engulfed by 'a priori'[110] planning

The traditional view of change typically involves setting goals and moving in ways (strategies) that are sequenced and conform to a predictable pattern. The challenge within quantum thinking arises when the goals start changing and the pathways towards them become circular or dead ends? "What if we decide the goal is no longer desirable?... Does goal setting even make sense in a context of fast paced change? Goals are obviously important but are ideally assessed with an open mind as to change" (Amundson, 2003, p. 95). This is the process of leaving 'room for miracles,'[111] being 'home on the road,' and 'dancing in the rain.'[112] It is being comfortable with God as Mystery in processes that invoke the Spirit of God alive and active in all things and practices.

---

[110] Planning in advance and in support of strategy and operations.
[111] Acknowledgement is given to Louise Cosgrove, a leader in Religious Education, for introducing the concept to the writer.
[112] Concepts drawn from Keynote Address, Bert Roebben (2018).

Being collaborative

The quantum perspective to life is that all is connected and interdependent. Humans are therefore co-creators in the Spirit with others. It is a process of "laying down what you want for other things to happen" (Dispenza, 2013). It is going beyond the natural survival instinct to engaging the supernatural, that which is beyond the immediate and the physical. It is not living with a cause and effect mentality but being open to possibilities and exercising proactive and constructive engagement. The challenge is not only to give energy through creation but to restore the energy balance through mutually beneficial relationships. The dilemma is summarised as "how to share energy and at the same time ensure that there is not an overall decline in energy for the person offering help" (Amundson, 2003, p.115).

Being present and respectful

Being present to others involves the process of personal engagement which allows for experiences to be shared and appreciated at multiple levels (information, behaviour, emotion and intuition). It is built on respect and dignity of the other and entails a conviction to engage the life of the Spirit within, among and beyond those present.

Being hope filled and trusting

The quantum field is infinite and within it there are endless options and possibilities. Values of hope and trust allow for perseverance and optimism when considering potential struggle and unresolved goals. Again, Norman Amundson, (2003, p.151) argues: "With hope, no matter what problems we face today, there are new possibilities for a better tomorrow ... We need to embrace the dream of the heroic and use this momentum to push aside the darkness of despair and cynicism."

Being committed to action

Behaviours indicative of creative responses within the quantum field entail a way of being. This is a commitment to a new life, a new way of thinking, feeling and behaving. It is a process that requires reinforcement, practice and repetition, less the impact be lost. It is maintaining a commitment to processes and being prepared to continuously "cross that river of change in you and your environment" (Dispenza, 2013 DVD). The process arises from knowledge, activates feeling, strengthens behaviours and is founded on intention and action.

Ministry

An appreciation of ministry flows out of the integrated nature of mind and Spirit. Notwithstanding, the concept of ministry is a relatively new one in the Church. It was not a specific topic for the Second Vatican Council which viewed ministry primarily in terms of the ordained: Deacon, Priest and Bishop. However, what was considered in depth by the Council was the role of the laity being "testimony of Christian life, by good works, by words to both non-believers and believers and by a special emphasis on charity" (AA, para. 6).

An acclaimed text on ministry (McBrien, 1988) begins with the invitation to 'scribble some definitions' about the topic but then concludes "Definitions of ministry are indeed hard to find." The suggestion follows that the best way to consider ministry is to examine some of its myriad of functions (p. 7). In categorical terms these are said to include formation, proclamation, service and celebration, each of which correlate with the universal goals of Church: Teaching the Word, serving the world, engaging in communion and celebrating the story. The reinforcement within the Decree on the work of the laity is clear.

Whenever there are people in need of food and drink, clothing, housing, medicine, employment, education; whenever people lack the facilities necessary for living a truly human life or are tormented by hardships of poor health, or suffer exile or imprisonment, there Christian charity should seek them out and find them, console them with eager care and relieve them with the gift of help. This obligation is imposed above all upon every prosperous person and nation (AA, para. 4).

The place and significance of ministry is that it is typically expressed within the overall pastoral practices of the Church as a response to the gifts of the Holy Spirit. It normally involves preparation through discernment, presumes formation and competence, possesses community recognition and support, and is given prominence through a process of public commissioning. The essence of ministry is captured holistically and practically as being called: by God, through Christ, in the Spirit, with others, and for others (Hahnenberg, 2014).

Ministry has a dual role within community through 'building up the life of the Church' and responding to the agenda of the world (Fox, 2011). The responsibility carries with it the goal of modelling a particular vision and set of values along with offering direct contributions to community development. Irrespective of the focus, the nature of ministry is said to be rooted in personal vocation, informed by charisms; is aligned to the vision of Jesus; and is integrated with the work of the Church. Authority for ministry arises from the Church and professional responsibility and accountability is to those served, the profession and the Church.

Professional vocation

The concept of ministry is an all embracing one which interfaces with notions about teaching, and vocation to teach. Teaching is the professional response which carries the expectations of the profession, school and community. Within this framework, vocation is the call to teach in accordance with the expectations of the institution within which it is carried out. The concept of Christian ministry further adds to this relationship by aligning vocation with sharing in the ministry of Christ within a Christian faith community.

The essence of ministry within the Catholic school is pastoral action within the mission and life of the Church. It involves and strengthens the building of communion within the school and the wider community. It is open to all and applies quality professional practices which engage the Spirit of Christ.[113] By definition, every staff member in a Catholic school is called to ministry and is in the broadest sense, a religious educator. Each and all staff contribute differentially, personally and communally, through witness, engagement and action in the religious education programme, the religious dimension to the curriculum, the religious life of the school, and the religious culture evidenced in structures, processes and systems.

The particular role of the religious education teacher includes engagement with the transcendent (Groome, 1998), support for students to better understand religion and to be religious (Moran, 1991), and, being responsive to the overall identity and mission of the Catholic school (Gleeson, Goldburg, O'Gorman and O'Neill, 2018). It is a role that Hindmarsh (2017) describes as "the heartbeat of the whole curriculum … inviting an encounter with mission that involves humility and openness of mind and heart; engaging a sense of mystery and sacredness in life; a passion like Jesus to heal the wounds of the world; respect and love for every person made in God's image; cherishing the natural order and web of life; and expressing gratitude for the gifts of God."

The ministry of the religious education teacher is to incorporate the essence of the tradition together with the process of doing applied theology. The approach is described by Gellel (2018) as Divine Pedagogy. It is the practice of religious education in a context of God walking with and being present to the teacher and students through relationships. It is premised on the dignity of all and the search for truth and the expression of love. The skills entail critical

---

[113] Archbishop Mark Coleridge when sharing perspectives on leadership and governance with leaders of Catholic schools within the Archdiocese of Brisbane described the challenge as being 'no longer business as usual'. It is a time to take stock and ensure the Spirit of truth and love are paramount in educative and organisational processes.

thinking, being familiar with ecumenical and inter-faith dialogue and a capacity to utilise teaching competencies in the arenas of spirituality and religious education. It is the practice of being in the world with intentionality, knowing the destination and being prepared to dialogue on the journey. It is a process of blending holiness with practical action and thereby applying theology within religious education practices mindful of the realities of the world.

The pedagogy of Religious Education calls for confidence and hope as the dialogue about religion and faith development challenge and confront established beliefs and values. The process is described as being 'home on the road' and being able to 'dance in the rain' (Roebben, 2018) as perspectives are exchanged, dissected and refined. The task invites teachers into practices of self-edification to first grasp their own and particular identity; transcending self in order to be open to others; and re-dedication to a paradigm which dares to receive and consider the possibility of God. This process is summarised by Roebben as 'theology in motion' where the Church as institution shares its traditions, and educators become responsive to the movements of the Spirit. In this way teachers do theology through demonstrating loyalty to the old and being open to the new.

The fundamental law of all catechetical method is that of fidelity to the Word of God and fidelity to the concrete needs of the faithful. This is the ultimate criterion by which catechists must appraise their work as educators. This is the fundamental inspiration of every proposal for renewal ... fidelity to God and fidelity to people. Here we are not dealing with two different concerns but with one spiritual attitude which leads the Church to seek out the most suitable ways of exercising its mediation between God and people. It is the attitude of the charity of Christ, the Word of God made flesh (Australian Episcopal Conference, 1970, para. 160).

Five-star aspirations

Modern marketing has created a sense of what might be expected within a 'five-star' facility or experience. Essentially, the assignment of five stars suggests the availability of the 'full package.' Similarly, establishing a 'five-star' benchmark for integrating a range of expectations and characteristics for Catholic school educators is worth considering.

It has been stated that we avoid elephants in the room. Yet, these elephants when opened can offer the seeds of individual and collective change. They are the kernels of

the underlying truth. They are most often avoided at all cost; yet in the exploration of these emotional realities we are invited into the truth of the resurrection, new life and the ongoing revelation of God's call. The more the elephants remain buried or negated, the more we continue to live in Good Friday or the grief of Holy Saturday blocking the new life of resurrection (Mark Clarke, 2016, p. 5).

Figure 15 identifies characteristics of a 'five-star' framework for teaching as ministry. While each aspect of the professional situation possesses uniqueness, the goal of an integrated, holistic and professional approach becomes the basis on which the 'faith-life-culture' relationship might be observed and supported. Within a Catholic school profile where Catholic faith is no longer universal, the elephant in the room is the question about how differing faith perspectives can engage mission, be supportive of one another, and provide a unified and consistent set of beliefs and values within an equally diverse culture. The challenge is real, potentially confronting, but one that needs to be addressed in light of every educator and every educational community desiring to offer a five-star professional service.

I would like to limit myself to recalling the features of an educator and his or her specific duty. To educate is an act of love, it is to give life. And love is demanding, it calls for the best resources, for a reawakening of the passion to begin this path patiently with young people. The educator in Catholic schools must be, first and foremost, competent and qualified but, at the same time, someone who is rich in humanity and capable of being with young people in a style of pedagogy that helps promote their human and spiritual growth. Youth are in need of quality teaching along with values that are not only articulated but witnessed to. Consistency is an indispensable factor in the education of young people! Consistency! We cannot grow and we cannot educate without consistency: consistency and witness! (Pope Francis, 2014).

Without being specific, the general descriptors that are identified in Figure 15 attempt to establish the overall ideal ministerial profile of an educator in a Catholic school. In the example offered, the teacher is called to be a competent and registered professional (Professional Competency); suitably engaged within a productive learning situation (Situational Stability); aware and committed to the mission of the school (Faith Connection); being a witness to this purpose (Personal Witness); and possessing a practical connection to a faith Tradition (Mission Commitment).

Figure 15. Five-star characteristics of a Catholic school educator

Spirit encounters

The power and expression of witness can be subtle and at times unpredictable. This was reinforced at a school commencement ceremony when a student impacted in ways other than expected. Since the ceremony was conducted by students, it was not surprising when one rose to do the opening scripture reading. The community in this instance, however, was particularly sensitive to the situation as the reader possessed a noticeable handicap. It was his courage and strength of composure that absorbed substantial interest. Witness was one of ability, acceptance and determination in the face of a challenging physical condition. In the aftermath of the ceremony those present stated that they had no idea of what was read, but certainly developed a clear appreciation of the characteristics of Spirit evident in the person doing the reading.

Action in the Spirit of love is identified in *Evangelii Gaudium* (EG, paras. 261-283) as a missionary impulse; a response entailing at least four core characteristics (Table 15). It is living the Gospel in practical form, being responsive to the Spirit and seeking alignment with the person and message of Christ.

Table 15. Ministry impulses from the *Joy of the Gospel*

Personal encounter with the saving power of Jesus	'Jesus' whole life, his way of dealing with the poor, his actions, his integrity, his simple daily acts of generosity, and finally his complete self-giving, is precious and reveals the mystery of the Divine life' (EG, para. 265).
The spiritual savour of being a people	'The word of God also invites us to be a people… God's people (1 Peter 2:10). Mission is at once a passion for Jesus and a passion for his people. 'All around us we begin to see nurses with soul, teachers with soul, politicians with soul, people who have chosen deep down to be with others and for others' (EG, para. 268).
The mysterious working of the risen Christ and his Spirit	'We need to recall that Jesus Christ has triumphed over sin and death and is now almighty. Jesus Christ truly lives…. we are invited to discover this, to experience this. Christ risen and glorified, is the wellspring of our hope, and he will not deprive us of the help we need to carry out the mission which he has entrusted to us' (EG, para. 275).
The missionary power of intercessory prayer	'One form of prayer moves us particularly to take up the task of evangelisation and to seek the good of others: it is the prayer of intercession (EG, paras. 281 and 283) … 'Intercession is like a 'leaven in the heart of the Trinity.' It is a way of penetrating the Father's heart and discovering new dimensions which can shed light on concrete situations and change them.'

The Spirit incorporates the dynamic and energising power of God operative in and through all processes and living things. The wonder and mystery of God revealed through the action of the Spirit is found in 'four great moments:' creation; grace; the incarnation; and the life of the Church (Edwards, 2011). It is the Spirit that brings grace, God's love, to all human activity and leads to liberation, transformation and salvation. In this way, Word and Spirit, Christ and the action of the Spirit make explicit the imagination of Christ in the life of the Catholic school. The Holy Spirit is, therefore, the 'guarantee of our inheritance' (Ephesians 1:3).

Love, when freed from egoism, is the way to fraternity and the reciprocal help towards perfection among people. Love is an irrepressible desire, inscribed into the nature of every man and woman on earth… Love is the individual's true nobility – above and beyond his or her belonging to any culture, ethnic group, social stratum or position.

> *It is the strongest, most authentic and most desired bond, which unites people among each other and makes them able to listen to each other, to pay attention to each other and to give each other's lives the esteem they deserve* (Congregation for Catholic Education, 2013, para. 41).

The Spirit is at the core of ministry. No one can predict how an individual or group will be moved to an appreciation of the transcendent and thereby grow in appreciation of God and one another. The particular impact of Scripture, liturgy, discussion, lectures, written material or the experience of another's help can never be foreseen, nor can it be fully understood in terms of what aspect of the encounter was most significant. Because of the difficulty of interpretation of any event or action, there will always be a degree of ambiguity. In this sense, actions, words, situations, events - happenings of every kind - can all have an effect of unknown proportion. What becomes important is the realisation that all experiences and words can speak, can evangelise, and it is in everything one does that the Spirit of Christ can be manifested.

Legends in the Spirit

The closing words of *Les Miserables* reveal the ability people have to manifest the saving power of Christ and the continuing presence of the Holy Spirit. "To love another person is to see the face of God," signals the importance of action that is real and healing. This is living the Gospel in practical and concrete ways and is evident in instances of care, promotion of justice and the search for truth. It is based on the inherent dignity of all and one's response through awareness and action, especially towards the most needy.

> *With hope, no matter what problems we face today, there are new possibilities for a better tomorrow... we need to embrace the dream of the heroic and use this momentum to push aside the darkness of despair and cynicism... the best opportunities come with the determination to live a balanced life* (Norman Amundson, 2003, p. 151).

Models in ministry are typically those colleagues, friends and known personalities to whom reflections default to when consideration is given to the 'how' and 'what' a response might entail, usually in relation to delicate or significant situations. They are the people who offer guidance through character and witness and so live the life of the Spirit as a life of faith. While examples are unique within the context of every ministry, the following are illustrative of a life-giving Spirit, often not recognised by the central character, but demonstratively observed by others.

The Monsignor's aura

Having joined James at a long term residential in-service (four weeks) we both learned quite early in the program that we, as married lay leaders, were very much in the minority as most participants were priests. Each day, the Eucharist would be celebrated and on each occasion, a different pastor was invited to lead the liturgy. After about three weeks, the invitation to 'Monsignor James' came and understandably had to be rejected. For some reason the majority of the group assumed James was a cleric, and even more so, a cleric with particular ecclesiastical status. While humorous at the time, my own reflection was about how the mistake would have been made and what characteristics precipitated the perception. Clearly, the spiritual orientation, the familiarity with Church, the adoption of traditions and the personal investment in relationships were a good start.

Adam's summary

I was first introduced to an Executive Summary for Catholic schools when a national administrator conveyed to Catholic school leaders that a particular government funded program was to be 'wound down' in resource terms. The 'speech' went something like "The government has decided to discontinue funding to a particular group of handicapped children and therefore asks school systems to take responsibility if the programme were to continue." Apart from being disappointed with the news, the chair of the forum offered the following response. "We are schools that are Christ centred and whatever the government funds or does not fund, will not move our focus from this very needy group within our communities." The two words 'Christ centred' for the mission of the school, together with a demonstrable stance for those in most need, summed up all that needed to be said about the focus of mission.

Bishop's plea

As a Catholic Education Office responsible for a group of schools, the necessary employment of area supervisors became a priority; particularly in terms of ensuring appropriate services were applied for support and accountability. For the staff engaged, the need to 'supervise' became quite paramount and yet the Bishop of the diocese was adamant that this form of supervision would take a particular form. In the Bishop's plea it was to be focused on professional and personal development; relationship over authority; and, presence over remoteness. The Spirit of leadership he desired was "Supervisors will not be successful if they first cannot relate. It is not about applying authority; it is more about building relationship and understanding, acting in ways that involve being present to people in ways that are mutually transforming."

The priest who saw goodness

Father Ben served the ministry of Catholic education for decades. Remembered because of immense personal skills and a litany of initiatives, this leader was known to the writer as someone who had fully integrated the characteristics of mission, spirituality and leadership. His uncompromising humility and ever-present affirmations of others typically ended in the same comment "That's good." The two words reflected a contemplative recognition that Catholic schools, in their small and not so small endeavours, entailed something quite sacred and deserved an affirmation that could otherwise be described as "that's God." His was a ministry that was able to step back, see the whole and be the silent witness to the sacred, which for him, was everywhere.

Everyday legend

The dramas and challenges of life in the Catholic school provide an extraordinary tapestry for being present with, to and for others. While not projecting any form of self-promotion, the following communication mirrored multiple engagements in just one day and echoed a similarity of engagement by other 'unknown legends' that staff Catholic schools and engage the Spirit in their not so ordinary ministry efforts. The communication went as follows. "Greetings Bill. It's Friday arvo, just got home - what a day. One of the students in Year 12 said he was going to be a dad. We chatted for a while but I had to run; will catch up with him on Monday. If that was not enough, my library supervision turned into a child protection concern. One of the lads mentioned that John was kicked out of home and is looking to friends for a place to drop. OMG, another for the counsellor! He is so alone and not the only one. We continue to try and reach these kids but how do we stop and be where they are at. My Science lesson followed - did it on automatic pilot, talk soon; in haste to pick up the children."

Fred - an expression of goodness in the world

Fred was not a Catholic by baptism nor a regular Church attender in any sense. He was, however, a faithful husband, a generous dad, a tireless worker who had a disposition to serve. Shy and retiring in social gatherings, he was engaged in multiple projects and requests made of him from the most unusual quarters. Single handed, he constructed (on weekends alone) a regional scouting headquarters; undertook aspects of construction in a fledgling Catholic school; provided extensions to convent quarters for local religious; and, throughout life was a generous contributor to small and seemingly unimportant 'handyman' tasks of all kinds. In this context, Fred was around, usually very quiet, mostly unnoticed and rarely acknowledged. Interestingly, 'jobs completed' rarely ended in invoices and never in ceremony. In short, Fred was a 'good person' doing 'good things' that enabled 'good to be done.' The community is rich with the presence of 'many Freds', doing good works, though not always recognised formally, and for the most part going unnoticed.

Legends in the Spirit are everywhere. They would be the first to decline recognition, but the first to engage the Spirit and mission of Christ. Their hallmark is service, their relationship is love, their intention is betterment, and their character one of holiness.

> *We are all called to be holy by living our lives with love and by bearing witness in everything we do, wherever we find ourselves. Are you called to the consecrated life? Be holy by living out your commitment with joy. Are you married? Be holy by loving and caring for your husband or wife, as Christ does for the Church. Do you work for a living? Be holy by labouring with integrity and skill in the service of your brothers and sisters. Are you a parent or grandparent? Be holy by patiently teaching the little ones how to follow Jesus. Are you in a position of authority? Be holy by working for the common good and renouncing personal gain* (GEE, para. 14).

Fruits of the Spirit

The practice of ministry is the enactment of the kingdom vision of Christ, and its measure of authenticity, the fruits of the Spirit which inspire and characterise this impulse.[114] *Evangelisation in the Modern World* (EN, para. 75) presents "the fruits made possible by the movement of the Spirit" are evident in being inspired by the Spirit, authentic witness, nurturing unity, seeking the truth and being animated by love.

Inspired by the Spirit

Just as Jesus was 'led by the Spirit' into the wilderness, so as to prepare himself for his mission; and it was 'through the power of the Spirit' (Luke 4:1) that he went into Galilee to begin his preaching (Luke 4:14). It was after the Holy Spirit came at Pentecost that the Apostles were able to go forth; and it was only after Peter was filled with the Holy Spirit that he could speak about Jesus as the Son of God (Acts 4:8). It was through the action of the Spirit that Paul (Acts 9:17) dedicated himself to the ministry of preaching Christ, and it is through the 'consolation of the Holy Spirit' (Acts 9:31) that the Church is able to increase.

---

[114] The concept of mission and ministry as an impulse in living the Gospel is outlined by Pope Francis in *Evangelii Gaudium*.

The first fruits of ministry involve engaging and drawing from the presence of the Spirit who invites, encourages and consoles. The gift of the Spirit is always present and yet its relevance is dictated by awareness and openness. This is seen in the extent to which connection is valued, openness exists, and the preparedness to wait upon outcomes without rushing to solution.

Authentic witness

Living authentically involves the correlation of action with words, activity with belief, lifestyle with holiness. The relationship between leaders and students is recorded by Pope Paul VI as one which gives primacy to witness: "The world is calling for evangelisers to speak to it of a God whom the evangelists should know and be familiar with as if they could see the invisible. The world calls and expects from us simplicity of life, the spirit of prayer, charity towards all, especially towards the lowly and the poor, obedience and humility, detachment and self-sacrifice" (EN, para. 76). The fruits of ministry are evident in witness and the stability, effectiveness and consistency that this witness offers.

Unity

Unity within the Catholic school is evidenced primarily in the unity of witness and life that accepts and acknowledges Jesus as the Lord who unites in the Spirit. The advantages of operating together, as one communion, are well known. Collaboration, however, within a spiritual context offers much more than mere association. The concept of communion seeks to reflect the Trinitarian life of God that is fundamentally relational. When we operate together within the Spirit, we are committing ourselves to what the Spirit offers and to the very existence of God. The fruits of the Spirit not only bind people together, they also direct their intentions on the basis of love and truth.

Servant of the truth

The Good News of Jesus is also news about the truth: truth about God, about humanity and about the world. Those engaged in ministry are therefore called to be people of truth, people who live and seek the truth. This is truth not only in the spiritual domain but in all its scientific and other forms. The fruits of the Spirit within a Catholic school context allow for a continuing search for God based on rationality. The gifts of intellect provide the means of searching that are innately present and powerfully motivating. Reason informs faith and so allows for deeper immersion in the Mystery of God.

Animated by love

Ministry is premised on love defined by the love of God who is self-giving (*agape*).[115] It is a love that knows no boundaries and has no favourites. It is based on the growth and needs of others and is observed in the love of a parent, the love of truth and the devotion to the proclamation of Jesus. Practical signs of love are seen in the respect shown to others as they are exposed to the Gospel, a determination to be clear about what is shared as the non-coercive nature of ministry takes shape. "This form of evangelisation not only is an expression of love for the evangelised but a source of joy and hope that is manifested in a life of optimism, courage, patience and fervour" (EN, para. 1).

Prayer and meditation

Prayer

An orientation to prayerful encounter, privately and liturgically, stems from a covenantal relationship with God in mission.[116] This sacred connection is an integrating principle which connects the practices of sacramental consciousness with formal experiences of Church life. In the language of Daniel O'Leary (2008), sacramental consciousness involves "being comfortable with the Mystery… seeing with the soul… putting on the eyes of Christ… looking into the heart of things… keeping the channel open… recognising the presence, power and grace of God in all." Complementary with this awareness is formal liturgy which breaks open the 'Word' through encountering Christ in Sacrament, Scripture, Proclamation and Service. It is in the multiple forms of prayer that connection with the Creator is enacted and where the Wisdom of the Spirit is awakened as the basis for pastoral action.

Much of the discretion, common sense, wisdom and intuition that are a necessary part of living can never be detailed. Life cannot be ordered, nor can the response to the multitude of situations ever be scheduled according to some predestined script. In this same way, responsibilities of people in Catholic schools cannot cover all the contingencies that arise. There are the unusual, the unpredictable, the non-rational, the unbelievable, and the ordinary circumstances of life that need to be addressed through living based on attention to the power and love of the Holy Spirit. It is this breadth of living that allows the 'God of Surprises' to be encountered and the wisdom of the Holy Spirit to be uncovered in ways that leave love, freedom and truth the beneficiaries.

---

115 *Agape* is selfless, sacrificial, unconditional love, the highest of the four types of love in the Bible. *Agape* perfectly describes the kind of love Jesus Christ has for his Father and for his followers.
116 Ronald Rolheiser in *Sacred Fire* provides an important distinction and advocates for each and the integration of both.

Connectivity with the Spirit of Christ provides the basis of spirituality in support of Catholic school identity. This form of engagement involves experiencing God before God is shared: The purpose of being with Jesus is to go forth from Jesus (Bishop Michael Putney, 2010, CD).

Meditation

Meditation in its broadest definition within the Tibetan culture is 'becoming familiar' (Dispenza, 2014). The process is potentially broad in its manifestations (mindfulness; visualisation; healing; questioning self; manifesting; body awareness; transcendent mantra) (Chopra, 2017) but is known for some common principles. While not exclusive these entail establishing a quiet place; creation of a meditative position; concentration on the breath; elimination of external stimuli; being present and becoming conscious of what consumes the mind; and accessing solitude (Lhundrup T - Rinpoche, 2006).

One of the main purposes of meditation is to move beyond the analytical mind. What separates the conscious mind from the subconscious mind is the analytical mind. As you slow your brain waves down, you move out of your conscious mind and thinking brain, past the analytical mind, into the operating system of the subconscious mind where all those automatic programmes and unconscious habits exist (Joe Dispenza, 2017a, p. 92).[117]

Meditation changes the functioning of the brain as the body becomes settled, less aroused and attends to the conscious and subconscious in more awakened ways. The process is said to 'flip the switch' (Benson, 2014) with effectiveness being enhanced through frequency of occurrence. While considered to be as essential as 'the air we breathe' (Harvey, 2014); it is a simple process that enables the reconditioning of the body to achieve a level of harmony and balance that is restorative. In the process, and in keeping with the lessons of neuroscience, meditation promotes an unwiring to new wiring of mind body and Spirit connections; moving from an unaware to an aware state; enabling planning and mental rehearsals to what might be; diminishing of necessary and limiting habits; replacing the energies of the past to invest in energies of the future; establishing new habits; and, replacing old genes with new genes (Dispenza, 2017).

---

[117] The conscious and analytical mind constitute 95 per cent of personal programmes and habits.

One characteristic indicative of lessons from neuroscience is the concept of becoming aware of the body and its parts in space and then establishing an appreciation of the space around this space (Dispenza, 2015). The argument is made that in the normal scheme of day-to-day events, the brain deals with significant breadth and analysis that potentially offer divisiveness to being and that the meditative state allows for the retrieval of a sense of coherence and relationship.

I should also add here that it is a real discipline to learn to be 'still.' If you have been going at breakneck speed and living within a somewhat chaotic situation, it takes a while for the mind to slow down. Think about past vacations that you have taken. Often it takes a day or two before you really start acting like you are on vacation. The same applies to 'stilling' our minds. We need to allow sufficient time for the noise to disappear. It is only within the stillness that conditions will be right for growing new ideas (Norman Amundson, 2003, p. 105).

The significance of meditation is summed up in the comment "If you don't have your mind in some sort of balance it doesn't matter how healthy you are" (Craig Duncan, 2014, DVD). Processes which support the mind, body, Spirit connections are many. "Just as there are scores of techniques that evoke the stress response, fight or flight, so there are scores of techniques that make the relaxation response" (Herbert Benson, 2014, DVD). Deepak Chopra (2017) comments that what becomes important in processes of selection is the practicality of techniques and their application in ways that support coherent signals among the brain, emotions and experiences. Notwithstanding the means, what is important is the goal of achieving a 'stress free state of being' or homeostasis. Otherwise known as 'a meditative state,' 'being at peace,' being awake,' 'relaxation response,' meditation shuts down stress by 'controlling the parasympathetic nervous system[118] and allowing for the conscious and the subconscious to be purified.' The chemistry of the experience is found in the body's release of cortisol[119] and other chemicals such as Immunoglobulin A,[120] (Dispenza, 2017 DVD), which enable 'mind corrections, breathing adjustments, and unshakeable peace' (Williamson, 2017, DVD).

---

[118] The parasympathetic nervous system (PNS) controls homeostasis and the body at rest and is responsible for the body's 'rest and digest' function. The sympathetic nervous system (SNS) controls the body's responses to a perceived threat and is responsible for the 'fight or flight' response. The PNS and SNS are part of the ANS, or autonomic nervous system.

[119] Cortisol is a steroidal hormone responsible for blood glucose regulation, immune functions, and anti-stress responses. It is also an anti-inflammatory and helps regulate blood pressure.

[120] The principal immunoglobulin in exocrine secretions such as milk, respiratory and intestinal mucin, saliva, and tears. It prevents pathogenic bacteria and viruses from invading the body through the mucosa of the gastrointestinal, pulmonary, and genitourinary tracts.

> *Create a new personal reality and a new person. Thoughts are the language of the brain, feelings the language of the heart. New emotions means new identity and this conditions the body to reflect ... be in command of a mind and body to make a new destiny ... believe in a future you can't experience just yet but you have thought about it enough for it to be real ... fire and wire in new patterns and behaviours ... the mental rehearsal installs new circuits ... give thanks to the new experience and so create the effect ... this is the quantum model the infinite possibilities within and beyond* (Joe Dispenza, 2017, DVD).

Living consciously

The invitation into a relationship with the universal Spirit of life involves the challenge to become aware of the continuing and unending nature of this sacred presence. In the context of this text it is the invitation to encounter; to attribute meaning and nurture transformation in the Spirit. It is the call to wholeness, one's personal growth and vocation, within the mission, life and culture of the Catholic school. It is an invitation that is inclusive and non-coercive, creative and not accusatory; one that responds with thankfulness and applies within the ordinary and the extraordinary. It is said to be characterised as the ultimate journey home and the acceptance of the final conclusion that all is connected (Myss, 2001 & 2017). It is "Where heaven is our father, earth our mother, all people our brothers and sisters and all things our companions" (Tu Weiming, 2015, DVD).

> *To me, God represents "All that is," the whole environment comprising the Universe. The cell engages in behaviour when its brain, the membrane, responds to environmental signals. In fact, every functional protein in our body is made as a complementary image of an environmental signal. If a protein did not have a complementary signal to couple with, it would not function. This means ...that every protein in our bodies is a physical/electromagnetic complement to something in the environment. Because we are machines made out of protein, by definition we are made in the image of the environment, that environment being the Universe, or to many, God* (Bruce Lipton, 2016, p. 207).

The acts of becoming awake, making conscious choices, 'tuning in' (Dyer & Hicks, 2014), are at the heart of living in the Spirit. A proactive spiritual approach to encounters in the everyday is offered by Ronald Rolheiser (2008, 2017) as a process of engaging 'blessing' over 'cursing.' In this view, it is a consciousness which engages a higher level of connection whereby affirmation takes precedence over actions indicative of a negative and disconnected disposition. In contrast, a cursed consciousness involves shutting down one's creative energy and connection with the source of life.

The significance of 'blessing' over 'cursing' is defined by Rolheiser (2008)[121] as 'a visible, perceptible, reflective proximity to God.' It is a process of seeing the sacred in all, releasing confidence, building relationships, confirming directions and reinforcing gifts of the Spirit. It incorporates behaviours that reveal at least three elements: to look for and notice people and their actions; speak well of those people and situations; and, offer commentary that gives 'life.' It is the process of recognising the sacred in life as a reflection of the source of all life and in the process to mirror freedom, joy and love (Dyer & Hicks, 2014). Manifestations of a blessed consciousness are shared by Rolheiser (2017) through a set of dispositions that make practical the sacred in life and provide a platform for relationship and blessing (Table 16).

Table 16. Dispositions of a Spirit centred consciousness

Surrender and Trust	Surrender and trust in the relationship with the Creator are clear and unequivocal about what faith promises and demands
Beyond Evidence	Trust beyond evidence and so live in hope that the resurrection means that God delivers on a promise and that our task as Christians is to celebrate and live in this conviction
Second Naiveté	Move towards a second naiveté and return to a second childlike trust in God
Contemplation	Engage in contemplative practice so as to ground oneself in something beyond the complexity and busyness of life
Do What Is Right	Never grow weary of doing what is right and so engage in proactive forgiveness as a source of healing and renewal
Sweat Blood	Be prepared to 'sweat blood' and accept the 'crosses' in love and look to their meaning for learning and development
Live With Difference	Acknowledge moods and individuality and seek to go beyond them
God's Healing	Know that nothing is impossible for God as grace and community will heal
Be Inspired	Lean on inspiration, diminish cynicism and use good stories to engage memory and energy
Bless Others	Proactively bless others through overt and appreciative acts of affirmation and support

---

[121] The significance is drawn from a definition of blessing offered by the German theologian, Dietrich Bonhoeffer.

"Why was it so?"

The practice of ministry occasionally invokes the reflection "I think I did that quite well." Alternatively, a comment from a more objective observer might be "That was really valuable." The experience with this kind of feedback is typically one of quiet satisfaction but it often begs the question as to why it 'felt so right' and 'why do others acknowledge the efforts so appreciatively?' The reflection is only further compounded when some deeper analysis of the 'why' leads to the conclusion that the leadership process did not necessarily follow a particular operational model or engage a predictable pattern in its delivery. It was performed more naturally and yet was perceived so favourably.

Conversations with those who have experienced positive responses to their behaviours invariably lead to consideration of relationship and process factors as being important. As one teacher put it "I just work for their welfare and they know I care;" while another noted "This is not about me; we are there for them and with them." These are the ministry practices which embody the 'fruits of the Spirit.' That is, exchanges based on love, truth, authenticity and unity. They are the powerful forces that herald productive outcomes; not necessarily conscious, but integrated. They are the deeper and pervasive gifts that reflect the Spirit in ministry; deep relational engagements that make all the difference. They are the natural outcomes of an integrated faith where teaching moments draw upon the 'natural me' awakened to the Spirit.

Let us be spurred on by the signs of holiness that the Lord shows us through the humblest members of that people which shares also in Christ's prophetic office, spreading abroad a living witness to him, especially by means of a life of faith and charity (GEE, para. 8).

Ministry: Perspective and capabilities

Renewing perspective

Perspective is key to quality ministry; something that is not to be left unattended when the 'busyness and commitment to ministry life' presents as enough. Wicks (2009) points out that renewal of perspective not only integrates capabilities; but attends to the primary role of one's meaning system as the basis for choice and motivation. Perspective is said to be advanced through behaviours of meditation – nurturing an awareness of self and the creative Spirit within; awakening – being context conscious and 'glancing again' at what might lie hidden; presence – being fully present to the circumstances of the moment and not 'somewhere else' in mind or desire; blessing – engaging experiences as situations of blessing and opportunities to bless; and choice – activating conscious choices for engagement or disengagement based on one's personal meaning system.

A reflective, challenging and insightful contribution on the Church 'rebirthing' itself is offered by the Bishop of Parramatta, Vincent Long Van Nguyen OFM Conv. Delivering the keynote address at the Ann D Clark Memorial Lecture (September 2017), Bishop Long Van Nguyen advanced that with challenge there also comes opportunity, for the gift of the Spirit is always with the Church.[122] Against a backdrop of a reputational crisis through the Royal Commission into Institutional Child Abuse, the pervasive and divisive debate on marriage laws, the decline in religious practice, and the minimal vocations to the priesthood, Bishop Long Van Nguyen underlined the renewal in Church particularly in keeping with the vision of Pope Francis.

Less a role of power, dominance and privilege but more a position of vulnerability and powerlessness; Less an enclosure for the virtuous but more an oasis for the weary and downtrodden; Less an experience of exclusion and elitism but more an encounter of radical love, inclusiveness and solidarity; Less of an attitude of "we are right and you are wrong" and more of an attitude of openness to truth wherever and whoever it is to be found; Less a leadership of control and clericalism but more a 'diakonia' of a humble servant exemplified by Christ at the Last Supper; Less a language of condemnation but more a language of affirmation and compassion; and Less a preoccupation for its own maintenance but more a concern for the kingdom of God (Bishop Long Van Nguyen).

Personal wholeness

Integral to a perspective on teaching as ministry is the maturation of both the staff member and the students. The commentary on the overall outreach of the religious educator by O'Shea (2017) is a helpful reminder that in its essence, the process of education is about wholeness, one that applies equally to the educator and those educated. "It is only when our students have become completely human, only when their religious experience has been fully nourished – in the body, heart and mind, can we expect to see a living faith in living human beings" (p. 205).

---

122 Delivering the Ann D. Clark Lecture, Bishop Long Van Nguyen of Parramatta Diocese in western Sydney observed that the Australian Church is living a 'watershed' moment in the wake of a series of recent crises.

The journey in ministry has more to do with 'being' than 'doing' and this being is in 'relationship' with God, self, others and the world. This is a journey with God that entails abandonment to the will of the Father, letting go of things that distract from a life of love and truth. The personal reflection of Richard Rohr in this light speaks persuasively. Commenting on his own ministry over decades he speaks of the progressive awareness of 'who was doing the work.' It started with a passion as a young priest as 'working for Christ,' moved to 'being in partnership with Christ,' to a stage of becoming aware of 'the Spirit of Christ working in and through him.' Ministry in this sense is not about the self, but the Spirit of God working through self and others.

Exemplars

Personal and observational examples of people exercising the integration and renewal of perspective exist in real and in fictional ways; both of which inspire and offer guidance as to the 'how of the practice.' As a confessed television tragic and someone who has delighted in the Hollywood series of M.A.S.H.; the fictional character of Major Sidney Freedman is one such example. As a psychiatrist his interactions hold special significance as he 'goes beyond the obvious and the physical' to explore deeper realities for people and for himself. He is portrayed as someone who is mature to a point, a fellow traveller with experience, and yet one with human needs who values integration. His character and name: Major Sidney Freedman, suggests something special and different. The viewer might ask "Why Major and why Freedman?" Is it too much to suggest that within this character there are insights from someone who is accomplished (major) and 'free' to engage and integrate life as a whole, to possess perspective.

In one particular M.A.S.H. episode the Major is experiencing challenges of full client loads, loneliness and challenges in the role. He reaches out to a known community and ventures to the 4077th to regain perspective. What is of interest is the process he uses to 'get himself back on track,' to renew and connect again as a whole person. His disposition is one of self-reflection; observing the 'craziness' of his friends; being present to the frivolities of practical jokes, looking again at what motivates his colleagues; and interpreting his own motivations. At the same time the group values him and seeks his commentary on their particular circumstances (his blessing) and, in turn, provide an atmosphere of respect and dignity, they too bless. After a period of renewal and recovery Sidney moves on and in the process signals a clarity of intention that underpins his choice to serve. What presented as important in his gathering of perspective was his own courage and initiative to 'look more closely,' engage trusting relationships, and draw from everyday life and experience as a source of wisdom.

Multiple ministry situations reflect 'Sidney Freedman' characters, those who present as 'majorly freed' and/or are in need of intervention as stress levels are high and processes of integration are not what they should be. Robert Wicks speaks of such people as functioning at a sub-clinical level, or, in his conversational terms, those in need of intervention without the formal processes of diagnosis and treatment. In these instances, he advocates 'renewing perspective,' interventions of the kind that Sidney Freedman experienced. These are encounters that entail a standing back, observing and attempting to understand the deeper motivations and realities that contribute to one's role within a supportive community.

Researching capabilities

The call to serve in the many and varied roles within the Catholic school is demanding and requires support and continuing formation. A challenge within this context is to explore what might constitute the capabilities; the basic knowledge, skills, behaviours and dispositions that can empower service as a spirit-centred contribution to mission, life and culture.

An exploration of capabilities underpinning Catholic school ministry entailed two basic steps. First, the identification of literature that might inform the inquiry; and second, the systematic examination of what might be suitably generic in support of a range of ministry endeavour. In response to step one, ten pieces of research were selected on the basis of relevance to Catholic education, recency of presentation, and, the implications for formation. The second step of examining the selected literature was pursued through a discourse analysis process: Interpretative Phenomenological Analysis (IPA).

IPA attempts to 'unravel the meaning contained in narrative accounts through a process of interpretative engagement with the text of transcripts' (Smith, Jarman, & Osborn 1999, p. 218). Three stages are involved in the process: (a) Data observations (identifying and exploring themes, summaries, questions, use of words, metaphors, etc.); (b) Generating thematic titles (nominating themes which capture the essence of what the text displays); and (c), Connecting themes (considering their relationship and recording a superordinate integrating principle).

The selected literature, together with the main ideas and core themes from the discourse process are presented in Table 17.

Table 17. Discourse data relevant to the practice of ministry

SOURCE	MAIN IDEAS	CORE THEMES
Duncan (1990)	Integral characteristics of leadership: **Faith** - Spirituality, prayer and theology **Learning** - Child development and adult education **Organisational** - Organisational theory and development	❖ Faith ❖ Learning ❖ Organisation
D'Orsa and D'Orsa (1997)	Principal in the Church of the third millennium: **Vista One:** Re-configuring the school's mission in the Church; Being responsible stewards; Inviting parents into a school partnership **Vista Two:** Re-defining the mission and driving it down into the school's structures; Structuring to serve the emerging Church; Developing leadership and management skills **Vista Three:** Setting the parameters for lasting school improvement	❖ Personal vision ❖ Knowledgeable ❖ Initiative, courage and tenacity ❖ Communicates forcefully ❖ Uses power for improvement ❖ Solves 'knotty' problems in engaging vision
Sergiovanni (2000)	Lifeworld of the Principal: Democratic values; Subsidiarity; Engagement in decision making; Empowerment to common good; Use of valid and useful information; Action that is free and informed	❖ Beliefs and Norms ❖ Community: Connections, affections, and obligations ❖ Needs and competencies
Crowther et al. (2002)	A parallel leader: Articulates a clear view of the world; Models trust; Confronts barriers; Builds networks; Applies authentic pedagogy	❖ Self-Awareness ❖ Social Skills ❖ Social Awareness ❖ Self-Management

SOURCE	MAIN IDEAS	CORE THEMES
Sharkey (2002)	**Building Capacity:** Commitment to Catholic ethos; Development in religious domain; Professional formation accords with role; Specialist roles in schools; Outreach; Training and resourcing.	❖ All Staff: Extension Experiences and Leadership Specialisation
USA Bishops (2005)	**The Invitation:** Human maturity and self-awareness; Call to role and call to spirituality; Engage the Catholic intellectual tradition; Strengthen Catholic identity and mission and formation within context	❖ Fields of Formation: ❖ Human; Spiritual; Intellectual; Pastoral
Fullan (2008)	**Principal Priorities:** **Leading Legacies:** Leading for others; Developing collaborative cultures; Linking to the outside; Leaving fond memories **Leading Knowledgeably:** Opening the 'black box' of instruction; Pursuing the precision quest; Linking the results; Developing a culture of improvement; Learning during performance **Leading Learning Communities:** The knowledge base; The action base **Leading Systems:** Purposeful peer interaction; Relationships within the district; Total system connection	❖ School Based Practices: De-privatise teaching; Model instructional leadership; Build capacity first; Grow other leaders; Divert the distractors; Be a system leader ❖ System Based Practices: Elevate and invest in instructional leadership; Combine direction and flexibility; Mobilise the power of data; Use peers to change district culture; Address the managerial requirements; Stay the course
D'Orsa and D'Orsa (2010)	**Leadership of Christ:** With authority that was not his own; With common sense; Situational theology (detail, small things, little people); To build up the community; With self-respect and respect for others; With criteria for good theology (sustainability, appropriateness, empowerment, challenge)	❖ Discipleship: Doing Theology as Jesus did Theology

SOURCE	MAIN IDEAS	CORE THEMES
Fullan (2014)	**Principal's Focus:** Leading Learning: Utilising research, Encouraging professional capital; Fostering being a District and System Player: Looking out to improve within; Engaging intra and extra district development; Becoming a Change Agent and being mindful of errors	❖ Leading Learning ❖ A District and System Player ❖ Becoming a Change Agent
Thornber and Gaffney (2014)	**Governance Formation:** Leadership development within Church; Formation varies for some roles; Commitment and appropriate resourcing; Possesses own language and traditions; Involves choices and ethical dilemmas; Presumes a level of maturity; Vocational across life; Being open to the Word of God; Different needs in different contexts; Teachings of Vatican II; Formation as support for Ministry; Value the place of holiness; Explore Catholic identity; Evolve and evaluate programs	❖ Appreciation of the meaning of formation ❖ Identifies formation needs ❖ Mission based criteria for selection ❖ Understands formation as more than a course ❖ Adult learning approach ❖ Considers time commitment ❖ Addresses generational changes
Neidhart and Lamb (2016)	**Faith Leadership:** authentic Catholicity and the person of the leader; leadership in the ecclesial identity; synthesis of issues and opportunities **Policy:** initiatives in new roles such as Identity and Mission **Research Insights:** Welcoming community and community building **Vocational Focus:** Faith leadership from baptismal commitment and lifelong process inclusive of formation for all staff as a 'bottom up' process	❖ **Context:** Historical and cultural foundations, parish relationships and new models of organisation and pastoral activities; system priorities ❖ **Content:** Facilitated academic study with an emphasis on Religious Education, Theology and Scripture

SOURCE	MAIN IDEAS	CORE THEMES
Neidhart and Lamb (2016)	**Moral and ethical frameworks:** for decision making and communication **Strategic:** Desire to meet individual needs through targeted formation activities **Formation Process:** based on symbolic interactionism, entailing formal study and reflective practice based on self-reflection and social interaction and incorporating knowledge acquisition, attitudinal change and skill development **Overall Goal:** Development of a new equilibrium of shared meaning and social action that not only responds to individual and local community needs, but is consistent with Catholic tradition and teaching	❖ **Skills:** Knowledge of Scripture and Theology; leadership skills in communication, relationships and staff management ❖ **Process:** Desire for conversational and network opportunities; social interaction and opportunities to take the role of another; as well as reflective practice with an interest in creative problem solving ❖ **Start:** Begin with identification of the problem situation (inclusive of prayerful self-reflection)

The third stage of the analysis, the generation of overall principles to integrate the main ideas and core themes, reflected ministry characteristics such as the integrity of the leader; co-operative endeavour and quality relationships; the context of education; and, the importance of perspective beyond the immediate situation. In this light, four principles were selected; 'personal,' 'relational,' 'professional,' and 'communal.' These principles, when applied to the development of formation experiences provide a focus on 'fields of endeavour' on which formation for ministry might focus. These are fields defined by personal, relational, professional and communal dimensions which emerge from preformed dispositions (genetically and spiritually) and provide for the integration of faith, life and culture (Figure 16).

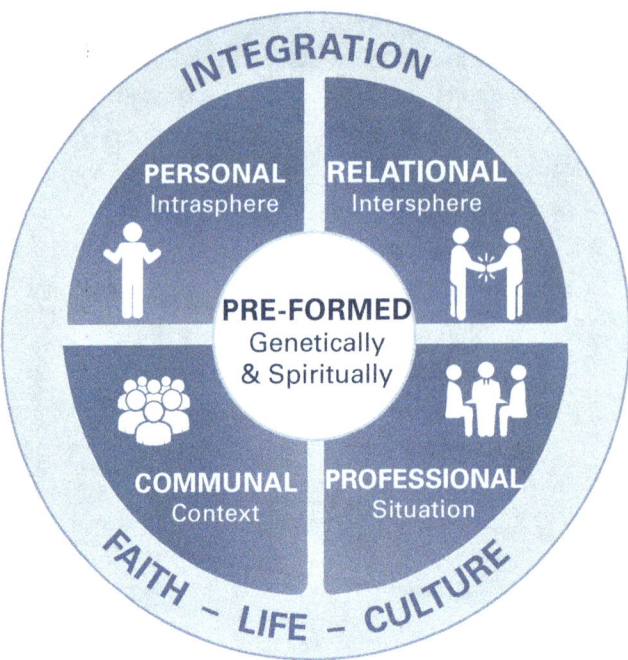

Figure 16. Fields of engagement and interaction in processes of formation

The establishment of fields that offer a focus for ministry formation still leaves open the question as to what capabilities (knowledge, skills, behaviours and dispositions) might apply within these overall fields of endeavour. The knowledge capability covers the technical information necessary to perform a leadership role, the skills dimension identifies the abilities central to the carriage of responsibilities, the behaviours indicate the observable characteristics which the leader would be seen to be performing, and, the dispositions integrate the knowledge, skills and behaviours by identifying overall orientations (ACARA, 2013, p. 5).[123]

Drawing from the definitions of capabilities, and applying these within the generic fields of personal, relational, professional and communal support; content knowledge, skills, behaviours and dispositions were developed in support of ministry preparation and service (Table 18). These formation fields and capabilities provide a background canvas to consider formation for ministry. They invite an interpretation of how particular roles can be enhanced and identify the breadth, subtlety, complexity and opportunity that ministry provides.[124]

---

[123] The capabilities identified in the ACARA framework parallel the Australian Qualifications Framework (AQF) dimensions of Knowledge, Skills and Application of knowledge and skills. The AQF is the national policy for regulated qualifications in Australian education and training.

[124] The challenge to recognise dimensions of teaching that are broad in nature, are reflected in national statements on school leadership by The Australian Institute for Teaching and School Leadership (AITSL, 2014) in their comment that "Contemporary classrooms call for more than educators who simply know the content and how to teach it".

Table 18. Examples of ministry capabilities within generic formation fields

KNOWLEDGE	SKILLS	BEHAVIOURS	DISPOSITIONS
PERSONAL			
❖ Self-concept ❖ Needs and aspirations ❖ Mind and spirit connection	❖ Reflection ❖ Contemplation ❖ Holistic living	❖ Praying ❖ Profiling ❖ Renewing	Personal awareness and engagement through meaning, affect and behaviour grounded in a Catholic Christian view of life and living
RELATIONAL			
❖ Social conditioning ❖ Group dynamics ❖ Sharing wisdom	❖ Inter-personal skills ❖ Sharing wisdom in groups ❖ Work-life integration	❖ Relating ❖ Teaming ❖ Balancing	Respect for the inherent dignity of others and engaging the life of the Spirit in social and group situations
PROFESSIONAL			
❖ Religious Education ❖ Wider curriculum ❖ Religious life of school	❖ Curriculum development ❖ Pedagogy ❖ Culture	❖ Planning ❖ Teaching ❖ Evaluating	Engaging and witnessing to mission through differential practices within religious education, wider curriculum and the religious life of the school
COMMUNAL			
❖ School community ❖ Church community ❖ Wider community	❖ Systems ❖ Engagement ❖ Dialogue	❖ Communication ❖ Facilitation ❖ Transformation	A commitment to dialogue on beliefs and values and the implementation of systems congruent with school, Church and wider community expectations

Ministry formation reflects the nature of ministry in terms of its breadth and depth. Preparation, facilitation, participation and evaluation of formation is therefore quite daunting for participants and facilitators. As seen in Figure 17, formation entails at least the nominated connections across elements of Fields, Capabilities, and Integration expectations[125] of participants, school and the accountable system authority. In this light, conversation about formation for ministry is challenged to be clear and simple lest communication suffer from the complexity of the process and compromise the quality of delivery for unique participants, communities and authorities.

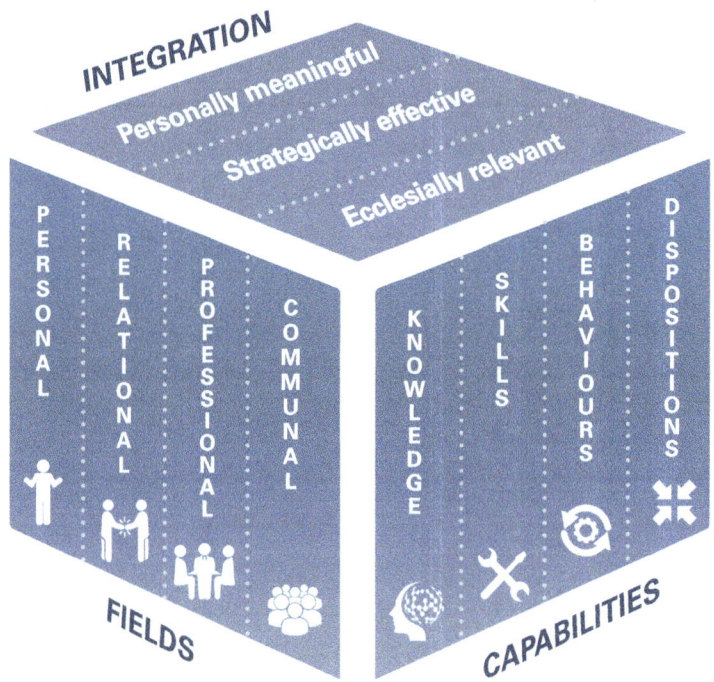

Figure 17. Formation elements integral to Catholic school mission

A metaphor for capabilities

An analysis of progressive research studies by Neidhart and Lamb (2016) point to a convergence of opinion on the nature and integration of knowledge, skills, behaviours and dispositions significant within ministry and indicative of formation needs. Moreover, the challenge of O'Shea (2017) to avoid dualism argues the inseparability of specific capabilities and invites a perspective that is holistic.

---

[125] The characteristics of integration are those nominated in the research of Gowdie, 2017.

The argument of O'Shea is that while it might be convenient to examine complex and important phenomena through separation of concepts within particular mental models; the reality is that people operate from an integrated base where aspects of knowledge, skills, behaviours and dispositions all come together in one form. Seldom does a ministry worker stop and ask whether an intervention is one of 'knowledge,' 'skill,' 'behaviour,' or 'disposition.' Rather, ministry activity typically reflects an integration of all capabilities with particular situations requiring different emphases.

Drawing on the metaphor of golf; within the experience of a 'game' there exist a similar combination of capabilities that majestically and automatically come together within the 'proficient player.' Knowledge of the game might speak to history, legendary players, rules, and etiquette expectations. Skills entail the competencies on club selection, stance, head position, swing and the like. Behaviours entail 'playing a round' and executing a level of personal and social satisfaction within an environment that is appealing. Dispositions include one's enjoyment of the experience and perhaps sharing the value of the game with others. In this light, the overall game reveals a number of capabilities that come together as holistic and integrated.

Within the field of ministry, the capabilities of knowledge, behaviours, skills and dispositions apply in a similar way. For example, educators and support professionals bring together an array of competencies into specific functions and in the process advance mission. In this instance, knowledge may entail an awareness of history, context and systems; skills may be evident in empathy, pedagogy and interpersonal relationship; behaviours include being present and exercising sound management; and dispositions might reflect motivation and the meaning system underpinning the call and commitment to mission.

While specific capabilities become integrated within the practice of ministry, it is the Spirit that shapes and guides thinking and action. Again, using the metaphor of golf, the choice to 'play a round' derives from the value one accords to the experience. Within ministry, choice is also informed by a meaning system. Choice is the action to progress ministry because of a deeper, often hidden reality that is at the core of decision making. The recorded exchange between Mother Teresa and a visitor to her Calcutta Hospice illustrates the concept. The visitor comments "I couldn't do what you are doing for a million dollars." Mother Teresa's response "Nor could I for a million dollars, but the love and engagement of Christ is so much more and provides the inspiration for what I do."[126]

---

126 Exchange drawn from James Martin's audio presentation of *My Life with the Saints*.

Gauging priorities

Formation for ministry is a process of integrating faith, life and culture. It is a process that is formal and informal, the subject of systematic planning, the readiness and requirements of the participant, and the application of methods and resources supportive of a host of experiences.

Appendix One provides an example of an instrument that explores priorities in ministry formation. A self-report questionnaire, the *Catholic School Formation Index* (CSFI), contains a series of statements on the Catholic school across the four generic fields of ministry formation: personal, relational, professional and communal; and asks respondents to identify the extent to which these statements evoke a priority for formation. The statements have been formulated from the research on Catholic school identity and mission (Sultmann, 2014; Hall, Sultmann & Townend, 2018) and reflect aspects of knowledge, skills and behaviours relevant to each of the generic fields. The definition of outcomes within each formation field is taken from the overall disposition statements discussed within this text.

The CSFI offers a practical means for applying the research on formation fields and capabilities in the development and delivery of formation experiences. Scores from the CSFI include the overall priority of formation for a respondent at a particular stage in ministry; a breakdown of this priority across the formation fields of personal; relational; professional and communal; and, the priority of formation across capabilities of knowledge, skills and behaviours relevant to the mission, life and culture of the Catholic school. The outcomes from the CSFI provide a gauge on the priorities of formation for individuals and groups and allow for processes of integrated preparation generated from an appreciation of needs.

> *True education of faith means the education of the entire personality of a 'person.' It is directed at all that a 'person' is, both by nature and grace. For this reason, a person to person relationship is established, involving the person in all spheres of life. This education will embrace the intelligence of a Christian, the capacity and need to act, 'with' emotions, 'with' faith, 'with' hope and charity. In a word it has to do with the whole spiritual make-up of the Christian believer and 'his and her' concrete vocation in the Church and in the world* (Australian Episcopal Conference, 1970, para. 131).

INTEGRATION

Executive Summary

Ministry in the Catholic school entails the integration of spirituality, mission and leadership shaped by foundations in faith. Ministry practice reflects oneness of the mind and Spirit and is evidenced in multiple forms. As a vocation endorsed by the Church, ministry is central to Catholic school mission, life and culture. It is underpinned by generic capabilities of knowledge, skills, behaviours and dispositions and is expressed within personal, relational, professional and communal living. Key to ministry development and practice is the renewal of perspective and the process of formation that enlivens this focus.

Reflection: The essence of ministry

Soon after the public announcement of a move from one Diocese to another, the leader was asked about the vision that would underpin the new ministry. "What will you take to this new position?" the reporter inquired. "I will take the message of Jesus and try to live it as Christians have done for centuries and are called to do everywhere," came the response. Not daunted by the seemingly brief and curious reply, the reporter attempting to search for more 'news,' began once more. "But what will your vision entail?" Once again, the respondent was to echo the mindset which underpinned the sweep of involvement for the many 'faces' of Church activity. "The Kingdom of Christ in a world so desperate for hope and meaning is what we will endeavour to live," the leader said. Still not satisfied with the dialogue and seeming to desire some 'scoop' as to a dramatic alteration to the life of the community, the reporter tried once more. "And your goals, what will they be?" Exercising patience while drawing upon the wisdom of the Spirit and the experience of many years, the answer came. "I will, with others, try to give life through the message of Christ for us in our modern age." Realising that the interview was not achieving the 'news' that would make headlines, the reporter turned the focus elsewhere, not appreciating the level of significance and possibility the responses possessed.

Questions

1. **Head:** What does the word 'ministry' mean to you?
2. **Heart:** Within your context, how is ministry experienced?
3. **Hand:** How would you see ministry success within your community?

Activities

Theme: Psychodynamic review of ministry

Goal: Professional renewal in ministry

Task: Privately complete the reflection exercise and share outcomes with a colleague.

Step One – Personal reflection

- This is how I see myself in ministry (my current situation);
- This is my ideal of ministry (where I see myself heading);
- What will block my reaching the ideal?;
- This is what I can do about the blockages.

Step Two – Shared discussion

- Presentation of reflection;
- Commentary from colleague;
- Refined and or developed position.

Step Three – My ministry profile is summarised as:

- Beliefs
- Values
- Image
- Symbol
- Behaviours

Theme: The CReATE Cycle[127]

Goal: Application of a problem solving strategy

Task: Identify a challenging matter and apply the steps of the integrated processes: Concern, Reflect, Action Plan, Try Out, and Evaluate (the CReATE cycle).

---

127 Strategy drawn from David Hunt in *The Renewal of Personal Energy*.

Activities

- *C (Concern)* Summarise the concern using prompts of: who, what, when, where, how and why;

- *Re (Reflect)* Consider the concern in terms of your thinking, feeling, and behaving;

- *A (Action Plan)* Nominate possibilities for resolving the concern and select a strategy or strategies that might work;

- *T (Try Out)* Implement the strategy/ies in terms of goals, process, timing, resources, personnel, outcomes;

- *E (Evaluate)* Identify the outcomes in relation to goals and ask what lessons existed with the process.

Theme: Living encounters

Goal: Reflection on 'the face of God'

Task: The task invites reflection on the 'Face of God' experiences in life.[128]

- What touched me that was unusual and unexpected today?
- Where did I experience the Spirit of Christ touching me today?
- How was I Christ to another today?

Theme: One on one

Goal: Places, times and situations for reflection

Task: Consider the typical day and identify places, times and situations that permit a settling of the mind through a meditative state.

- The best time for me to engage in meditation is…
- The most suitable place for meditation is…
- The situations that provide for meditation include…

---

[128] The nomination of a Year of Grace by the Australian Episcopal Conference incorporated the goal of reflecting on a 'thousand opportunities and experiences' through which the grace of God might be seen.

CHAPTER SIX
'To experience is to know: Open the window and let in the world'

Chapter Outline

CHAPTER SIX	198
TO EXPERIENCE IS TO KNOW: OPEN THE WINDOW AND LET IN THE WORLD	198
INTRODUCTION	198
Reflection	198
At a glance	198
Focusing Story: Piercing the cocoon	199
From your experience	199
THEMES AND MAIN IDEAS	199
Glance again	199
Known for what?	200
Responding personally	201
Stepping up and stepping out	204
Why as a basis for how?	205
ENGAGING HOLISTICALLY	206
Conclusion	208
A dynamic tradition	208
Blessing in a sacred place	209
An unfinished symphony	210
Reflection: "No more fences"	211
Activities	212

CHAPTER SIX

To experience is to know: Open the window and let in the world[129]

INTRODUCTION

Reflection

"As Jesus walked by the Sea of Galilee, he saw two brothers, Simon who is called Peter and Andrew his brother, casting a net into the sea; for they were fishermen. And he said to them, "Follow me and I will make you fishers of men." Immediately they left their nets and followed him" (Matthew 4:18-20).

At a glance

'To experience is to know: Open the window and let in the world' revisits the title theme of each chapter and highlights a characteristic from each that holds special significance.

Foundations in faith record the significance of Christ and the Church as central to the life of the Catholic school summarised in the phrase "known for what?" Spirituality of engagement is characterised as "responding personally;" prophetic mission is an invitation to "step up and step out;" leadership as Christian praxis involves imagining "why as a basis for the how;" and, ministry is summarised through "engaging holistically." The chapter concludes that these characteristics portray the Catholic school as serving within a living tradition; one that renews within and without through engaging the mission of God under the guidance of the Spirit. It is a sacred place in which the Spirit of Christ is experienced and shared; where encounters are not pre-defined, nor responses found 'in the manual;' and where a continuing search and appreciation of God's presence becomes the norm.

---

129 The introductory sentence of 'to experience is to know' arose in conversation with reverend John Auram CP. The emphasis was given to ministry as a process of engagement of the Spirit of Christ within self and others.

Focusing Story: Piercing the cocoon

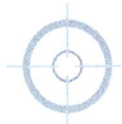

This text had its beginnings in the confines of a 'high rise,' the seventeenth floor of an inner-city apartment with all the attendant characteristics of closed windows and doors, confined spaces, controlled ventilation, and provision of the essentials; all of which provided something of the atypical and constituted a potential shield from the world outside. Even communications with visitors were screened through security features ensuring that only the very familiar could get through. The setting of the apartment provided a cocoon, a sheltered existence that protected inhabitants from the outside. It was only when the doors and the windows were opened, when people visited, wrote or phoned that a fuller appreciation of the wider environment could be experienced.

Piercing the cocoon of self-absorption and separation from the world are fundamental to the development of mission, life and culture in the Catholic school. Experience, reflection and commitment enable learning from the wisdom 'already within' and the 'lessons' available 'from without.' Attributes of optimism, exploration, dialogue, trust, faith and love characterise the process. It is the experience of coming to know more fully what is already integrated and engaging the new in hope through reflection and action. It is believing in the Spirit to guide and support in an environment of abundance.

From your experience

1. How is your educational service informed through self-reflection?
2. How are processes of engagement evidenced in your community?
3. How do you view your responsibilities and witness in the Catholic school?

THEMES AND MAIN IDEAS

Glance again

This final chapter revisits key themes and offers brief and integrative commentary on material introduced in the text. The words of the acclaimed writer Thomas Stearns (TS) Eliot (1888 - 1965) set the context "We shall not cease from exploration and the end of all our exploring will be to arrive where we began and to know the place for the first time."[130] The invocation is to keep looking and

---

130 Retrieved from: http://www.columbia.edu/itc/history/winter/w3206/edit/tseliotlittlegidding.html

ideally, by glancing again, to uncover insights that provide a deeper level of meaning not easily arrived at or first recognised.

The text expanded on the scriptural passage "I am the way, and the truth and the life" (John 14:6). The manifestation of discipleship through walking his way (spirituality), telling his truth (mission), and living his life (leadership) are the 'doors and windows' through which the Spirit of Christ is encountered. However, these emphases are not exhaustive, the final or only words on how the Spirit might be interpreted and lived within the mission, life and culture of the Catholic school. They do however offer a framework and a beginning to this appreciation and application. Moreover, the integration of these characteristics within ministry reveals the Spirit as dynamic in the day-to-day, the ordinary and the extraordinary, the expected and unexpected gifts of life within the Catholic school.

Known for what?

Chapter One, 'Knowing his story: Foundations in faith' examined themes and main ideas relevant to the fertile question of Christ as the cornerstone of the Catholic school. This was developed in terms of the revelation of God, the vision and mission of Jesus as the Christ, the insights of Vatican II, and being Church today. The goal of the chapter was to identify the foundations for encountering the Spirit of Christ and what the Catholic school might be known for.

A story elaborated by David Pivonka TOR and Ralph Poyo (2014) speaks of the final wishes of the American founding father, Thomas Jefferson (1743 - 1826). Jefferson, the principal architect of the *Declaration of Independence* and the third President of the United States, was intentional and precise when framing the words that were to appear on his gravestone.[131] While the words were significant, what was reflected was not a host of achievements, but a simple statement as to his life's purpose. The few carefully chosen words captured his passion and interest in a context of extraordinary and expansive engagement and contribution. It was what he wanted to be known for, as distinct from a summary of what he achieved publicly.

The example of Jefferson invites the reflection as to how anyone might want to be remembered. That is, what could be said to constitute the essence of one's life and relationships that are so important to be assigned to one's grave. For people for whom the Christian faith is central, the final statement in *Encounter Jesus: From Discovery to Discipleship* (Pivonka & Poyo, 2014), records a powerful example: "To live a life of love, grow in faith, and experience the peace of God" (2014, CD). The summary reveals the breadth and depth of what might constitute

---

[131] Here was buried Thomas Jefferson, Author of the Declaration of American Independence of the Statute of Virginia for religious freedom & Father of the University of Virginia.

the essence of Christian discipleship. The concepts recall the nature of God as love, the development of faith as a journey, and the reward of peace as a gift of the Spirit.

A response to the personal question of 'being known for what' invites the additional reflection on the Catholic school and the work of the Spirit. As a ministry within the church, and considering the church as giving support to the expression to God's mission in the world (Lennan, 2018a), the 'known for what' in relation to the Catholic school is to recognise, affirm and engage God's mission already present. This particular mission entails invitation not imposition, being benefactor and beneficiary, acting as a sacrament of Christ's love, recognising the gap between the ideal and the real, accepting difference and rejecting division, and, offering an alternative to 'win lose' models. To an inspiring litany of aims, Lennan adds "We embody the Spirit when we look like Jesus … a church in and for the world … a model of communion connected through the Word of God, the life of Jesus, and the gift of the Spirit."

The experience of the Spirit as fundamental to the life of the Catholic school invites an awareness of the centrality of the Holy Spirit in mission as "presence and power" (Coleridge, 2017, DVD). The challenge is to engage in ways that give life to the mission of God in the world. It is a conviction born of reflection and experience, one that was outlined in the narrative of Chapter One. It is founded on 'Knowing his story: Foundations in faith' and draws from the significance of the Spirit in defining purpose, offering privilege in service, nurturing communion, and advancing possibility in the community that is the Catholic school.

Responding personally

Chapter Two began the first of a three-chapter elaboration of "I am the way, and the truth and the life" (John 14:6). Specifically, this chapter considered spirituality in terms of life as graced and gifted and a response in Christian faith as incorporating sacramental living and discipleship. Within this interpretation of spirituality, the words of Christ "I am;" and, "No one comes to the Father except through me," ring out. These are the emphatic reminders by Jesus that he is the anointed and that engagement with the Father is through him. The invitation is to not only follow and engage a spiritual relationship with God, but to do so in ways that arise from a personal relationship with the Lord. The words of the acclaimed theologian highlight the position "You see, you're only dealing with Jesus when you throw your arms around him and realise right down to the bottom of your being that this is something you can still do today (Karl Rahner, 1983, p. 23).

Personal encounters with Christ engage the total self and are found in a host of situations and circumstances: nature, birth, death, interpersonal love, commitment to truth, a passion for justice and friendship (Shea, 1987, p. 16). The synthesis of the potential encounters by John Shea names Jesus as the one who is able and welcoming of relationships that are 'one on one,' and allow for the bringing of our experiences and concerns to Christ "for acceptance, transformation and hope" (p.18). This is a journey in relationship that moves from 'fascination, to discipleship to friendship' (p. 19).

The reminders of a spiritual director address the limitations of thought and isolation in contrast to the development of a personal relationship with Christ. The comments "It is so easy to be attracted to knowledge of Jesus and not the engagement of the person through the heart … the Christian life is easy if you let the Spirit lead you … God loves you personally and so allow yourself to encounter this unbelievable gift … recognise and act on this as if you are uniquely named and loved." The challenge is to respond to the encounter with Christ in a personal way as distinct from possessing knowledge about an historical figure or an ideology. The theologian Leonardo Boff[132] notes the difference: "A theology, any theology, not based on spiritual experience is mere panting, religious breathlessness" (1984, p. 2).

Forming a relationship with Christ is at first curious, for how is a personal relationship fashioned with the historical Jesus? However, faith in his commitment to be present in Spirit (Matthew 28:20), recognition of God as love and truth, experiencing this love in the circumstances of one's life, together with the practices developed and offered by the believing community of the Church, are a 'good start.'[133] Notwithstanding these means, seeking and asking for a personal relationship and pursuing it as already present are significant.

An illustration of building a deeper and personal relationship with Christ was shown in the reaction of the community to the death of the legendary cricketer, Don Bradman. As tributes flowed and the significance of the man became clear, levels of relationships moved from the abstract to the personal. The first wave of media tributes recognised family and circumstances of work, life in retirement, interests and so on. Soon after these initial details, comments took the form of an avalanche of information as to his achievements. Not to downplay those extraordinary endeavours, a third set of tributes simply recognised his person, for as one commentator stated, "I knew the man." Similarly, the challenge to encounter Christ is to not only know the history, aspirations and practices of Christ, but to

---

132 Leonardo Boff is a Brazilian theologian and writer, known for his active support for liberation theology. He currently serves as Professor Emeritus of Ethics, Philosophy of Religion, and Ecology at the Rio de Janeiro State University .

133 Developing a relationship with Christ is argued to entail core steps: prayer, reading Scripture, immersion in the tradition, engaging in the wider mission of the Church, and finding nourishment in the Sacraments (Chaput, 2001, p. 47-53).

experience and be present to the person of Jesus as saviour, friend, companion and mentor. It is to possess a relationship that goes beyond knowing the facts of the story to a point where "I know and engage the person of Christ through the action of the Spirit".

The documentaries produced by the acclaimed media journalist Malcolm Muggeridge have captured outstanding people and issues of the twentieth century. The story of Mother Teresa of Calcutta, *Something Beautiful for God*, was one such classic that inspired the world. It brought to public awareness the Spirit that motivated her service to others, specifically the underprivileged, desperate and dying people of the slums of Calcutta. Mother Teresa has now 'gone to God' and yet her service remains in the hearts, minds and hands of others. Just prior to her death, the following story revealed the underlying Spirit that empowered the extraordinary.

During one of her visits to Rome, reporters gathered around Mother Teresa in the outer courtyard of her convent on the Coelian Hill, and one of them was known to have stated publicly "Mother, you are seventy. When you die, the world will be exactly as it was before. What has changed after so much effort?" Mother Teresa could have reacted with a touch of righteous indignation, but she merely gave one of her luminous smiles, as if he had kissed her affectionately, and replied "You see, I have never tried to change the world! I have only tried to be a drop of clear water in which God's love can shine. Do you think that is nothing?" The reporter was speechless, and Mother Teresa became the centre of an attentive, moving silence. She spoke to the reporter again. "You, too, try to be a drop of clear water through which the love of God might shine, and then there will be two of us. Are you married?" "Yes, Mother." "Then tell your wife, too, and then there will be three of us. Have you any children?" "I have three, Mother." "Then tell them, too, and like that, there will be six of us." [134]

The experience of 'Calcutta's saint' registers an incredible humility drawn from a life of experience and engagement with the most destitute. The relationship of Mother Teresa with God through the Spirit can never be fully known nor can the personal relationship anyone has with the person of Christ; it is personal. What is known for sure is that there is such a relationship and at times it emerges more publicly. On one occasion a reporter was known to have said "Mother, I couldn't do what you do for a million dollars." "No, ... I couldn't do it

---

134 Cardinal Pio Laghi, Prefect for the Congregation for Catholic Education, provided the foundation for the story. It is reproduced with some minor editing from the *Proceedings of the International Conference on Catholic Education, India*, 1998.

for a million dollars either, but it is engagement with the Spirit of Christ, present in all, that carries me on."[135]

Stepping up and stepping out

Chapter Three traced the prophetic mission of the Catholic school in Australia from its humble beginnings to an expansive presence characterised by a distinctive philosophy informed through experience and Church exhortations. The commentary by Joseph Komonchak (2001)[136] reflected its mission as incorporating 'God's gift and our task.'

Ministry in the Catholic school is a blend of 'theory and practice' to which the whole body is called to participate, to step up and step out through the guidance of the Spirit. It is the invitation to believe and respond. "If there were no believers, no one who hoped in Christ and the Spirit, no one in whom the love of God for us had created love for God and for our fellows, there would be no Church. We are the body of Christ, incorporated to him by the Spirit of God; but we ourselves also build up the body of Christ. We are brought into the temple of the Spirit, but we ourselves are the living stones of which it is to be created" (Komonchak, 1987, p. 740).

Catholic schools are called to share vision and mission and so offer the world the Good News as light and leaven within the 'new normal.' In being open, the school community not only reaches out, but also is embraced and influenced by the world and the universal presence of the Spirit. The invitation is to be open, personally and communally, to form and be formed. It is about being a servant and, paradoxically, through that service, coming to experience being served.

Dialogue and history provide a basis for mission. Drawing from the perspective of Church history, Massimo Faggioli (2018) points out history is important to understanding the Church and where it might go. "History teaches who we are and the world we live in ... Do not look for the golden age - it never really existed. The process is one of continuity and discontinuity ... The past was neither all wonderous nor all bad." Dialogue through listening constitutes respectful engagement as the Catholic school enriches and is enriched by the community it serves. The task is one of responding to the challenge and exercising trust and hope in what are unknown situations in potentially untravelled locations.

Pilgrims have walked the Camino de Santiago trails across Europe for centuries, making their way to Santiago de Compostela in Galicia, North-West of Spain. A publicly acclaimed song written for pilgrims, *Somewhere Along the Way*,[137]

---
135 The story is taken from Martin, J. (2009). *My Life with the Saints*.
136 A celebrated theologian and Catholic Priest.
137 Written and sung by Dan Mullins: see Dan Mullins music.com

narrates experiences and relationships. The song is an invitation to meet and support fellow pilgrims while finding and exploring 'something more' while on the journey. It is a metaphor for walking with Christ and finding Christ within self and others. It is a process of 'stepping up' and 'stepping out' in the hope of enriching and being enriched in the journey of mission within the Catholic school.

Why as a basis for how?

Chapter Four addressed leadership within the Catholic school through introducing theoretical streams of endeavour and concluding with an interpretation of leadership as Christian praxis characterised by service and communion. Personal, relational, organisational and communal arenas were identified as places for transformation underpinned by an understanding of 'why.' Knowing the 'why' of leadership empowers leaders in establishing, managing and persevering with multiple 'how's.'

The two most recent documents from the Congregation of Catholic Education; *Educating to Intercultural Dialogue in Catholic Schools Living in Harmony for a Civilization of Love* (2013), and, *Educating to Fraternal Humanism* (2017) speak of proactive processes which educate through relationship based on dialogue. The relationship draws from the relationship with Christ, incorporates relationship with others, and is lived within the community where relationships are abundant. The 'why' of leadership is the enactment of the vision of Christ within the mission of the Catholic school. It is an interactive, relational and transformational experience (Branson & Marra, 2019) that supports the many 'how's.'

Individual and collaborative leadership ministry while responsive to Christ is challenged to go beyond itself to embrace the oneness and relationship that life entails. The questions that the 'living stones' are challenged to answer in ways that resonate with the person and message of the cornerstone are summed up by Faggioli (2018b) as "Does religion make you more human or less a person?" and, put another way, "Is there a religious dimension to leadership that makes the community more human?" This is the challenge of encountering the Spirit of Christ in leadership through ministry which integrates and seeks to integrate spirituality and mission in supporting the mission of God in the world (Figure 18).

Figure 18. Encountering the Spirit of Christ in the Catholic school

Engaging holistically

The integration of the Spirit of Christ manifested in spirituality, mission and leadership was pursued in Chapter Five through a discussion of ministry. Themes of oneness in mind and Spirit, the concept of ministry, examples of living in Spirit and developing perspective and capabilities were woven together and argued to inform formation based on fields of endeavour and capabilities.

The nature of ministry as an integrative response to spirituality, mission and leadership was highlighted by a personal experience that summed up how it might be viewed in complex and adapting environments. The experience was a recent walk in a national park during which I encountered a young family and in the process became privy to an exchange between a mother and her youngest. With the motivation to enthuse her child about possibilities, the mother was overheard to say, "Come on, let's go into the day." The words stayed with me and I wondered if it were more accurate to say "Let's exist within the day" for it is never about entry and energy alone. This more expanded thought also presented as insufficient and invited a further consideration. Could we not say "Let's go into, exist within, and through the day make a difference?"

The prepositions 'into,' 'within,' and 'through' suggest something more integrated and comprehensive about life in the day-to-day. Without over simplification, they appear to sum up the theme of this overall narrative. *Cornerstone: Encountering the Spirit of Christ in the Catholic School* is about entering the life of the Catholic school from a perspective on life; engaging in the experience through the lens of the Spirit; and operating through it in ways that make a difference. 'Into,' 'within,' and 'through' sum up the characteristics of mission, spirituality and leadership when encountering the living Spirit of Christ. In this light, the words of Robert Greenleaf bear reflection for they acknowledge the essence of all encounters that are individually and collectively entered into, operate within, and through our engagement, make a difference.

I do not want to define or explain Spirit. There is, in my theology, a mystery before which I simply stand in awe. At the threshold of the Mystery, I ask no questions and seek no explanations. I simply bow before the Mystery, and what it wants to say to me comes as gently as doves, as I achieve the quiet (Robert Greenleaf, 1998, p. 143).

Participation in the mission, life and culture of the Catholic school is a journey inspired and accompanied by the Spirit of Christ. It is a journey of known and unknown paths; a journey with multiple encounters with the life of Christ as model, the Spirit of Christ as companion, the leadership of Christ as compass, and the generosity of friends and colleagues who make a difference through activation of the Spirit within their ministry.

Pope John Paul II, Karol Wojtyla, was well known for his journeys to nations of the world and his love of journeying in the outdoors. The image of journeying is captured in his often-quoted line "It is necessary to have the courage to walk in a direction no one has walked so far."[138] Such is the encounter with the Spirit of Christ in the Catholic school. It is a personal journey of courage supported by hope and joy, a journey of encounter that is guided by and accompanied by the Spirit. It is a journey that people have taken before, and within changing times, it calls for new 'tracks' as hope sustains. "Hope is like a road in the country; there was never a road, but when many people walk on it, the road comes into existence."[139]

Richard Lennan (2018b) in a series of lectures on *Leading Ecclesial Communities* advances ministry as essentially reflecting on and building on the work of God

---

138 The statement is reported in a tribute, Courier Mail Newspaper, April 7, 2005, p. 3
139 The quotation is from Lin YuTang, as extracted from Jackley, 2015, p. 184.

in the world. More particularly, ministry is founded on co-operative support and seen as a Sacrament of God's reign, based on the model of Jesus (teacher, healer, reconciler), exercised through the action of the Spirit, responsive to the needs of the world, distinct but not separated from a baptismal vocation to discipleship, and nurtured by Word, Sacrament, and life of the worshipping community. It is being sent out, requires discernment of gifts, involves ongoing formation, is endorsed through ecclesial recognition, is performed on behalf of the community, and, is formalised in structures which remain open to the Spirit. Lennan concludes that ministry is that part of Christian faith that is shaping itself based on emerging needs and this in turn is shaping the Church as it goes.

Conclusion

A dynamic tradition

The integrating theme of this manuscript has been the call to serve through a relationship of encounter with Christ the cornerstone. This is a relationship of significance but is one where specific guidelines from a manual are not available. The response of the Christian to the encounter with Christ through discipleship is a response to the living Spirit of Christ that draws from his story, his prophetic voice and his leadership within the Kingdom. It is not something we get to the end of; it is a work in progress (Lennan, 2018). In this light the Church and the Catholic school within the life of the Church is a living body that grows and changes as a pilgrim community. This is a dynamic community that carries the living tradition and in the process forms and reforms itself.

The Spirit nurtures the Church's journey in faith, service and communion. This is invitational in nature and assisted through resources of Word, Sacrament and community. Lennan (2018) adds that as a human community, the Church possesses structures to hold together the parts and that nobody gets the Church they design for themselves. The Church is God's work and not anyone's. It is built on complexity and there is no perfect model. Through the Spirit, the Church exercises discernment in its movement towards God. Responsibility involves faithfulness and creativity in the mission.

Faith foundations, spirituality, mission, leadership and ministry have been proposed as offering lenses on the work of the Spirit in the Catholic school. While not exhaustive of purposes, possibilities, places, situations, and responses that a Catholic school community might activate, they do represent immediate and achievable means within which the actions of the Spirit might be observed. They provide the platform for a living tradition (Johnson, 2003) for continuing the experience of Christ within a place and culture that reflect his vision and mission in the world. In this light, the Catholic school is a sacred place; a community in which the Spirit of Christ is found, explored, understood and applied in ways that give life, meaning and purpose.

Blessing in a sacred place

The evangelists Matthew (7:24-27) and Luke (6:48-49) contrast buildings that are founded on rock and sand and, in times of rain, flood and wind become tested. Clearly, the implication for the Catholic school is that its foundation is secure when it is centred on Christ, through the Spirit. The vision of the Catholic school is, therefore, sacred in origin, magnificent in intention and profound in application. It is a source of joy and hope for those who become its community and a means of light and leaven within the environment it serves. It is a place where the Spirit of Christ dwells, a community that gives expression to, and literally is challenged to become, a sign and instrument of God in the world, a face and place of Church, a community constituting a new temple in the Lord.

The invitation of mission within the Catholic school is a call to holiness in a sacred place. Christian faith tells us that life is a gift and that, in the journey of life, we move towards God, towards the good. As people of faith, we seek to live an aligned life and attempt to understand and deepen the mystery of God within it. We do this in relationship to the cornerstone who, in turn, reveals and shares the very nature of God.

Much of the discretion, common sense, wisdom and intuition that are a necessary part of living can't be detailed and logically laid out. Not everything is in the manual. Life cannot be ordered, nor can the response to the multitude of situations ever be scheduled and programmed. There are the unusual, the unpredictable, the non-rational, the unbelievable, and the ordinary circumstances of Catholic school life that need to be addressed through living within the power and love of the Spirit. It is this breath of life that allows the 'God of surprises' to be encountered and the wisdom of the Spirit to be uncovered in ways that leave love, freedom and truth the beneficiaries.

The acclaimed movie, *A Few Good Men*, not only showcases the talents of Jack Nicholson (Colonel Jessup) and Tom Cruise (Lieutenant Caffey), but highlights a culture of routine and order over openness and encounter. One scene records the interactions of a witness displaying faithfulness to the code of conduct by Marines while the defence lawyer is attempting to demonstrate that not all behaviours are necessarily programmed. The court scene depicts Caffey interrogating the witness and, in the process, revealing the pedantic and almost slavish approach to the procedures in the manual that a 'good Marine' must adhere. Question after question from Caffey extracts from the witness the predictable rebuttals that are all aligned to the expectations in the 'trusted book' until Caffey's frustration reaches a highpoint, "And what about meals, what does the book say about going to the 'mess' tent?" "Well, Sir, the way to the mess tent is not in the manual," comes the response; only to have Caffey reply "That's right, it's not in the manual. Not everything is in the manual, not all is outlined, planned and predicted."

An unfinished symphony

Ronald Rolheiser in a series of works (1995, 1998, & 2014) introduces the concept of insufficiency and the notion of a 'holy longing' that underpins many 'unfinished symphonies.' That is a natural sense of incompleteness, a feeling of 'unfinished business.' In managing this insufficiency, Rolheiser suggests that concerns about unfinished works might well give way to extending the desire for a deeper and more enduring spiritual life which is the ultimate symphony, one that can be experienced in the here and now. The image is not dissimilar to the image in the well-known movie, *Mr Holland's Opus*, in which Mr Holland was always going to finish his *American Symphony*, but never quite did. The crescendo comes at the end of his career as a teacher when he realises that his symphony was in fact how he lived his life. The 'notes he wrote' were the influences he gave to the students in his care.

The concept of searching for the Divine, living in the Spirit, recognising one's contemporary symphony is integral to the development of a maturing faith. It is a foundational concept that is developed in theory and practice by spiritual writers. One imaginary approach offered by Richard Rohr is his retelling of the search for the 'holy grail.' At its deepest level, it is the story about resolving a deeper restlessness for the sacred. It is the 'holy longing' that Rolheiser describes; a process that entails a search and discovery of a treasure that is already available but not necessarily recognised, understood or accessed.

The story of the grail, the search for the cup used by Jesus at the last supper, is the source of legend and myth. The cup symbolises the presence of Christ, the gift he invited his followers to celebrate. The knight Percival enters the grail search but after much travel fails to locate the treasure. Upon re-entering Camelot, Percival is told of the whereabouts of the cup within the castle, in a far room, and in a chamber behind a door. Committed to these final advices, Percival eventually finds and opens the chamber, only to be disappointed once more. However, in the process he becomes awake to the reality there is no cup, for the search for the Divine, the quest for the grail, is the search of the Spirit of God within. It is the process of opening doors into an 'inner castle' to experience the Spirit that shapes, guides, comforts and renews.

The conclusion of Rolheiser about being awake to the Spirit of God within, foreshadows a response that the love and the presence of God is just the beginning. The fuller experience of the grail story relates to an appreciation that goes beyond the presence of the gift, to the enjoyment and satisfaction with the gift itself. It is the presence of God; always beckoning, inviting, disturbing and enriching. It is the presence of God coming to us disguised as our life and accompanying us on the journey of life.[140] It is the realisation that the language God speaks to us is the experience God writes into our lives if only we might be attentive and appreciative of the richness it offers.[141]

The implication of the grail search is that within the gift of the Catholic school, there is also something to be recognised, valued and lived with appreciation, joy and hope. Catholic school mission and ministry is therefore not just an idea or concept to search for but is a place in which the Spirit of Christ is already present and offering answers to offset insufficiencies. It is a place in which to take delight and invokes an integrated response "To stop studying, stop preparing, stop searching, and to start teaching, doing, manifesting, and producing. The rehearsals are over, the show is on."[142] This is the invitation to engage a living agenda, where the Spirit of Christ not only informs but supports performance. It is the practice of integrating thinking, feeling and behaving in ways that build from encounters, and support the development of the temple of the Lord within each person and group comprising the community, the living stones of the Catholic school.

Reflection: "No more fences"

The seminar had come to 'break time' and allowed the participants to move to the 'urns.' Encounters were everywhere, and differing accents soon led to a discussion about country of origin and those special places that were prized. As the seminar had relevance to Catholic schools and faith practice, it wasn't too long before the dialogue turned to views about Church, the mission of Catholic schools, and the challenges that appeared universal. For some reason the conversation focused on a comparison of rural landscapes in two very different settings. The first image recalled the 'blue grass' region of Kentucky where the fields are deep green, the fences vivid white, the barns red roofed and the landscape overall, simply a 'picture.' In this environment, the fences constitute the mechanisms for safety, security and identification. The second landscape imaged the outback region of Australia where the property sizes are so great that

---

140 The concept is drawn from the writing of Daniel O'Leary.
141 A saying of the Christian mystic, John of the Cross.
142 An extract from an Immersion Journal in sacred places in India during 2015.

fences are not an option. In these settings the flocks and herds remain together, not because of the presence or absence of fences, or even because of the identification with structures and landscapes, but by reason of the water that exists or is made available through underground supplies, artesian and sub-artesian bores.

The comparison between a Kentucky ranch and an Australian outback cattle station, is that in one environment the means for sustaining life were appearance, structure and order; whereas in the other, life was based on a fundamental resource, water, and care about its provision. While in both environments, order and organisation are important, the images led to the propositions "Would it not be ideal if the Catholic school were able to be sustained through the mission they provide rather than allow externally driven features of rule, appearance and regulation to become the motivation for participation?" Moreover, "Could not the 'living waters' that Jesus promised be the means to enhance life, to value add to personal growth, social well-being, and educational transformation?" This is the 'project' into which the living stones of the Catholic school are invited into through the Spirit of Christ. It is in the encounters of knowing his story, living his Spirit, engaging his mission, and integrating his life within and for the agenda of God's action in the world, that the 'Spirit of the cornerstone' is built.

Activities

Theme: Perceptual Positions

Goal: Facilitating understanding from multiple perspectives

Task: Identify an issue of significance and reflect on your perspective drawn from the following perceptual positions:

- *Position One* – What I observe and think
- *Position Two* – What the other person observes and thinks
- *Position Three* – What a third party observes and thinks
- *Position Four* – What observations emerge when the wider context is considered?
- *Position Five* – What observations arise from a transcendental (Kingdom) perspective?

Activities

Theme: What becomes important?[143]

Goal: Values identification

Task: Reflect on the invitation by Oriah of what gives life and identify what inspires and gives energy, purpose and focus to your professional situation.

The Invitation by Oriah[144]

"It doesn't interest me what you do for a living. I want to know what you ache for and if you dare to dream of meeting your heart's longing.

It doesn't interest me how old you are. I want to know if you will risk looking like a fool for love, for your dream, for the adventure of being alive.

It doesn't interest me what planets are squaring your moon. I want to know if you have touched the centre of your own sorrow, if you have been opened by life's betrayals, or have become shrivelled and closed from fear of further pain. I want to know if you can sit with pain, mine or your own, without moving to hide it or fade it or fix it. I want to know if you can be with joy, mine or your own, if you can dance with wildness and let the ecstasy fill you to the tips of your fingers and toes without cautioning us to be careful, to be realistic, to remember the limitations of being human.

It doesn't interest me if the story you are telling me is true. I want to know if you can disappoint another, to be true to yourself. If you can bear the accusation of betrayal and not betray your own soul. If you can be faithful and therefore trustworthy. I want to know if you can see beauty even when it is not pretty every day. And if you can source your own life from its presence. I want to know if you can live with failure, yours and mine and still stand at the edge of the lake and shout to the silver of the full moon, "Yes."

It doesn't interest me to know where you live or how much money you have. I want to know if you can get up after the night of grief and despair, weary and bruised to the bone and do what needs to be done to feed the children.

It doesn't interest me who you know or how you came to be here. I want to know if you will stand in the centre of the fire with me and not shrink back.

It doesn't interest me where or what or with whom you have studied. I want to know what sustains you from the inside when all else falls away. I want to know if you can be alone with yourself and if you truly like the company you keep in the empty moments."

---

143 The writer was made aware of the invitation of Oriah through the impact it possessed on a creative and loving teacher who experienced its power personally as a values beacon for life and living.

144 Drawn from The Invitation by Oriah published by HarperOne, San Franciso, 1999.

Activities

Theme: Jesus off the bench

Goal: Identifying the Spirit of Christ already present

Task: The exhortations of an experienced Catholic school principal was often to include the statement "Does Jesus get a jersey in this experience?" From your own engagement, how can you relate to the position "Jesus is off the bench."

Theme: Three-phase power

Goal: Activating the gifts of spirituality, mission and leadership

Task: Three phase power is an electrical concept that is translated as 'enough electricity to light up the neighbourhood'. In light of ministry as a process of integrating the gifts of spirituality, mission and leadership, what three core characteristics 'light up your ministry in relation to the immediate and wider community of the world?'

EPILOGUE: LIVING AGENDA

A friend asks, "what is the take home message of this work?" It is a way of saying that in the mix of what has been narrated, drawn, tabled, questioned, experienced and felt; what is it that stands out as significant? An accurate response, in view of several interactive themes within the text, is virtually impossible. However, as an Epilogue does offer an opportunity to give expression to things already stated, the temptation to try holds some appeal.

An experience within my early years of ministry within Catholic Education entailed attending an intensive six-day retreat with Drs Joe and Eileen Connolly on 'Leadership for a Better World.' The course was profound in many ways with one procedural aspect continuing to hold attention. The presenters were insistent that there was to be no taking notes. In fact, when people did try to 'jot briefly,' the refrain was always: "No notes, you are the living agenda for this experience."

The meaning of 'living agenda' was simply about the process of integration as distinct from the aggregation of written material which may or may not 'ever be seen again.' It was also about recognition of individual differences in people and context that each participant brought to the encounters and would take away. The message was clear: "You take away what you have considered, accommodated and integrated."

Cornerstone: Encountering the Spirit of Christ in the Catholic School offers the same opportunity. The work is the invitation to think, feel and experience and, in the process, to ideally integrate and apply 'reflections, feelings and actions' in unique ways. The material itself holds no 'magic,' but in light of the Spirit, is another resource in support of service and communion within the Catholic school.

Come Holy Spirit,
fill the hearts of your faithful
and kindle in them the fire of your love.
Send forth your Spirit
and they shall be created.
And You shall renew the face of the earth.

O, God, who by the light of the Holy Spirit,
did instruct the hearts of the faithful,
grant that by the same Holy Spirit
we may be truly wise and ever enjoy His consolations,
Through Christ Our Lord.[145]

---

145 The Prayer Come Holy Spirit - Prayers - Catholic Online https://www.catholic.org/prayers/prayer.php?p=3269

REFERENCES

Abbott, W. (1966). *The documents of Vatican II*. New York: America Press.

Actuarial Eye (2016). *The latest statistics on public and private schools*. Retrieved from: http://www.actuarialeyecom/2016/02/07the-latest-statistics-on-public-and-private-schools

Amundson, N. E. (2003). *The physics of living*. British Columbia: Ergon Communications.

Anderson, M. & Coates, H. (March 2009). Balancing act: Challenges for educational leadership. *Professional Educator*, 8(1) 32-37.

Arbuckle, G. (2017). Building intentional faith communities in Catholic education: Understanding culture. Paper presented at the *Catholic Mission and Identity symposium: Honouring the Call to Prophetic Leadership in Catholic Education*. Broken Bay Institute: The Australian Institute of Theological Education, Brisbane, October 26.

Australian Bureau of Statistics (2017). *Schools, Australia 2016. Summary of findings*. Retrieved from: http://www.abs.gov.au/AUSSTATS/abs@.nsf/mf/4221.0.

Australian Curriculum, Assessment and Reporting Authority (2013). *Website data*. Retrieved from: https://www.australiancurriculum.edu.au/f-10-curriculum/general-capabilities.

Australian Episcopal Conference, (1970). *The renewal of the education of faith*. Sydney: E. J. Dwyer.

Australian Government Department of Education, Employment and Workplace Relations (2012). *Schools in Australia: report of the Interim Committee for the Australian Schools Commission, May 1973*. Retrieved from: http://apo.org.au/node/29669.

Australian Institute for Teaching and School Leadership (2014). *Website data*. Retrieved from: https://www.aitsl.edu.au.

Australian Qualifications Framework (2017). Retrieved from: *https://www.aqf.edu.au*.

Balasuriya, T. (1991). Right relationships: De-routeing and re-rooting of Christian theology. *Logos*, 30(3-4), 1-244.

Barron, R. (2016). Reflecting on the image of God. *Saint Anthony Messenger Press Newsletter*, 124(5) p. 32.

Bathersby, J. (2010). *Closing Address*. Launch of the Chair in Identity and Curriculum. Brisbane: Australian Catholic University.

Bays, B. (2006). *Freedom is: Liberating your boundless potential*. (Audio). London: Hodder and Stoughton Audio Books.

REFERENCES

Beckwirth, M. (2017) Interview. In, K. Noonan, *Heal: Change your mind, change your body, change your life* (DVD). Hillsboro, Oregon: Beyond Words.

Begley, P. T. (2006). Self-Knowledge, capacity and sensitivity: Prerequisites to authentic leadership by school principals. *Journal of Educational Administration*, 44(6), 570-589.

Begley, P. T. (2011). Leading with moral purpose: The place of ethics. In M. Preedy, N. Bennett & C. Wise (Eds.), *Educational Leadership: Context, Strategy and Collaboration*. Melbourne: Sage Publications Ltd.

Benjamin, A. (2002). Leaders in Catholic schools in the third millennium: Engaging with hope. In Duncan, D.J. & Riley, D. (2002). *Leadership in Catholic Education*. Sydney, N.S.W, Australia: Harper Collins Publishers.

Benjamin, R. (1999). *Catholic Education: An intervention statement to the Synod of Bishops for Oceania in Rome*. Rome: Vatican City.

Bennett, V. & Mathieson, I. (2002). *The effective leader: how to balance the mind, body and spirit at work and at home*. Australia: Harper Collins Publishers.

Bennis, W. & Nanus, B. (1985). *Leader strategies for taking charge*. New York: Harper & Row.

Bevans, S. (2009). The mission has a church: Thinking missiologically about ministry and the shortage of priests. *Compass, 3-15*.

Bevans, S. (2012). *Mission and prophetic dialogue*. Keynote address. Religious Formation Conference: Transformation of religious life. An Action Oriented Initiative.

Bevans, S. (2013). Partnering with the missionary God: A vision of mission today. *Mission: one heart many voices. A multi-sector celebration and dialogue of living and leading mission better*. Sydney, Australia: 29 April – 1 May.

Bishops of NSW & ACT. (2007). *Catholic schools at a crossroads*. Pastoral Letter. Bishops of NSW and ACT in association with Catholic Education Office, Sydney.

Boevre, L., & Bloechl, J. (1999). Sacramental considerations. Opening of Junior Scholar's Conference. Leuven encounters in systematic theology. *Sacramental presence in a postmodern context: Fundamental theological approaches*. 2nd International L.E.S.T – Conference, Nov. 3-6. Catholic University of Leuven, Belgium.

Boff, L. (1984). *Salvation and liberation*. New York: Maryknoll.

Bonhoeffer, D. (2003). *Dietrich Bonhoeffer works, volume 4*. Minneapolis: Fortress Press.

REFERENCES

Braden, G. (2017). *Human by design: from evolution by chance to transformation by choice.* Carlsbad, California: Hay House.

Braden, G. (2017a). Interview. In, K. Noonan Gores, *Heal: Change your mind, change your body, change your life.* (DVD). Hillsboro, Oregon: Beyond Words.

Braden, G. (2018). Science and spirituality co-operating for our new world. *Holistic Bliss.* 102, 20-21.

Braden, G., & Dispenza, J. (2014) *Get your shift together* (Vol. 2). (DVD). Seattle: Encephalon.

Bradley, Y. (1994). Working in the shadow: Machiavelli and biblical and secular leadership models. *Journal of Christian Education*, 37(1), 15–36.

Bradley, Y. (1999). Servant leadership: A critique of Robert Greenleaf's concept of leadership. *Journal of Christian Education*, 42(2), 43–54.

Branson, C., & Gross, S. (Eds.) (2014). *Ethical educational leadership.* New York: Routledge.

Branson, C., Marra, M. & Buchanan, M. (2019). Re-Constructing Catholic school leadership: Weaving together mission, identity and practice. *International Studies in Catholic Education*, in press.

Brennan, F. T. (2018). *Social cohesion or social division.* Panel discussion: Annual dinner, Australian Catholic University, Brisbane, May, 24.

Brennan, P. J. (1987). *The evangelizing parish: Theologies and strategies for renewal.* Allen, Texas: Tabor Publishing.

Briody, P.M., Ruddiman, W. & Doherty, J. (2003). *Not so distant voices: A brief history of the Catholic education office.* Toowoomba, Australia: Catholic Education Office.

Brogan, K. (2017). Interview. In, K. Noonan Gores, *Heal: Change your mind, change your body, change your life.* (DVD). Hillsboro, Oregon: Beyond Words.

Brown, A. (2017, October). The war against Pope Francis. *The Guardian.* www.thegurardian.com/news2017/October 27.

Brown, B. (2010). The gifts of imperfection: *Let go of who you think you're supposed to be and embrace who you are.* Centre City, Minnesota: Hazelden.

Brown, R. (1986). *The gospels.* Lecture Series (video production).

Buchanan, M.T., & Gellel, A. M (Eds.). G*lobal perspectives on Catholic religious education*, Volume 2. London: Springer.

REFERENCES

Buckingham, J. (2010). *The growth of religious schooling.* Retrieved from: http://www.abc.net.au.

Burford, C. (2017). *Leading self and leading communities.* Learning community professional development experience. Townsville, Queensland.

Burke, K. (2009). *Challenge, change faith: Catholic Australia and the Second Vatican Council.* Melbourne: Burke Family Trust.

Burns, J.M. (1978). *Leadership.* New York: Harper & Row.

Caldwell, B. J. (2006). *Re-imagining educational leadership.* Camberwell, Victoria: ACER Press.

Campion, E. (1987). *Australian Catholics: The contribution of Catholics to the development of Australian society.* Middlesex: Penguin.

Canavan, K. (1999). The mission of the Catholic school. *Bulletin 50.* Sydney: Catholic Education Office.

Cannato, J. (2006). *Radical amazement.* Notre Dame, Indiana: Sorin Books.

Canon Law Society of Great Britain and Ireland. (1983). *The Code of Canon Law.* London: Collins.

Catechism of the Catholic Church. (1994). Homebush, N.S.W.: St Pauls Publications.

Cattaro, G. (2017). Encountering leadership making the word flesh: Creating a culture of dialogue. Catholic leadership: *Inspiring leaders in a globalised 21st century Melbourne symposium.* Australian Catholic University.

Celli, C. (2011). Keynote Address. Being effective communicators and carriers of Christ in a digital culture. *Inspiration and Identity, National Catholic Education Convention.* Adelaide, South Australia.

Chaput, C. (2001). *Living the Catholic faith: Rediscovering the basics.* Cincinatti, Ohio: St. Anthony Messenger Press.

Chittister, J. (2003). *Twelve steps to inner freedom: Humility revisited.* Erie, PA: Benetvision.

Chopra, D. (2015). The stillness is you: Whispering the mystery. In G. Malkin, *Wisdom Films: Contemplative Media for Human being.* www.wisdomoftheworld.com.

Chopra, D. (2017). Interview. In, K. Noonan Gores, *Heal: Change your mind, change your body, change your life.* (DVD). Hillsboro, Oregon: Beyond Words.

Chopra, D. (2018). AZ Quotes. Retrieved from: http://azquotes.com/author/deepak chopra

REFERENCES

Chopra, D., & Tanzi, R. (2018). *The healing self: Supercharge your immune system and stay well for life.* London: Rider.

Clarke, M (2014). *Envisioning the future of religious life as a pioneer community.* Indianapolis, IN: Community Works Inc.

Clarke, M (2015). *Spiritual leadership for the pioneer community.* Indianapolis, IN: Community Works Inc.

Clarke, M (2016). *Discerning a future based on a smaller community.* Indianapolis, IN: Community Works Inc.

Coleridge, M. (2008). The word of God as vital source for preaching. *In the new evangelisation: Developing evangelical teaching.* J. Porteous (Ed). Proceedings of the Third Colloquium on the New Evangelisation. Ballan, Victoria: Connor Court Publishing.

Coleridge, M. (2017). Claiming the call to prophetic leadership. In, *Catholic Mission and Identity Symposium: Honouring the Call to Prophetic Leadership in Catholic Education.* Broken Bay Institute: The Australian Institute of Theological Education, Brisbane, October 26.

Coleridge, M. (2018). *Leadership and governance.* Video address to Principals of Catholic schools. Archdiocese of Brisbane.

Coleridge, M. (2018a). *Social cohesion or social division.* Panel discussion: Annual dinner, Australian Catholic University, Brisbane, May, 24.

Collins, J. (2001). *Good to Great.* (CD). London: Harper Collins.

Congregation for Catholic Education. (1977). *The Catholic school.* Homebush, N.S.W.: St Paul Publications.

Congregation for Catholic Education. (1982). *Lay Catholics in schools: Witnesses to faith.* Homebush, N.S.W.: St Paul Publications.

Congregation for Catholic Education. (1988). *The religious dimension of education in a Catholic school: Guidelines for reflection and renewal.* Homebush, N.S.W.: St Paul Publications.

Congregation for Catholic Education. (1998). *The Catholic school on the threshold of the third millennium.* Homebush, N.S.W.: St Paul Publications.

Congregation for Catholic Education. (2007). *Educating together in Catholic schools: A shared mission between consecrated persons and the lay faithful.* Homebush, N.S.W.: St Paul Publications.

REFERENCES

Congregation for Catholic Education. (2013). *Educating to intercultural dialogue in Catholic schools: Living in harmony for a civilization of love.* Rome: Vatican City.

Congregation for Catholic Education. (2017). *Educating to fraternal humanism: Building a civilization of love 50 years after Populorum Progressio.* Rome: Vatican City.

Convey, J.J. (2012). Perceptions on Catholic identity: Views of Catholic school administrators and teachers. Catholic Education: *A Journal of Inquiry and Practice,* 16(1), 187-214.

Cook, T. J. (2015). *Charism and culture: Cultivating Catholic identity in Catholic schools.* Arlington, VA: National Catholic Education Association.

Cooke, B. (1983). *Sacraments and sacramentality.* Connecticut: Twenty Third Publications.

Council for the Australian Federation. (2007). *The future of schooling in Australia.* Victoria: Department of Education.

Covey, S. (1989). *The 7 habits of highly effective people.* Melbourne: The Business Library.

Covey, S. (1992). *Principle centred leadership.* Audio collection. London: Simon & Schuster.

Craven, G. (2018). *Social cohesion or social division.* Panel discussion: Annual dinner, Australian Catholic University, Brisbane, May, 24.

Croke, B. (2007). Australian Catholic schools in a changing political and religious landscape. In G. R. Grace & J. M. O'Keefe, (Eds). (2007). *International handbook of Catholic education: Challenges for school systems in the 21st century. Parts one and two.* The Netherlands: Sprenger.

Crowther, F. (1999). *Parallel leadership.* Address, Annual General Meeting, Australian College of Education. Toowoomba, Queensland. Darling Downs Chapter.

Crowther, F. (2001). *The teaching profession: The dawn of a new era.* G.W. Bassett Memorial Oration. Brisbane. Australian College of Education, Queensland Chapter.

Crowther, F., Kaagan, S. S., Ferguson, M., & Hann, L. (2002). *Developing teacher leaders: How teacher leadership enhances school success.* Thousand Oaks California: Corwin Press.

Curti, E. (2009). More than the material world. *The Tablet,* July, 10-11.

REFERENCES

Deal, T. E. & Kennedy, A. A. (Eds). (1984). *Corporate cultures: The rites and rituals of corporate life*. California: Addison-Wesley.

Delio, I. (2011). *The emergent Christ: Exploring the meaning of Catholic in an evolutionary universe.* Maryknoll, New York: Orbis Books

Dempster, N. (2009). Leadership for learning: A framework for synthesizing research. *Edventures.* ACT: Australian College of Educators.

Dispenza, J. (2007). Evolve your brain. *The science of changing your mind.* (DVD). Sydney: Encephalon.

Dispenza, J. (2012) *Breaking the habit of being yourself: How to lose your mind and create a new one.* (CD). Sayed Alamy, Seattle, USA: Audio Books.

Dispenza, J. (2014). *Understanding the power of your mind:* Intensive workshop notes. New York: Encephalon.

Dispenza, J. (2015) *Meditations for breaking the habit of being yourself: How to lose your mind and create a new one.* New York: Hay House.

Dispenza, J. (2017). Interview. In, K. Noonan Gores, Heal: *Change your mind, change your body, and change your life.* (DVD). Hillsboro, Oregon: Beyond Words.

Dispenza, J. (2017a). *Becoming supernatural: How common people are doing the uncommon.* New York: Hay House.

Dixon, R. (2017). *Video address: The Australian church in 2030.* St Thomas More Forum, Campbell, A.C.T., on 26th April 2017. Retrieved from: http://www.catholica.com.au/forum/index.php?id=198247

Dixon, R. (2017a). *The Catholic community in Australia: A profile.* Retrieved from: http://catholicschoolsguide.com.au/catholic-education-featured-articles/faith-andspirituality/the-catholic-community-in-australia

Doidge, N. (2008). *The brain that changes itself.* Carlton North, Victoria: Scribe Publications.

Doidge, N. (2010). *The brain that changes itself.* (DVD). Canada: 90th Parallel Productions Ltd.

D'Orsa, J. & D'Orsa T. (1997). Reimagining Catholic school leadership for the third millennium. In R Keane & D. Riley, (Eds.). *Quality Catholic schools: Challenges for leadership as Catholic education approaches the third millennium.* Brisbane: Brisbane Catholic Education.

REFERENCES

D'Orsa, J. & D'Orsa, T. (2010). *Explorers, guides and meaning-makers: Mission theology for Catholic educators*. The Broken Bay Institute Mission and Education Series. Mulgrave, Victoria: John Garratt Publishing.

D'Orsa, J. & D'Orsa T. (2013). *Leading for mission: Integrating life, culture and faith in Catholic education*. Mulgrave, Victoria: Vaughan Publishing.

Dreyer, E. (1996). Spirituality more easily found in the world than in churches. *National Catholic Reporter*, 9-11.

Dreyer, E. (1998). Earth crammed with heaven: An everyday spirituality, *Conference*, 15(2), 1-10.

Drucker, P. (1997). Leadership challenges today. *Management*. July.

Drucker, P. (1998). How to prosper in the new economy. *Forbes Global Business Finance*. October, 52-63.

Dubrin, A. J. & Dalglish, C. (2003). Leadership an Australasian Focus. Sydney, Australia: John Wiley & Sons.

Duchesne, S., McMaugh, A., Bochner, S.; & Krause, K. L. (2013). *Educational psychology for learning and teaching* (4th Ed.). South Melbourne, Victoria: Cengage Learning Australia.

Duignan, P. (1987). Leaders as culture builders. *Unicorn*, 13, 208-213.

Duignan, P. (1998). *Leadership*. Opening address at the International Working Seminar and Inter Visitation Program for Catholic leaders. Sydney, Australian Catholic University.

Duignan, P. (2002). *The Catholic educational leader: Defining authentic leadership; caritas, veritas, gravitas*. The vision and the reality: Issues and challenges facing Catholic educational leadership. Sydney, Australia.

Duignan, P. (2007). *Leadership* Keynote Address. The fourth international conference on Catholic educational leadership. Australian Catholic University, Flagship for Creative and Authentic Leadership. Sydney, 29–31 August.

Dulles, A. (1985). *Vatican II and the extraordinary synod*. Collegeville, Minnesota: The Liturgical Press.

Duncan, D. J. (1990). The preparation for leaders of Catholic education. In M. McMahon, H. Neidhart, J. Chapman, A. Lawrence, & L. Angus. *Leadership in Catholic Education*. Melbourne: Spectrum Publications.

Durka, G. (2002). *The teacher's calling: A spirituality for those who teach*. New Jersey: Paulist Press.

REFERENCES

Dyer, W. W. (1995). *Your sacred self: Making the decision to be free.* Pymble, N.S.W.: Harper-Collins Audio Books.

Dyer, W. W. (2004). *The power of intention: Learning to co-create your world your way.* Carlsbad, California: Hay House Publications.

Dyer, W. W. (2005). *Staying on the path.* (CD). New York: Hay House Publications.

Dyer, W. W. (2006). *Your life begins now.* (CD). Carlsbad, California. Hay House Publications.

Dyer, W. W. (2007). *Change your thoughts – change your life: Living the wisdom of the Tao.* New York: Hay House Publications.

Dyer, W. W. (2009). *Tales of everyday magic: My greatest teacher.* (DVD). www.hayhouse.com. Hay House Publications.

Dyer, W. W. (2010). *Excuses be-gone. How to change lifelong self-defeating thinking habits.* Carlsbad, California: Hay House Publications.

Dyer, W. W. (2014). *I can see clearly now.* (DVD). www.hayhouse.com. Hay House Publications.

Dyer, W. W. (2018). *Quality control for your head.* Retrieved from: https:wwwdrwaynedyer.com/blog/tag/memes.

Dyer, W. W. & Hicks, E. (2014). *Co-creating at its best: A conversation between master teachers.* (DVD). Carlsbad, California: Hay House Publications.

Edmund Rice International (2016). *Walking the human story.* Geneva: Congregation of Christian Brothers.

Edwards, D. (1987). *Called to be church in Australia.* Homebush, N.S.W.: St Paul Publications.

Edwards, D. (1990). Can every member be a leader: Theological reflections on Christian leadership. In, G. Everett, W. F. Sultmann, & K. Treston (Eds). *Called to serve: Reflecting and visioning about contemporary Christian leadership.* Brisbane, Brisbane Catholic Education.

Edwards, D. (1995). *Jesus the wisdom of God.* Homebush, N.S.W.: St Paul Publications.

Edwards, D. (2011). *The Holy Spirit: Giver of life.* National eConference, Broken Bay Institute. Retrieved from: http:// holyspirit.vividas.com.

Elliott, M. & Rush, K. (2011). *The new religion curriculum: Strategic plan 2011-2015.* Brisbane, Australia: Catholic Archdiocese of Brisbane.

REFERENCES

Fagan, S. (1976). Sacraments today. *Doctrine and life*, 26(4), 264–70.

Faggioli, M. (2017). From Vatican II to post Vatican Catholicism. In, Lecture Series. *Leading for mission and Catholic identity: Insights from Vatican II*. Sydney, Australia. Broken Bay Institute: The Australian Institute of Theological Education.

Faggioli, M. (2017a). Principles of Catholic ecclesiology for mission and identity. From Vatican II to post Vatican Catholicism. In, Lecture Series. *Leading for mission and Catholic identity: Insights from Vatican II*. Sydney, Australia. Broken Bay Institute: The Australian Institute of Theological Education.

Faggioli, M. (2017b). What and who is 'Catholic laity' in the church and world of today. In, Lecture Series. *Leading for mission and Catholic identity: Insights from Vatican II*. Sydney, Australia. Broken Bay Institute: The Australian Institute of Theological Education.

Faggioli, M. (2018). History of ecclesiology of church communities. In, Lecture Series. *Leading ecclesial communities*. Brisbane, Australia. Broken Bay Institute: The Australian Institute of Theological Education.

Faggioli, M. (2018a). Ecclesiology of Catholic communities. In, Lecture Series. *Leading ecclesial communities*. Brisbane, Australia. Broken Bay Institute: The Australian Institute of Theological Education.

Faggioli, M. (2018b). The recent ecclesial past and its effect on the ecclesiology of Vatican II. In, Lecture Series. *Leading ecclesial communities*. Brisbane, Australia. Broken Bay Institute: The Australian Institute of Theological Education.

Feeney, J. J. (1997). Can a worldview be healed? Students and postmodernism. *America*, 177 (15), 12-16.

Fisher, A. (2006). *Purposes of Catholic secondary schools today*. Catholic Secondary Schools Association of N.S.W. Sydney, Australia: Catholic Education Office.

Fitzgerald, P. (1990). The Leader of the Catholic school community: reflections on the primary documents. In M. McMahon, H. Neidhart, J. Chapman J., A. Lawrence, and L. Angus. *Leadership in Catholic Education*. Melbourne: Spectrum Publications.

Flynn, M. (1985). *The effectiveness of Catholic schools*. Sydney: St Paul Publications.

Flynn, M. (1989). The culture of Catholic schools. *Catholic School Studies*. 62(2), 22–29.

Foley, G., & Schmaltz, T. (1987). *Connecting faith and life: Holiness of ordinary life*. Kansas City: Sheed & Ward.

REFERENCES

Forman, C. (2018). *An interview with Colbey Forman.* Retrieved from www.beurin university.org.

Forrestor, K. G. T. (2018). *Christianity as a nondual spiritual path.* Retrieved from: https://progressingspirit.com/2018/04/05/christianity-as-a-nondual-spiritual-path/

Fox, Z. (2011). On sacred ground: lay leadership. Conference, *Lay leaders of Catholic institutions serving the church and the world.* Seton Hall University. September 21st.

Freeman, L. (2010). *What is contemplative prayer?* (CD). Keynote Address. Pray 2010. Brisbane: Catholic Archdiocese of Brisbane.

Freire, P. (1998). *Pedagogy of the oppressed.* New York: Continuum.

Fullan, M. (2008). *What's worth fighting for in the principalship (2nd Ed.).* Columbia University, New York: Teachers College Press.

Fullan, M. (2014). *The principal: Three keys to maximizing impact.* San Francisco, California: Jossey-Bass.

Gellel, A. M. (2018). Re-thinking Catholic religious education. In M. T. Buchanan & A. M. Gellel, (Eds.). *Global Perspectives on Catholic Religious Education Volume II: Learning and Leading in a Pluralist World.* Netherlands: Springer Press.

Gillard, J. (Nov 2008). *Leading Transformational Change in Schools.* Keynote Address. Melbourne, Australia: Department of Education, Employment and Workplace Relations.

Gillard, J. (Oct 2009). *Valuing the future: building skills for recovery.* Address to the Per Capita annual conference. Canberra, Australia: Department of Education, Employment and Workplace Relations.

Gittins, A. J. (1994). Missionary myth making. In J. A Scherer & S. B. (Eds.). *New directions in mission and evangelisation 2.* Maryknoll, New York: Orbis Books.

Gleeson, G. (2017). *Identity and curriculum in Catholic education.* Summary Report. Australian Catholic University.

Gleeson, J., Goldburg, P., O'Gorman, J., & O'Neill, M. (2018). Characteristics of Catholic schools as seen by teachers in the USA and Queensland, Australia. *Journal of Catholic Education.*

REFERENCES

Goldburg, P. (2018). *Pedagogical content knowledge: A missing piece in the puzzle that is Religious Education in Catholic schools*. In M. T. Buchanan & A. M. Gellel, (Eds.). Global Perspectives on Catholic Religious Education Volume II: Learning and Leading in a Pluralist World. Netherlands: Springer Press.

Goleman, D. (December 2013). The big idea: The focused leader. *Harvard Business Review*, 50-60.

Good News Bible. (1978). New York: American Bible Society.

Gonski, D. (2018). *Through growth to achievement. Report of the review to achieve educational excellence in Australian schools*. Canberra: Australian Government Department of Education and Training.

Gowdie, J. (2009). *Catching fire staff with Spirit: Spiritual formation framework for the mission of Catholic education*. Brisbane: Brisbane Catholic Education.

Gowdie, J. (2017). *Stirring the soul of Catholic education: Formation for mission*. Mulgrave, Victoria: Vaughan Publishing.

Gowdie, J. (2017a). Formation and Leadership. In, *Catholic mission and identity symposium: Honouring the call to prophetic leadership in Catholic education*. Broken Bay Institute: The Australian Institute of Theological Education, Brisbane, October 26.

Grace, G. (1997). *School Leadership: Beyond education management an essay* in policy scholarship. London: Falmer Press.

Grace, G. (2010). Renewing spiritual capital: an urgent priority for the future of Catholic education internationally. *International Studies in Catholic Education*, 2(2), 117-128.

Grace, G. R., & O'Keefe, J. M. (Eds). (2007). Catholic Schools Facing the Challenges of the 21st Century: An Overview. *International Handbook of Catholic Education: Challenges for School Systems in the 21st Century. Parts One and Two*. The Netherlands: Springer.

Greenfield, S. (2000). *Brain story: Unlocking our inner world of emotions, memories, ideas and desires*. London: BBC Worldwide Ltd.

Greenleaf, R. K. (1977). *Servant leadership*. New York: Paulist Press.

Greenleaf, R. K. (1998). *The power of servant leadership*. San Francisco: Berrett-Koehler Publishers.

Gregory, B. (2003). Viewing the Church as a communio three challenges. *Origins*, 33(4), 410–13.

Grenyer, B. (2018). *Newsletter*. Issue 22. Psychology Board of Australia.

REFERENCES

Grocholewski, Z., & Brugues, J. L. (2009). *Circular*. Rome: Congregation for Catholic Education.

Groome, T. H. (1980). *Christian religious education: Sharing our story and vision*. San Francisco, United States of America: Harper and Row Publishers.

Groome, T. H. (1996). What makes a school Catholic? In T. McLaughlin, J. O'Keefe & B. O'Keefe, (Eds.). *The contemporary Catholic school: Context, identity and diversity*. London: Falmer Press.

Groome, T. H. (1998). *Sharing faith: A comprehensive approach to religious education and pastoral ministry. The way of shared praxis*. Oregon: Wipf and Stock Publishers.

Groome, T. H. (2006). Bringing life to faith and faith to life: for a shared Christian praxis approach and against a detractor. *Compass*, 40, 17–24.

Groome, T. H. (2018). *Catholic Religious Education: Educating for faith*. In M. T. Buchanan and A. M. Gellel, (Eds.). *Global Perspectives on Catholic Religious Education Volume II: Learning and Leading in a Pluralist World*. Netherlands: Springer Press.

Habermas, J. (1984). *The theory of communicative action: The critique of functionalist reason*. Vol. 1 and 2. Boston. USA: Beacon Press.

Hahnenberg, E. P. (2014). *Theology for ministry. An introduction for lay ministers*. Collegeville, Minnesota: Liturgical Press.

Hall, D. & Sultmann, W. F. (2018). Formation for mission: A systems model for advancing the formation of the religious educator within an Australian context. In M. T. Buchanan and A. M. Gellel, (Eds.). *Global Perspectives on Catholic Religious Education Volume II: Learning and Leading in a Pluralist World*. Netherlands: Springer Press.

Hall, D., Sultmann, W.F., & Townend, G. (2018). *Constants in Context: An examination of magisterium documents on Catholic schools in the conciliar and post-conciliar period*. Sydney: Research Report 2. La Salle Publications. Australian Catholic University.

Hamilton, D. (2017).Interview. In, K. Noonan Gores, Heal: *Change your mind, change your body, change your life*. (DVD). Hillsboro, Oregon: Beyond Words.

Harpaz, Y. (2005), Teaching and learning in a thinking community. *Journal of Curriculum and Supervision*, 2(2), 136-157.

Harvey, S. (2014). *The connection: Mind and body*. Elemental Media. www.theconnection.tv.

REFERENCES

Haslam, A. S., Reicher, S. D. & Platow, M. J. (2012). The new psychology of leadership: Identity, influence and power. *Administrative Science Quarterly*, 56(3) 477-479.

Hersey, P. & Blanchard, K. (1982). *Management of organisational behaviour: Utilising human resources.* (4th Ed). New Jersey: Prentice Hall.

Hicks, E. & Hicks, J. (2007). *The teachings of Abraham: The law of attraction in a ction.* New York: Hay House Publications.

Hindmarsh, P. (2017). RE as the heartbeat of the whole curriculum: RE transcends RE. In, *Catholic mission and identity symposium: Honouring the call to prophetic leadership in Catholic education.* Broken Bay Institute: The Australian Institute of Theological Education, Brisbane, October 26.

Hirst, E., Renshaw, P. & Brown, R. (2009). A teacher's repertoire of practice in a multi-ethnic classroom: The physicality and politics of difference. In M. Cesar & K. Kumpulainen (Eds), *Social interactions in multicultural settings*, 329–48. Rotterdam, The Netherlands: Sense Publishers.

Hock, D. (1999). *Birth of the chaordic Age.* San Francisco: Berrett-Koehler Publishers.

Hodgens, E. (2008). New Evangelisation in the 21st Century. Voices. *Quarterly essays on religion in Australia.* Vol 1, No 3. Mulgrave, Victoria: John Garratt Publishing,

Holohan, G. (1999). *Religious education in Catholic schools.* Canberra: National Catholic Education Commission.

Holohan, G. (2009). *Evangelisation.* Keynote Address. Meeting of Directors. Sydney, Australia: National Catholic Education Commission.

Hughes, G.W. (1994). *God of surprises.* London: Darton, Longman & Todd.

Hunt, D. (1991). *The renewal of personal energy.* Toronto: OISE Press.

Independent Schools Council of Australia (2016). Socio-Economic Profile of Schools. *Independent Update*, Issue 7.

Jackley, J. (2015). *Clay, Water, Brick: Finding inspiration from entrepreneurs who do the most with the least.* New York: Spiegel & Grau Random House.

Jackson, R. (2018). *Teaching about religious diversity: Policy and practice from the Council of Europe.* In M. T. Buchanan & A. M. Gellel, (Eds.). *Global Perspectives on Catholic Religious Education Volume II: Learning and Leading in a Pluralist World.* Netherlands: Springer Press.

REFERENCES

James, S. (2017). *Psychoneuroimmunology: What every psychologist should know about the mind body connection.* Australian Psychological Society Workshop, June 17, North Coast Branch, Queensland Australia.

Johnson, E. (2003). *Consider Jesus: Waves of renewal in Christology.* (CD). Cincinatti, OH: Franciscan Media.

Kasper, W. (1989). *Theology and Church.* New York: Crossroad.

Kelly, G. B; & Godsey, J. D. (Eds.). (2003). *Dietrich Bonhoeffer works, volume 4.* Minneapolis: Fortress Press.

Kelly, P. (2017). A new secularism thrashes tradition. *Weekend Australian*, April 15-16.

Kelly, T. (1993). *An expanding theology: Faith in a world of connections.* Newtown, Sydney: E. J. Dwyer.

Kennedy, J., Mulholland, J, & Dorman, J. (2010). *Queensland Catholic education commission consultancy project.* An investigation of the issues that affect the decisions of Catholic families in low socio-economic circumstances in Queensland when choosing schools for their children. Banyo, Brisbane: Australian Catholic University.

Kleinman, P. (2012). Psych 101: *Psychology facts, basics, statistics, tests and more.* Avon, Massachusetts: Adams Media.

Komonchak, J. (1987). The church: God's gift and our task. *Origins*, 16(42), 735–41.

Komonchak, J. (2001). The Church: God's gift and our task. In, *Perspectives on leadership and catechesis.* R. I. Colbert & J. A. Krauss (Eds.). Arlington, Virginia: National Catholic Education Association.

Kouzes, J. M. & Posner, B. Z. (2003). *A leadership challenge resource.* San Francisco, CA: Pfeiffer.

Lane, D. A. (2015). *Catholic education in the light of Vatican II and laudato si.* Dublin, Ireland: Veritas.

Larkins, G. & Weatherill, M. (2018). *An examination of how the Enhancing Catholic SchoolIdentityProject(ECSIP)isimpactingonreligiouseducation, curriculum and pedagogy in the Catholic diocese of Sandhurst.* In M. T. Buchanan & A. M. Gellel, (Eds.). *Global Perspectives on Catholic Religious Education Volume II: Learning and Leading in a Pluralist World.* Netherlands: Springer Press.

Lennan, R. (2001). *The nature of Church.* Keynote lecture. Diocesan Assembly, Diocese of Toowoomba, Australia.

REFERENCES

Lennan, R. (2018). Locating the church. In, Lecture Series. *Leading ecclesial communities*. Brisbane, Australia. Broken Bay Institute: The Australian Institute of Theological Education.

Lennan, R. (2018a). Mission and the life of the church. In, Lecture Series. *Leading ecclesial communities*. Brisbane, Australia. Broken Bay Institute: The Australian Institute of Theological Education.

Lennan, R. (2018b). Ministry in the church. In, Lecture Series. *Leading ecclesial communities*. Brisbane, Australia. Broken Bay Institute: The Australian Institute of Theological Education.

Leximancer Manual (2017). Retrieved from: *https://www.leximancer.com. Version 2.23*.

Lhundrup, T. (2006). *Practical meditation with Buddhist principles*. (DVD). China: Hinkler Books.

Lipton, B. (2016). *The biology of belief*. (10th Ed). New York: Hay House.

Lipton, B. (2017). Interview. In, K. Noonan Gores, *Heal: Change your mind, change your body, change your life*. (DVD). Hillsboro, Oregon: Beyond Words.

Livingstone, T. (2017). Controversial reforms of Pope Francis may destroy him. *Weekend Australian*, April 20.

Lovat, T. (2018). *Theological underpinnings of Catholic Religious Education: A role for public theology and a case instance concerning Islam*. In M. T. Buchanan & A. M. Gellel, (Eds.). *Global Perspectives on Catholic Religious Education Volume II: Learning and Leading in a Pluralist World*. Netherlands: Springer Press.

Lucchetti-Bingemer, M. C. (2001). Sacramentality and the poor. Leuven encounters in systematic theology. *Sacramental presence in a postmodern context: Fundamental theological approaches*. 2nd International L.E.S.T–Conference, Nov. 3-6. Catholic University of Leuven, Belgium.

Maddix, M. A. & Estep, J. R. (2017). *Practicing Christian education: An introduction for ministry*. Grand Rapids Michigan: Baker Academic.

Maher, A. (2017). The journey to Vatican II and movements beyond. In, Lecture Series. *Leading for mission and Catholic identity: Insights from Vatican II*. Sydney, Australia. Broken Bay Institute: The Australian Institute of Theological Education.

Maher, A. (2017a). Mission and Catholic identity for contemporary institutions. Lecture Series. *Leading for mission and Catholic identity: Insights from Vatican II*. Sydney, Australia. Broken Bay Institute: The Australian Institute of Theological Education.

REFERENCES

Maher, A. (2017b). A 21st century incarnational spirituality: Envisioned for mission and identity in an Australian context. Lecture series. *Leading for mission and Catholic identity: Insights from Vatican II.* Sydney, Australia. Broken Bay Institute: The Australian Institute of Theological Education.

Mann, R. D. (1959). A review of the relationship between personality and performance. *Psychological Bulletin*, 56, 241-270.

Martin, J. (2009). *My life with the saints.* Cincinatti, Ohio: Franciscan Media.

Martos, J. (2009). *The sacraments: An interdisciplinary and interactive study.* Collegeville, Minnesota: Liturgical Press.

Mason, M., Singleton, A. & Webber, R. (2008). *The spirit of generation Y: Young people's spirituality in a changing Australia.* Mulgrave, Victoria: John Garratt Publishing.

McBrien, R. P. (1988). *Ministry: A theological pastoral handbook.* San Francisco: Harper & Row.

McDonald, (2016). *Trinity Sunday reflection.* Personal circulation of Scripture commentary within the Church's calendar for weekly Eucharistic worship.

McDonald, (2017). *Trinity Sunday reflection.* Personal circulation of Scripture commentary within the Church's calendar for weekly Eucharistic worship.

McElvee, J. (2017 October). Honest interviews: A pastoral risk. *National Catholic Reporter.* Retrieved from: Nconline.org/news/Vatican/new book Francis calls honest interviews – pastoral risk.

McGrath, A. (2018). *God, science and the human quest for meaning.* Keynote address: Dialogue Australia Network Conference, April 13-15. Sydney, Australia.

McKay, H. (2018). *Beyond belief: How we find meaning, with or without religion.* Keynote address: Dialogue Australia Network Conference, April 13-15. Sydney, Australia.

McKinney, M. B. (1987). *Sharing wisdom.* Chicago: Falcon Publications.

McLaughlin, G. D. (2000). (Ed.) *The purpose and nature of catholic education.* Canberra, Australian Catholic Commission for Industrial Relations.

McLay, A., Coghlan, D., Corkeron, P., & Druery, A. (1979). *Project Catholic School.* Brisbane, Queensland: Queensland Catholic Education Office.

REFERENCES

McLay, A., Druery, A., Murphy, M., & Shaw, F. (1982). *A tree by the waterside: A practical guide for building community in Catholic Education.* Brisbane, Queensland: Queensland Catholic Education Office.

Merton, T. (1975). *The Asian journal of Thomas Merton.* New York: New Directions.

Miller, J.M. (2007 video recording). *Directions for Catholic educational leadership in the 21st century.* The Fourth International Conference on Catholic Educational Leadership. Sydney Australia: ACU National.

Miller, M. (2010). *The Holy See's teaching on Catholic schools.* Strathfield, N.S.W: St Paul's Publications.

Ministerial Council on Education, Employment, Training and Youth Affairs (MCEETYA) (2008). *Melbourne declaration on educational goals for young Australians.* Retrieved from: http://www.curriculum.edu.au/verve/_resources/National_Declaration_on_the_Educational_Goals_for_Young_Australians.pdf on 23 July 2017.

Moore, T. (1994). *Care of the soul: A guide for cultivating depth and sacredness in everyday life.* New York: Harper Perennial.

Moore, T. (2008). Foreword. In H. Nouwen, *Out of solitude: Three meditations on the christian life.* Notre Dame, Indiana: Ave Maria Press.

Moran, G. (1991). Understanding religion and being religious. *Professional Approaches for Religious Educators*, 22, 249-252.

Morwood, M. (1997). T*omorow's Catholic: Understanding God and Jesus in the new millennium.* Melbourne: Spectrum Publications.

Morwood, M. (2007). *From sand to solid ground: Questions of faith for modern Catholics.* New York: Crossroad Publishing.

Moses, G. & Lizzio, J. (2011). *The four pillars of stewardship.* Induction of New Teachers and Pastoral Workers Seminar. Cairns, Australia: Catholic Diocese of Cairns.

Mulford, B. (2007). *An overview of research on Australian educational leadership 2001–2005.* Winmalee, N.S.W: Australian Council for Educational Leaders.

Myss, C. (2001). *Anatomy of the spirit.* (CD). Boulder Colorado: Sounds True Audio.

Myss, C. (2017). *Choices that can change your life.* TEDx Findhorn Salon.

National Catholic Education Commission (2015). *Annual report.* Retrieved from: http://www.ncec.catholic.edu.au/resources/publications/424-2015-annual-report/file.

REFERENCES

National Catholic Education Commission (2016). *Annual report*. Retrieved from: *http://www.ncec.catholic.edu.au/resources/publications/460-2016-annual-report/file*

National Catholic Education Commission (2016a). *Catholic schools in Australia*. Retrieved from: *http://www.ncec.catholic.edu.au/resources/publication/401-catholic-schools-in-australia-2016/file*.

National Catholic Education Commission (2017). *A framework for formation for mission in Catholic education*. Retrieved from: *https://www.ncec.catholic.edu.au/images/stories/documents/AFramework4Formation.pdf*.

National Catholic Education Commission (2017a). *Home - preamble*. Retrieved from: http://www.ncec.catholic.edu.au/index.php?option=com_contentandview=articleandid=16.

National Catholic Education Commission (2018). *Framing paper: Religious education in Australian Catholic schools*. Canberra: National Catholic Education Commission.

Neidhart, H. (1997). Spirituality and the ministry of leadership-icing or leaven? *Catholic School Studies*, 70(1), 20-22.

Neidhart, H.,& Lamb, J. (2016). Australian catholic schools today: School identity and leadership formation. *Journal of Catholic Education*, 19(3), 49-65.

Newbigin, L. (1994). The Logic of Mission. In J. A Scherer & S. B. (Eds.), *New Directions in Mission and Evangelization 2*. Maryknoll, New York: Orbis Books.

Nolan, A. (1987). *Jesus before Christianity*. London: Darton Longman & Todd.

Nolan, A. (2006). *Jesus Today: A spirituality of radical freedom*. Cape Town: Creda Communications.

Noonan Gores, K. (2017). *Heal: Change your mind, change your body, change your life*. (CD). Hillsboro, Oregon: Beyond Words.

Nouwen, H. (1991). *In the name of Jesus: Reflections on Christian leadership*. New York: Crossroad Publishing.

O'Donohue, J. (1997). *The divine imagination*. [Audio Tape] Series: Sounds True.

O'Leary, D. J. (2008). *Already within: Divining the hidden spring*. Blackrock, Dublin: Columbia Press.

O'Loughlin, F. (2007). The new evangelisation of the twenty-first century. *Australian Catholic Record*, 84(4), 401–13.

REFERENCES

O'Murchu, D. (1995). *The kingdom dimension*. Disarming Times. London: Mercier Press.

O'Shea, G. (2017). Confronting dualism in religious education. *Journal of Religious Education*, 64, 197-206.

Pagola, J. A. (2011). *Jesus: An Historical Approximation*. Miami, Florida: Convivium Press.

Pascoe, S. (2007). Challenges for Catholic education in Australia. In G. R. Grace & J. M. O'Keefe, (Eds). (2007). *International handbook of Catholic education: Challenges for school systems in the 21st century. Parts one and two*. The Netherlands: Sprenger.

Pell, G. (2007). Religion and culture: Catholic schools in Australia. In G. R. Grace and J. M. O'Keefe, (Eds). (2007). *International handbook of Catholic Education: Challenges for school systems in the 21st Century*. Parts One and Two. The Netherlands: Sprenger.

Pencak, S. (2018). Leadership myths de-bunked. *Leadership Breakthrough*. Retrieved from: https://silviapencak.com/top-ledership-myths-debunked.

Perry, L. (2018). *Social cohesion or social division*. Panel discussion: Annual dinner, Australian Catholic University, Brisbane, May, 24.

Pich, D. (August, 2017). The leadership road less travelled. *Leadership Matters*, 29-31.

Pich, D. (May, 2018). The shift to the intentional leader. *Leadership Matters*, 23.

Pivonka, D. & Poyo R. (2014). *Encounter Jesus: From discovery to discipleship*. (CD). Cincinatti, OH: Franciscan Media.

Pollefeyt, D. (2011). Keynote address. Assessing and enhancing Catholic school identity. *Inspiration and Identity, National Catholic Education Convention*. Adelaide, South Australia.

Pollefeyt, D. & Bouwens, J. (2010). Framing the identity of Catholic schools: Empirical methodology for quantitative research on the Catholic identity of an education institute. *International Studies in Catholic Education*, 2(2), 193-211.

Pontifical Council for the Family. (1995). *Truth and meaning of human sexuality*. Rome: Vatican Press.

Pope Benedict XVI (April 2008). *Meeting with Catholic educators*. Washington DC: Catholic University of America.

REFERENCES

Pope Benedict XVI (October 2009). *Pope encourages personal relationship with Christ*. Retrieved from: http://www.zenit.org/article-27296?l=english.

Pope Francis (2013). Address of Pope Francis. Apostolic journey to Rio De-Janeiro on the occasion of the XXVIII World Youth Day. Meeting with the bishops of Brazil (28 July). Retrieved from: https://w2.vatican.va/content/francesco/en/speeches/2013/july/documents/papa-francesco_20130727_gmg-episcopato-brasile.html.

Pope Francis (2014). *Address of Pope Francis to participants in the plenary session of the Congregation for Catholic Education*. Retrieved from: https://w2.vatican.va/content/francesco/en/speeches/2014/february.

Pope Francis (2015). *Homily preached at the daily mass at Casa Santa Marta*. Retrieved from: https://w2.vatican.va/content/francesco/en/cotidie/2015/documents/papa-francesco-cotidie_20151106_to-serve-not-to-be-served.html.

Pope Francis (2017). *Catholic schools and universities make a great contribution to the mission of the Church when they are at the service of growth in humanity, in dialogue and in hope*. Address of Pope Francis to Congregation for Catholic Education. Retrieved from: https://zenit.org/articles/popes-address-to-congregation-for-catholic-education.

Pope Francis. (2017a). Pope's address. *Audience with the participants in the plenary of the pontifical council for promoting new evangelisation (29 September)*. Vatican Apostolic Palace.

Pope Francis (2018). *Happiness in this life: A passionate meditation on material existence and the meaning of life*. Natalie Benazzi (Ed). London: Bluebird.

Pope John Paul II. (1979). *Redeemer of humankind*. Homebush, N.S.W.: St Paul Publications.

Pope John Paul II (1984). *Address to Catholic educators*. September 17. Rome: Vatican City.

Pope John Paul II. (1986). Address to parents, teachers and students of the federation of institutes of education activities on the role of the Catholic school in modern society'. *The Pope Speaks*, 30, 4.

Pope John Paul II. (1987). *On social concern*. Homebush, N.S.W.: St Paul Publications.

Pope John Paul II. (1991). *The vocation and the mission of the lay faithful in the church and in the modern world*. Rome: Vatican City.

Pope John Paul II. (1996). *Agenda for the third millennium*. London: Harper-Collins.

REFERENCES

Pope John Paul II. (Nov. 2001). *Ecclesia in Oceania: Post-synodal apostolic exhortation*. Homebush, N.S.W.: St Paul Publications.

Pope John Paul II. (April 7, 2005). A magnificent mission. *The Courier Mail, 16 page commemorative tribute*.

Pope John XXIII. (1962). Apostolic Exhortation *Sacrae Laudis* of the Second Ecumenical Vatican Council. Rome: Vatican City.

Pope Paul VI. (1967). *Encyclical letter Populorum Progressio*. Rome: Vatican City.

Pope Paul VI. (1975). *Apostolic exhortation evangelii nuntiandi, on evangelisation in the modern world*. Homebush, N.S.W.: St Paul Publications.

Pope Pius XI. (1929). *Divini illius magistre* (christian education of youth). Official Vatican Text, Derby, New York: Daughters of St Paul.

Pope Pius XI. (1931). *Quadragesimo anno*. Rome: Vatican City.

Population Reference Bureau (2005). *The changing demographics of Roman Catholics*. Retrieved from: http://www.prb.org/Publications/Articles/2005/TheChangingDemographicsofRomanCatholics.aspx.

Porteous, J. (2008). (Ed.). *The new evangelisation: Developing evangelical preaching*. Ballan, Victoria: Connor Court Publishing.

Porteous, J. (2013). *New evangelisation. Mission: one heart many voices. A multi-sector celebration and dialogue of living and leading mission better*. Sydney, Australia: 29 April -1st May.

Porteous, J. (2018). *Intentional discipleship*. Address to Catholic principals in Tasmania. Tarreleah, June 1st.

Powell, R. & Pepper, M. (2016). Religion and Spirituality in Australia. *Australian community Survey*. Sydney, Australia: NCLS Research.

Putney, M. E. (2010). *Prayer and evangelisation*. (CD). Keynote Address of Pray 2010. Brisbane: Catholic Archdiocese of Brisbane.

Rahner, K. (1971). How to receive a sacrament and mean it'. *Theology Digest*, 19, 227-234.

Rahner, K. (1983). *The love of Jesus and the love of neighbour*. New York: Crossroad.

Ranson, D. (2008). A service shaped by Catholic identity. In *Identity and Mission in Catholic Agencies*. Neil Ormerod (Ed.), Strathfield, Sydney: St Paul Publications.

REFERENCES

Reeves, D. B. (2008). Leadership and learning. *William Walker Oration.* Melbourne, Australia: Australian Council for Educational Leaders.

Riley, J. (2009). *Lecture notes: A silent advent retreat.* Brisbane, Queensland: Santa Teresa Retreat Centre.

Robinson, G. (1997). *Travels in sacred places.* Blackburn, Victoria: Harper-Collins.

Roebben, H. (2018). *New wine in new wineskins.* Keynote address, In M. T. Buchanan & A. M. Gellel, (Eds.). Global Perspectives on Catholic Religious Education Volume II: Learning and Leading in a Pluralist World. Netherlands: Springer Press.

Rohr, R. (1992). *Sermon on the mount.* (CD). Cincinnati, Ohio: St Anthony Messenger Press.

Rohr, R. (1996). *Jesus' plan for a new world: The sermon on the mount.* Cincinnati, Ohio: St Anthony Messenger Press.

Rohr, R. (1997). *Spirituality of imperfection.* (CD). Cincinnati, Ohio: St Anthony Messenger Press.

Rohr, R. (2003). *The path of descent.* (CD). Albuquerque. Centre for action and contemplation. Cincinnati, Ohio: St Anthony Messenger Press.

Rohr, R. (2004). *What difference does Trinity make?* (CD). Paper presented at the Religious Education Congress. Albuquerque, New Mexico: Center for Action and Contemplation.

Rohr, R. (2005). *Rebuild the Church.* (CD). Albuquerque. Centre for action and contemplation. Cincinnati, Ohio: St Anthony Messenger Press.

Rohr, R. (2012). *Adam's Return: the five promises of male initiation.* (CD). Cincinnati, Ohio: St Anthony Messenger Press.

Rohr, R. (2010). Building bridges toward healing. In R. Rohr, B. McLaren, C. Borgeault & S. Stabile. *Emerging Christianity: How we get there determines where we arrive* (CD). Cincinnati, Ohio: St Anthony Messenger Press.

Rohr, R. (2017). *The divine dance: The trinity and your transformation.* Interview with Mike Morrell. www.talks at google.

Rohr, R. (2018, Jan. 25). *Jesus of Nazareth.* Richard Rohr's daily meditation. Centre for Action and Contemplation. Retrieved from: http://cac.org.

Rolheiser, R. (1995). *Against an infinite horizon.* (CD). www.Franciscanmedia.org.

REFERENCES

Rolheiser, R. (1998). *Seeking spirituality: Guidelines for a Christian spirituality for the twenty-first century.* London: Hodder & Stoughton.

Rolheiser, R. (1998a). *The holy longing: The search for a Christian spirituality.* New York: Image Publications.

Rolheiser, R. (2008). *Blessings.* (DVD). Oblate Media. www.Franciscanmedia.org.

Rolheiser, R. (2010). *On not running with the crowd.* Retrieved from: http://www.ronrolheiser.com.

Rolheiser, R. (2011). *An anatomy and theology of trust – from paranoia to metanoia.* (CD). Los Angeles Religious Education Congress. Simi Valley, California: CSC Digital Media.

Rolheiser, R. (2014). *Sacred fire: A vision for a deeper human and Christian maturity.* New York: Image Publications.

Rolheiser, R. (2017). *Trust as living out of a blessed consciousness – living in trust as Jesus did.* LA Congress on Religious Education. Los Angeles, USA.

Romey, K. (2017, December). The real Jesus: What archaeology reveals about his life. *National Geographic.*

Rossiter, G. (2015). A case for a big picture re-orientation of K-12 Australian Catholic School Religious Education in the light of contemporary spirituality. The Person and the Challenges. *The Journal of Theology, Education, Canon Law and Social Studies inspired by Pope John Paul II,* 5(2) 5-32.

Ruddiman, W. (1999). *Challenge, crisis and response in the Roman Catholic Archdiocese of Brisbane.* Unpublished doctoral thesis, University of Queensland, Australia.

Rush, O. (2009). *The wisdom of God.* Diocesan Synod Presentation. Diocese of Cairns, Australia.

Rymarz, R. (2012). *The new evangelisation: Issues and challenges for Catholic schools.* Ballan, Victoria: Connor Court Publishing.

Salicru, S. (2017). Leadership in crisis. *Leadership Matters,* November, p. 35-37.

Schillebeeckx, E. (1963). *Christ the sacrament.* London: Sheed & Ward.

Schroeder, R. P. & Bevans, S. B. (2004). *Constants in context: A theology of mission for today.* Maryknoll, NY: Orbis Books.

Search Institute (2008). *With their own voices: A global exploration of how today's young people experience and think about spiritual development.* Minneapolis, Minnesota: Centre for Spiritual Development in Childhood and Adolescence.

REFERENCES

Seligman, M. (2007). *The search for happiness.* Keynote address. Brisbane, Queensland. Australian Institute of Management.

Senge, P. M. (1990). *The fifth discipline: The art and practice of the learning organisation.* Century Business: Random House. Kindle Edition.

Senge, P. M., Scharmer, C. S., Jaworski, J. & Flowers, B. S. (2005) *Presence: An exploration of profound change in people, organisations, and society.* New York: Doubleday.

Sergiovanni, T. J. (1987). *The principalship: A reflective practice perspective.* Newton, MA: Allyn & Bacon.

Sergiovanni, T.J. (1992). *Moral leadership: Getting to the heart of school improvement.* San Francisco: Jossey Bass.

Sergiovanni, T. J. (2000). *The lifeworld of leadership: Creating culture, community, and personal meaning in our schools.* San Francisco, California: Jossey-Bass.

Sergiovanni, T. J. (2005). The virtues of leadership. *The Educational Forum*, 69 (2), 112-123.

Shaduri, M. (2008). Principle of Holography in Complex Adaptive Systems. *Kybernetes*, 36 (6), 732–8.

Shapiro, J.P., Stefkovich, J.A. & Gutierrez, K.J. (2014). Ethical decision making. In C. M Branson & S. J. Gross (Eds.). *Handbook of Ethical Educational Leadership.* (210-228). New York: Routledge.

Sharkey, P. (2002). Building the capacity and commitment of staff for new evangelisation in Catholic schools. *Journal of Religious Education*, 50(3), 1-10.

Sharkey, P. (2017). Understanding the CECV Leuven research. In R. Rymarz & A. Belmonte (Eds.), *Religious education in Australian Catholic schools.* Mulgrave: Vaughan.

Sharkey, P. (2018). *Profiling and enhancing religious education in Catholic schools.* In M. T. Buchanan & A. M. Gellel, (Eds.). *Global Perspectives on Catholic Religious Education Volume II: Learning and Leading in a Pluralist World.* Netherlands: Springer Press.

Shea, J. (1987). *The Spirit master.* Chicago, Illinois: The Thomas More Press.

Sheridan, G. (2017). Is God dead? The west has much to lose in banishing christianity. *The Australian*, 26 August 2017.

Singer, P. (2018). *Ethics and the meaning of life.* Keynote address: Dialogue Australia Network Conference, April 13-15. Sydney, Australia.

REFERENCES

Smith, J. A., Jarman, M. & Osborn, M. (1999). Doing interpretative phenomenological analysis. In, M. Murray & K. Chamberlain (Eds.), *Qualitative Health Psychology: Theories and Methods*, (218–240). London: Sage.

Spry, V. G., & Sultmann, W. F. (1994). *Self-renewing Catholic schools: The self-renewing Catholic school process*. Brisbane, Brisbane Catholic Education.

Starratt, R. J. (1986). Human resource management: Learning our lessons by learning to learn. In, *Shaping Education*. Carlton, Victoria. A.C.E. (34-47).

Starratt, R. J. (1993). *The drama of leadership*. London: Falmer Press.

Stulberg, B. *Peak Performance*. Retrieved from: http://ow.ly/2NZr307eNOZ.

Sultmann, W. F. (2003). *Cornerstone*. Toowoomba, Queensland: Toowoomba Education Centre.

Sultmann, W. F. (2004). Cornerstone of the Catholic school. *Catholic School Studies*, 77(1), 26–30.

Sultmann, W. F. (2011). *Stones cry out: A gospel imagination for Catholic school identity*. Unpublished Doctoral Dissertation. Australian Catholic University.

Sultmann, W. F. (2014). *Stones cry out: A gospel imagination for Catholic school identity*. Saarbrucken, Germany: Lambert Academic Publishing.

Sultmann, W. F. & Brown, R. (2011). Modelling pillars of Catholic school identity: An Australian study. *International Studies in Catholic Education*, 3(1), 73-90.

Sultmann, W. F. & Brown, R. (2013). Magisterium perspectives on Catholic school identity. *Journal of Religious Education*, 61(1), 4-14.

Sultmann, W. F. & Brown, R. (2014). Catholic school identity and the new evangelisation. *Journal of Religious Education*. Retrieved from: http://link.springer.com/article/10.1007/s40839-014-0001-6.

Sultmann, W. F. & Brown, R. (2016). Leadership and identity in the Catholic school: An Australian perspective. *International Studies in Catholic Education*, 8(1), 73-90.

Sultmann, W. F. & Burton, A. M. (2004). *People skills for everyone*. Brisbane: Australian Academic Press.

Sultmann, W. F. & McLaughlin, D. (2000). *Spirit of leadership*. Toowoomba, Queensland: Catholic Institute of Education.

Sultmann, W. F., Thurgood, G. & Rasmussen, B. (2003). What parents are thinking: Some reflections on choices for schooling. *Catholic School Studies*, 76(2), 16–20.

REFERENCES

Swimme, B. & Berry, T. (1994). *The universe story: From the primordial flaring forth to the ecozoic era. A celebration of the unfolding of the cosmos.* San Francisco: Harper.

Swimme, B. (2008). *The Current Moment. A guided meditation.* Retrieved from: http://www.youtube.com/watch?v=Jw0RS2Tfk74.

Synod of Bishops. (1997). *Jesus Christ and the peoples of Oceania: Walking his way, telling his truth, living his life.* Sydney: St Paul's Publication.

Tacey, D. (1998). Toward a new theology of the Holy Spirit and divine immanence. *Conference*, 15(12) 17-22.

Tannock, P. D. (1975). *The organization and administration of Catholic education in Australia.* St. Lucia, Queensland: University of Queensland Press.

Tarrant, D. (May 2017). Pieces of the leadership puzzle. *Leadership Matters*, 22-25.

Thomas, .A. R. (1979). Preface. In A. McLay, D. Coghlan, P. Corkeron, P., & A. Druery. *Project Catholic School.* Brisbane, Queensland: Queensland Catholic Education Office.

Thompson, A. (2017). *Mindfulness and its effectiveness in regulating intellectual and emotional functioning of the brain.* Australian Psychological Society Workshop, June 17, North Coast Branch, Queensland Australia.

Thornber, J. H. & Gaffney, M. (2014). *Governing in faith: Foundations for formation.* Ballarat: Connor Court Publishing.

Timm, P. R., Petersen, D. D., & Stevens, J. C., (1990). *People at work: Human relations in organisations* (3rd Ed). St Paul. Minneapolis: West Publishing Co.

Tolle, E. (2004). *The power of now.* Vancouver, British Columbia: Namaste Publishing.

Tolle, E. (2005). *A new earth: Awakening to your life's purpose.* Victoria, Australia: Penguin.

Tolle, E. (2006). *Findhorn retreat: Stillness amidst the world.* Hong Kong: Eckhart Teachings Inc.

Treston, K. (1997). Ethos and identity: Foundational concerns for Catholic schools'. In R. Keane & D. Riley, (Eds.). *Quality Catholic schools: Challenges for leadership as Catholic education approaches the third millennium.*

Treston, K. (2018). *The wind blows where it chooses: The quest for a Christian story in our time.* Bayswater, Victoria: Coventry Press.

REFERENCES

Turner, K. (2017). Interview. In, K. Noonan Gores, *Heal: Change your mind, change your body, change your life.* (DVD). Hillsboro, Oregon: Beyond Words.

United States Conference of Catholic Bishops (2005). *Co-Worker's in the vineyard of the Lord.*

Versaldi, G. (2017). *Five keys to education in Catholic schools.* Chile's Sixth National Congress on Catholic Education, October 12-133, Catholic News Agency.

Walonick, D. S. (2010). *New Science as a Model for Organizational Development.* RAPIDBI. Retrieved from: http://rapidbli.com/management/new.

Weiming, T. (2015). *Returning home.* (DVD). In G. Malkin, Wisdom Films: Contemplative media for human being. www.wisdomoftheworld.com

Westley, D. (1996). *A theology of presence: The search for meaning in the American Catholic experience.* Mystic, Connecticut: Twenty-Third Publications.

Wheatley, M. (1992). *Leadership and the new science: learning about organizations from an orderly universe.* San Francisco: Berrett-Koehler Publishers.

Whelan, M. (1986). *The call to be.* Homebush, N.S.W: St. Paul Publications.

Whelan, M. (2015). *Developing your own spirituality.* Sydney, N.S.W: Aquinas Academy.

Wicks, R. (2009, July 02). *Riding the dragon.* You Tube Presentation retrieved from: www.youtube.com/watch?v=jRKJfkmovxI.

Wilber, K. (1997). *The eye of the spirit: An integral vision for a world gone slightly mad.* Boston: Shambhala.

William, A. (2017). Interview. In, K. Noonan Gores, *Heal: Change your mind, change your body, change your life.* (DVD). Hillsboro, Oregon: Beyond Words.

Williamson, M. (2004). *Spiritual principles.* Hay House Publications. (DVD). www.hayhouse.com.

Williamson, M. (2017). Interview. In, K. Noonan Gores, *Heal: Change your mind, change your body, change your life.* (DVD). Hillsboro, Oregon: Beyond Words.

Wilkinson, P. (2018). The Second Australian Provincial Council held between the 18th and 25th April 1869 in Melbourne. Article drawn from the *The Swag, Quarterly Journal of the National Council of Priests of Australia.* Retrieved from: http://www.catholica.com.au/gc4/pw/019_pw_120418.php.

REFERENCES

Willower, D. (1985) Philosophy and the study of educational administration. *Journal of Educational Administration*, 23(1), 5-22.

Winston, R. (2004). *The human mind and how to make the most of it*. London: Bantam Press.

Wirth, S. (2012). *The path of contemplative dialogue: Engaging collective awareness*. Retrieved from: contemplative dialogue.org.

Zani, A. V. (2018). *Five challenges for Catholic schools*. Address to a national gathering of Catholic school leaders initiated by the La Salle Academy, Australian Catholic University. March 6, Sydney, Australia.

APPENDIX 1.

Catholic School Formation Index
CSFI

CONTENTS
Catholic School Formation Index

PROFILING FORMATION PRIORITIES — 247
- Formation For Mission — 247
- Nature and Purpose — 247
- Process and Participants — 247
- Scoring and Reporting — 247

SELF-REPORT QUESTIONNAIRE — 248
- Contents — 248
- Instructions — 248

INDIVIDUAL PROFILE SUMMARY SHEET — 253

GROUP PROFILE SUMMARY SHEET — 254

APPENDIX ONE
Catholic School Formation Index

PROFILING FORMATION PRIORITIES

Formation for Mission

Catholic school formation entails the integration of faith, life and culture informed by the Catholic Christian Tradition. Processes include formal and informal encounters influenced by personal and group experiences, participant motivation, and capabilities of knowledge, skills, behaviours and dispositions.

Nature and Purpose

The Catholic School Formation Index (CSFI) is a self-report questionnaire for establishing formation priorities for individuals and groups. It explores priorities in four generic fields: Personal, Relational, Professional, and Communal. The purpose of the CSFI is to provide participants, school leaders, and facilitators with data to inform formation practices; meet accountability requirements; and, for personal and group planning and renewal. Significant to the application of the CSFI is its interdependence with school and system processes.

Process and Participants

The application of the CSFI includes group orientation; profile completion; planning; and, review. Participants will vary in accord with interest, and potentially include any member of the Catholic school community.

Scoring and Reporting

Results of the CSFI provide an overall formation priority score; and a breakdown of priorities within the generic fields of: Personal, Relational, Professional, and Communal; and priorities within the capabilities of Knowledge, Skills, Behaviours and Dispositions. Quantitative results of the CSFI are enhanced through shared reflection and summarised in a confidential individual report, complemented by an overall group summary.

Self-Report Questionnaire

Contents

The CSFI comprises 32 short statements on Catholic school mission, life and culture. Statements are clustered within fields of Personal, Relational, Professional and Communal, and reflect capabilities of Knowledge, Skills, Behaviours and Dispositions.

Participants are invited to respond to each statement in terms of its formation priority by indicating a score on a scale of 1 - 5. A score of 1 indicates a very low priority, whereas a score of 5 indicates a very high priority.

Example: An item relating to Catholic school mission, culture and life may appear as follows:

	Formation Priority Very Low to Very High
Personal witness is a means for reinforcing the mission of the school.	1 ② 3 4 5

Circling 2 reveals that this aspect of mission, life and culture holds a relatively low Formation Priority for the participant at this point in time.

Instructions

The questionnaire is able to be completed within a 10-minute period and there is no 'correct' or 'incorrect' response. Each response should reflect the participant's **current formation priorities**. To assist assessment of formation priorities within Personal, Relational, Professional and Communal fields, a brief description of each is given. This description should be read prior to responding to the statements that follow.

— CORNERSTONE —

PERSONAL

Personal Formation …

Personal awareness and engagement through meaning, affect and behaviour grounded in a Catholic Christian view of life and living.

Rating (For Information Only)
Personal Formation Priority
1. Very low
2. Low
3. Medium
4. High
5. Very High

Personal Formation Perspectives *Please consider and respond to the following in terms of your formation priority*	Formation Priority *(Circle one only)* Low → High				
1. Catholic Christian faith foundations are fundamental to the mission, life and culture of the Catholic school.	1	2	3	4	5
2. Christ is the cornerstone for spirituality, mission and leadership in the Catholic school.	1	2	3	4	5
3. Personal awareness of my beliefs, values and attitudes informs my role within the Catholic school.	1	2	3	4	5
4. Integrating what I think, feel and do within the Catholic school is significant to my professional service.	1	2	3	4	5
5. Reflection and contemplation are integral to personal and professional awareness and practice.	1	2	3	4	5
6. Balancing personal and professional requirements are key to quality practices.	1	2	3	4	5
7. Personal and community formation plans are developed to enhance my role.	1	2	3	4	5
8. Engagement with prayer, school story, faith symbols and liturgy are central to my professional practice.	1	2	3	4	5
TOTALS	Raw Score				
	Average				

RELATIONAL

Relational Formation …

Respect for the inherent dignity of others and engaging the life of the Spirit in social and group situations.

Rating (For Information Only)
Personal Formation Priority
1. Very low
2. Low
3. Medium
4. High
5. Very High

Relational Formation Perspectives *Please consider and respond to the following in terms of your formation priority*	Formation Priority *(Circle one only)* Low ⟶ High
1. Gospel values are significant to quality relationships.	1 2 3 4 5
2. Staff collaboration is foundational to mission, life and culture.	1 2 3 4 5
3. Compassionate presence is key to my relationships.	1 2 3 4 5
4. Staff relationships give witness to school mission.	1 2 3 4 5
5. Respectful and active listening characterise interpersonal behaviour.	1 2 3 4 5
6. Sharing wisdom is the basis of group engagement.	1 2 3 4 5
7. Affirmation and encouragement exist among staff.	1 2 3 4 5
8. Group prayer is a community priority.	1 2 3 4 5
TOTALS	Raw Score
	Average

PROFESSIONAL

Professional Formation …

Engaging and witnessing to mission through differential practices within religious education, wider curriculum and the religious life of the school.

Rating (For Information Only)
Personal Formation Priority
1. Very low
2. Low
3. Medium
4. High
5. Very High

Professional Formation Perspectives *Please consider and respond to the following in terms of your formation priority*	Formation Priority (Circle one only) Low → High
1. School mission is based on advancing and celebrating the mission of God in the world.	1　2　3　4　5
2. Curriculum is underpinned by a Catholic Christian view of life and living.	1　2　3　4　5
3. Teaching and learning practices are in accord with student levels of development, personal needs and system and national goals.	1　2　3　4　5
4. The religious life of the school is expressed through Scripture, Prayer, Sacrament, Liturgy, Catholic Social teachings, and outreach to those made poor.	1　2　3　4　5
5. Teaching and learning combine concrete experiences with theoretical understandings.	1　2　3　4　5
6. The Religious Education program is educationally challenging and personally formative.	1　2　3　4　5
7. Teaching and learning activities reflect the diversity of student needs in faith development and practice.	1　2　3　4　5
8. Dialogue and planning support the religious dimension of the curriculum.	1　2　3　4　5
TOTALS	Raw Score
	Average

COMMUNAL

Communal Formation …

A commitment to dialogue on beliefs and values and the implementation of systems congruent with school, Church and wider community expectations.

Rating (For Information Only)
Personal Formation Priority
1. Very low
2. Low
3. Medium
4. High
5. Very High

Communal Formation Perspectives *Please consider and respond to the following in terms of your formation priority*	Formation Priority (Circle one only) Low → High
1. Community engagement is proactive and transparent.	1 2 3 4 5
2. Parents are the primary educators who engage with staff in mutually beneficial ways.	1 2 3 4 5
3. The school learns from other similar faith-based schools and organisations.	1 2 3 4 5
4. School systems (eg finance, policy, industrial, student and staff performance), are aligned with mission.	1 2 3 4 5
5. The school explores particular relationship opportunities with those 'made poor.'	1 2 3 4 5
6. Policies are a key mechanism for promoting the mission, life and culture of the school.	1 2 3 4 5
7. The school is active in its dialogue with the community it serves.	1 2 3 4 5
8. Formation planning is realistic, adaptable and achievable.	1 2 3 4 5
TOTALS	Raw Score	
	Average	

– CORNERSTONE –

INDIVIDUAL PROFILE SUMMARY SHEET

Overall Formation Priority

Total Raw Score (   ) and Average Score (   )

Respondent Details				
Name:			Date:	
School:			Role:	

	Field	Priorities	
		Total	Average
Field Priorities	*Personal*		
	Relational		
	Professional		
	Communal		

	Capability	Priorities	
		Total	Average
Capability Priorities	*Disposition* (Items 1 & 2 across all fields)		
	Knowledge (Items 3 & 4 across all fields)		
	Skills (Items 5 & 6 across all fields)		
	Behaviours (Items 7 & 8 across all fields)		
Discussion Reflections			
Summary Priorities			

– CATHOLIC SCHOOL FORMATION INDEX –

GROUP PROFILE SUMMARY SHEET

Overall Group Formation Priority Score (   )

	Fields	Priority Score	
		Individual Averages	Group Averages
Field Priorities	Personal		
	Relational		
	Professional		
	Communal		
	Capabilities	**Priority Score**	
		Individual Averages	Group Averages
Capability Priorities	Disposition		
	Knowledge		
	Skills		
	Behaviours		
Discussion Reflections			
Summary Priorities			

Notes

Notes

www.ingramcontent.com/pod-product-compliance
Lightning Source LLC
Chambersburg PA
CBHW080345300426
44110CB00019B/2507